Reuniting The Neshamas

A Journey of Remembrance, Commemoration and Healing

by **Sheri Stern**

Mazo Publishers

Reuniting The Neshamas

ISBN: 978-1-956381-05-4

Published by

Mazo Publishers
www.mazopublishers.com
mazopublishers@gmail.com

•••

Neshama / neshamas (pl): Hebrew and Yiddish for soul / souls.

•••

The text of all correspondence in all forms included in this book are the personal opinions of the individuals as private citizens. They are not official statements of the individuals in their professional capacities representing or speaking for their places of work, unless otherwise apparent.

Individuals who accompanied the author while in Germany did so as private citizens, in their free time, and not as public officials, unless otherwise apparent.

•••

Excerpts from "Caste: The Origins Of Our Discontents" by Isabel Wilkerson (Oprah's Book Club) Copyright © 2020 by Isabel Wilkerson. Used by permission of Random House, an imprint and division of Penguin Random House LLC. All rights reserved.

First They Came ...

First they came for the Socialists,
and I did not speak out –
because I was not a Socialist.

Then they came for the Trade Unionists,
and I did not speak out –
because I was not a Trade Unionist.

Then they came for the Jews,
and I did not speak out –
because I was not a Jew.

Then they came for me –
and there was no one left to speak for me.

Friedrich Gustav Emil Martin Niemöller

CONTENTS

DEDICATION

In Memory of Groups 1 and 2

Group 1

Ralph Stern – my father-in-law, my "second Father", "Dad". He was named Rolf at birth in Germany, and he changed the name to Ralph when he came to America.

By the grace of G-d, and his insightful loving parents, he was one of the lucky ones who was able to flee Germany. He escaped to America to live with relatives there. His parents had been aware of what was happening in their country and made that incredulous decision that no parent or child should ever have to make: they did whatever it took to get at least one of their children out of Germany before it was too late, the remaining three of them planning to join Dad in America soon afterwards.

Can you imagine fleeing your homeland at the age of 15½, alone, due to persecution/the Holocaust, leaving your family, not knowing if you'd ever see them again, not speaking any English, connecting with a stranger on the ship who was a chaperone for you and many other children fleeing for their lives without their parents, not knowing anyone else – including the German-American relatives you were going to live with but had never met?!

Can you imagine never seeing your family again after 1938, never hearing from them again after 1941, and never finding out exactly what happened to them?

When asked to describe Dad and his life so that the participating German children could read it aloud at the Stolpersteine ceremony, Gail wrote: "After family, the most important thing to my dad was education. ... He was so proud of all of us, and so happy that his hard work made it all possible. The third thing that was important to my dad was charity.... He supported many charitable organizations, and taught my brother and me from an early age the importance of giving to others."

I think Dad was one of the dearest, kindest, supportive Mensches (Yiddish: a person of integrity and honor) I've known in my lifetime. He lived to make his family happy, and was very proud of us. He lived to enjoy his two grandchildren, watch them grow up, become Bar and Bat Mitzvahs in the traditions of our Jewish forefathers and now also our foremothers, and become independent adults. His words and actions made us feel like we were his "everything", and we were.

He lived through many hardships in his lifetime, among the most devastating: the German Nazi regime's persecution of him and his family, all Jews, and others, leaving his homeland and all who were dear to him – alone – to save his life by escaping to America, the grotesque inhumane murders of almost his entire family during the Holocaust, serving in WWII as an American soldier – stationed in Germany, seeing the Holocaust up close and personal when liberating Dachau concentration camp's survivors, and a miscarriage – loss of their first child (before Jeffrey was born). Yet I never heard him speak one word of anger about the Holocaust, his life-altering losses, or anger at G-d. His faith remained strong, and he continued to practice Judaism throughout his lifetime.

One thing that truly puzzled and disturbed him was that he could never understand why some families don't get along or speak to each other over "ridiculous things" (his phrase). Though I never heard him say the reason why, I know it's because of how his life experiences shaped him – for he would've done anything humanly possible to have been able to rescue his family to join him in America, and to have been able to age together gracefully throughout his lifetime with his younger sister, parents, and aunts and uncles.

He and Mom (Shirley Stern) welcomed me into their family decades ago, even before Jeffrey and I married in 1975. They both made me feel like their "second daughter", always. I miss having them both in my life.

Dad, in your memory this book covers all three of those things that you shared with us that were important to you, *L'Dor v'Dor*. [1] This book is about:

---

1   Hebrew: "From generation to generation".

1) Family (Mishpacha in Yiddish).

2) Education.

3) Supporting charitable organizations: The profits from this book are being donated to these organizations, to support their Values and Missions which we support:

- The United States Holocaust Memorial Museum in Washington, DC. The USHMM educates with facts, evidence, and compassion, to help assure that "Never again" will hatred breed, multiply, and create another genocide. Yet tragically, genocides do continue through the present day. Together, let's take Action to *prevent* hatred and ongoing genocide, instead of mourning the victims.

- The Stolpersteine Initiative. The Stolpersteine Initiative "reunited" and "returned" our family to us, and commemorates all victims and survivors of the Holocaust. Their goal is to remember everyone's loved ones, so that collectively we "Never forget".

- HIAS is the Hebrew Immigrant Aid Society. HIAS supported Dad's parents in desperate times by assisting with Dad's passage to America in 1938. Dad supported HIAS thereafter. Jeffrey, Gail, and I support HIAS in its mission to "Welcome the Stranger. Protect the Refugee."

Margot Stern – Dad's sister. Four years younger than Dad, she was 15½ years old (the same age Dad was when he'd fled Germany four years earlier) when she was deported with her parents and 1161 other Jews by the Nazis. The cattle car conditions were not even fit for animals, much less humans, much less for the number of human beings cramped together without any hygiene or sanitary arrangements.

Until the day Dad died in 2009, despite his multiple efforts to find out the ultimate fates of Margot, his parents, and other family members, he never knew. Margot never lived to become "sweet-16". In Jewish tradition, Gail is named after her (Gail Marsha, the M for Margot), as is our daughter Michelle.

Dad's nuclear family pre-Holocaust – Dad (Rolf/Ralph), Auguste – Mother/Wife, Julius – Father/Husband, and Margot – daughter and Dad's younger sister in their garden at home in Hohenlimburg, pre-Holocaust.

Julius and Auguste Stern – Rolf-Ralph's parents, who were deported and murdered together with their teenage daughter Margot (Dad's sister) and many others by the Nazis. These are the grandparents that Jeffrey and Gail never knew.

Of note, Julius Stern was born on February 2, 1886. Ralph and Shirley Stern, my second-parents/in-laws (Jeffrey and Gail's parents) were married on February 2, 1952 – 66 years later on the same date. I wonder if they did that on purpose.

Aunt Jenny Weil – Auguste's younger sister, who we learned was transported between a number of different Nazi concentration camps before dying in Sobibor. As well, this book is dedicated to the memories of the rest of Dad's family who endured countless atrocities and were all murdered at the hands of Nazis during the Shoah (the Hebrew term – "catastrophe" – used for the Holocaust, the mass murder of Jewish people under the German Nazi regime).

Group 2

• The 6,000,000 Jews who were tortured, starved, enslaved into forced labor, experimented on, separated from their families, raped, beaten, shot, gassed, burned, and buried in mass graves that they themselves were often forced to dig while the Nazis looked on.

• All those other human beings in addition to Jews who were tortured, imprisoned, and murdered by the Nazis because they were not deemed to be "perfect Aryans" by Hitler: the Romas and Sintis (Gypsies), political prisoners, homosexuals, the physically and mentally disabled, the elderly, babies and young children, Jehovah's Witnesses, Poles, Soviet POWs, and Soviet citizens and those unfit to work.

• All those courageous Jewish and non-Jewish souls who resisted Nazi power and fought back. Their efforts were valiant and made a difference in people's lives. They followed their moral compass.

• All those with tattooed numbers burned into their arms who survived and went on to lead relatively healthy and productive lives after the Shoah, despite their physical and invisible emotional scars. How did they do it?!

– How could my father-in-law, who was able to get out of Germany before becoming a Jewish prisoner and getting a number tattooed on his arm, still believe in G-d and worship and praise Him till the day he died – after Hitler was responsible for the orders that senselessly murdered his entire family?

– My girlfriend's mother was a Jewish Holocaust survivor. She was unusual only in the sense that she would tell anyone her stories of captivity in the concentration camp. My friend relates this story that her Mom told her: One day, her Mom was ordered by a Nazi soldier to go inside a building for something. Carrying her young baby in her arms, she began to follow his orders immediately. However, the Nazi stopped her, told her to hand her baby over to one of the other imprisoned women in line outside who would take care of her baby until she returned. Reluctantly, she handed her baby over to another prisoner. As soon as her mother disappeared inside the building, the Nazi grabbed the baby from the prisoner's arms and threw the baby into a nearby blazing fire. Her mother was informed by the other prisoners when she returned outside.

Besides hatred, that Nazi felt further empowered and entitled by his "dominant caste" position in Hitler's Nazi regime, knowing there would be no retribution, and even possibly a reward for his actions. Once liberated from the horror of the camps in 1945 at the end of the war, her Mother went on to marry, have children (among them, my friend) and grandchildren, practice Judaism, and lead a full life. How could she carry on?!

– How could that Nazi perpetrator throw that baby to its fiery excruciating death?!

– I remember the photographer for my Bat Mitzvah (a Jewish coming of age religious ritual for girls at 12 or 13 years old). He had a series of numbers on his arm. I knew exactly what they were. At 12 years old, it was hard not to stare. At 68, it's still hard.

• All those human beings, both unnamed or named on the Mount of Remembrance in Jerusalem. The Avenue of the Righteous among the Nations honors ... "the non-Jews who acted according to the most noble principles of humanity and risked their lives to save Jews during the Holocaust. Before entering the Holocaust History Museum, which presents the story of the Shoah, the visitor is reminded that there was an alternative: there were individuals who chose to walk the righteous path and shine a glimmer of light amidst the darkness." [2]

---

2 www.yadvashem.org.

In Honor of Groups 3 and 4

Group 3

Without whom, we would continue to have so many more unanswered questions about our family and the Shoah, and our lives would not have been changed so significantly: our "Significant 4" who we call our German "Mishpacha" (Yiddish for family, pronounced Mish-pah'-cha), and our other Stolpersteine Friends who also became Mishpacha:

- Our Significant 4, Mishpacha: Ira (pronounced Ear'ah), Oliver, Rolf and his wife Christina. Rolf was the Leader of the Meinerzhagen Stolpersteine Initiative chapter in 2014 when we initially met.
- Herbert (formed the Meinerzhagen Stolpersteine Initiative) and his wife Gretel.
- Dietmar and "his" Christina – They are the new Leaders of the Meinerzhagen Stolpersteine Initiative chapter for several years.
- Shaked – our Israeli Mishpacha.
- Gudrun – the retired teacher who taught her students about acceptance and peace; a member of the Meinerzhagen chapter of the Stolpersteine Initiative.
- Barbara and Heinz – the Rexingen couple who created a Holocaust Museum.
- Gunter Demnig – the creator of the Stolpersteine Initiative Art Project, the Artist who lays the Stolpersteine throughout Europe.

Group 4 (*Last, but certainly not least*)

• My husband Jeffrey: for his enduring love and friendship, for always making me laugh, for his support throughout my life of "giving back" (which he "kvells" about to others (Yiddish: to be extraordinarily proud and rejoice; brags)), and for always readily accepting my answer of "you know – I'm doing stuff, checking emails, purging" when he frequently asked what I was doing so long at the computer every night (When in fact, during

2021, I was completing this book and researching editors and publishers!). He is my best friend, my first and only love, and the wind beneath my wings.

• Our children Ryan, Michelle and John: Each of you are special to me in your own unique ways. Giving birth to Ryan and Michelle, and motherhood, remains one of my top peak life experiences, alongside marrying Jeffrey; and then came the grandchildren! John joined our family when he "married in", but became our son-from-another-mother, our "third child", even when he was dating Michelle.

– A memory: Our daughter Michelle, at 8 years old, sat on my lap after coming home from Hebrew school and first learning about the Holocaust. She asked in all her innocence and naivety: "Mommy, what did Pop-Pop (Ralph Stern) and his family ever do to Hitler that made Hitler so angry that he killed Pop-Pop's whole Family?"

• My sister Gail (in-law; Jeffrey's sister): Though a sister-from-another-mother, Gail and I have become true sisters over the years since Jeffrey and I met as teens. I admire her loving generosity to her family, friends, and people in need, her strength, courage, passion for justice, and her ability to speak the truth – even when it is difficult.

• Our two delicious granddaughters: Rowan and Sydney, the youngest next generation, our future and legacy. May they learn about the Shoah, "know" their family roots, treasure and practice their Jewish heritage, "Never forget", stay kind and compassionate, and never have to bear witness in their lifetimes to any acts of man's inhumanity to man.

PREFACE

Once home from our 2014 journey to Germany, I began to process all that had occurred before and during it. We continued to stay in touch with our Significant 4, and they independently chose to continue researching our family and sent new information whenever they found it. Once home, I told everyone who would listen about my experiences, singing the praises of our Significant 4 and the other Germans we'd met, marveling at their ongoing compassion and commitment to their "cause". I passively thought about writing a book, which I'd never done, but I think I got distracted both by the emotional satisfaction of "telling the story" to others, as well as the "busy-ness" of our lives. After I retired in 2015, in addition to my ongoing activism for social justice, veterans who are homeless, and voting rights for all, and further compounded by bearing witness to vile rhetoric and many ongoing acts of hate and violence within my own country and abroad, I realized that "telling the story" to others, verbally ...was simply not enough.

I feel "called" to write this book for a number of reasons:

This is my written Legacy Gift to our Significant 4, our German Mishpacha: Rolf and Christina, Ira, and Oliver. As well, it is for these others who also have become Mishpacha: Herbert and Gretel, Gunter Demnig, Dietmar and "his" Christina, Barbara and Heinz, Gudrun, Stefan, the members of the Stolpersteine Initiative, and so many other Germans – for all they've given to me, our family, and so many other Jewish people. This is my written Legacy Gift to them so that you, too, will come to know them as Mensches (Yiddish: a person with integrity and honor).

"When You Listen To A Witness, You Become A Witness." (Elie Wiesel). I write this despite all those who deny that the Holocaust ever occurred, or who minimize it ("Oh, they're exaggerating the numbers, it wasn't that bad."). I write this because of them, so the truth continues to be told, *L'Dor v'Dor* (Hebrew: from generation to generation), so we "never forget", and so "never again" should this happen.

It is my responsibility. I have a duty to tell this story, not only to bear witness and share what I've learned about the tragedies of the Shoah, but also to bear witness and share what I've experienced: countless kindnesses, compassion, atonement and amends from a number of German people.

I owe it to the countless Germans who were and are accepting of others and peaceful, some of whom may still bear the pain and shame for what their ancestors and countrymen did to other human beings.

Perhaps you and others reading this might finally be able to start thinking of Germany and German people now – as just that: Germany, and people – fellow human beings – rather than some people who may still think of all of them ONLY as "Nazi" Germany and "Nazis" – because there is a significant difference. If we think that all Germans are Nazis, then we are only repeating the past beliefs and behaviors of Hitler's and the Nazis' hatred and intolerance towards us and anyone else labeled "other" by White Supremacists and other groups.

I am privileged to live in the United States of America, Land of the Free, and practice my beliefs, religion, and values openly without fear of persecution, harm, or death – all this, because of the Brave men and women who choose and chose to serve and protect our freedoms as USA Military Service Members and Veterans.

It frightens, hurts, and angers me when I confront the reality of today's ongoing increasing anti-Semitism, systemic racism targeting people of color, anti-Muslim, anti-Asian false beliefs and actions against them, and intolerance and scapegoating of anyone who is "different" or "other"- everywhere in the world. However, I do not feel helpless. I do not stand by silently. I stand up, speak out, participate in protest marches, donate to and join activist organizations with similar missions. I am a proud member of the Sisterhood of Salaam Shalom (www.sosspeace. org), an organization of Muslim and Jewish women who come together in peace to learn about each other and rise up together against hatred of any kind. I partner with ADL (Anti-Defamation League), ACLU (American Civil Liberties Union), LWV (League of Women Voters), Everytown for Gun Safety, BZD (Baltimore Zionist

District), AIPAC (American-Israel Public Affairs Committee), and similar organizations. I contact my legislators. Once, during the prior US Administration that promulgated "the Muslim Ban", I called all 535 US legislators in Congress to voice my opposition and strongly encourage their taking appropriate action. I found that I was unable to send email messages through many of the other 49 states' legislators' websites, because when asked to enter my zipcode – my message was not accepted because I was not their constituent. Hence, the 535 individual phone calls. Took me two weeks to get it done, but "oh, what a feeling!" That "Muslim Ban" was finally repealed once the new Administration of our 46th President Joe Biden and Vice-President Kamala Harris began, within their first 100 days in office.

There are good kind decent human beings in this world we live in, mensches – and people need to hear their stories, replicate them, create their own, and perform more acts of "*Tikkun Olam*" (Hebrew: repairing the world). "Think globally, act locally."

"See one, do one, teach one." Let's DO this, People! Be a Role Model for anyone who's "watching" you, especially your children and grandchildren! We each have 24 hours in a day, one lifetime to live, and TOGETHER – WE CAN AND DO MAKE A DIFFERENCE!

I am guided to be an Instrument of Love, Forgiveness, Healing, and Peace.

I am one, but I am only one.
I cannot do everything, but I can do something.
And because I cannot do everything,
I will not refuse to do the something that I can do.

Helen Keller

PROLOGUE

Von (From): Oliver
Gesendet: Freitag (Friday) 3. Januar 2014 16:47
An (To): Gail Stern
Cc: Rolf; Herbert; Ira
Betreff (Subject): Information on Erwin Stern's family in Baltimore, MD

Dear Ms. Stern,

I am a German historian living in Paris, France, and I am sending you this request on behalf of an association of volunteers based in Meinerzhagen, Germany, my home town. This association commemorates the fate of the town's Jewish inhabitants under Nazi rule when they were deported to concentration camps or had to leave Germany to survive. In front of the houses where the victims were living (that is, the last address chosen by themselves and not imposed by the authorities), small commemorative brass plaques with the names of the inhabitants and the date of their escape or deportation are embedded into the sidewalk. This initiative is part of a nationwide commemorative project (for more information, see http://www.stolpersteine.eu/en/), and a first series of plaques were set in Meinerzhagen in 2013.

In 2014, this association would like to set further plaques, among others for Erwin Stern, his sister Erna (Stern) Schwarz and his brother-in-law Siegfried Schwarz, who had been living in the same house on the main street in Meinerzhagen. As their descendants are to be invited to attend this event, I was asked to find out whether there are still relatives alive in the US.

I am sending you this e-mail because I found a photograph on the internet which was taken in 1979 when you graduated from Baltimore Law School. As this photograph shows Erna Schwarz and Erwin Stern on the left, I concluded that they must have been relatives or close friends of your family. In "The Baltimore Sun", I also found an obituary of one of Erwin's sons ... which mentions two brothers, ... but I have not been able to find any information on them. Erwin Stern had apparently come to Meinerzhagen in the 1980s, but the town hall in Meinerzhagen did not jot down his address, unfortunately.

Therefore, I would like to know whether you still have the contact details of the Stern and Schwarz families in Baltimore and whether you could provide me with an e-mail address, a phone number or the like, so that I could forward this information to the association which would contact the families afterwards and send them information on its commemorative activities in 2014. If you should have any other information on Erwin's and Erna's families I would be very glad to learn about them, too. In fact, I found very interesting material in the archives of the American Jewish Joint Distribution Committee and in the New York review "Aufbau", among others, and I am interested in any document which may contribute to a full picture of Erwin Stern's escape to Baltimore via Lisbon in 1941 and of his sister's prior emigration to the US. Thank you very much in advance for your efforts, best wishes for 2014 and with kind regards from Europe. ... Oliver

Gail's 1979 Law School Graduation picture, which helped Oliver find Gail. L-R, back row: cousins Erwin Stern, Erna Stern Schwarz (Erwin's sister), Jeannette Stern (Erwin's wife), Jeffrey Stern (Face is blocked in photo; Ralph and Shirley Stern's son; Sheri's husband), Mom – holding purse (Shirley Stern, Dad's wife, Jeffrey and Gail's mother), Sheri (Jeffrey's wife; Gail's sister-in-law; Mom and Dad's daughter-in-law). L-R, front: Gail (Mom and Dad's daughter), Dad – Rolf/Ralph Stern – wearing a tie.

Chapter 1

IN THE BEGINNING

It began with that one intriguing email to my sister-in-law Gail on January 3, 2014, from a "self-described" (Jeffrey and I didn't know if he really was a German historian!) German historian named Oliver – asking if Gail was related to or knew any of these three individuals from Germany – Erna Schwarz and her husband Siegfried Schwarz, and Erwin Stern – Erna's brother.

Spoiler Alert: Yes, of course we knew all three of them – they and their children are our cousins, on Jeffrey and Gail's side! Erna, and Erwin and his wife Jeannette, had celebrated Rosh Hashanah and Passover Holiday gatherings with us for decades, celebrated Bar and Bat Mitzvahs and weddings with us, supported us during challenging times, ever since Gail and Jeffrey were children, and they danced with us when Jeffrey and I married. In fact, their grown children, grandchildren, and great-grandchildren still gather with us, and vice-versa, at significant Holidays and life events!

We knew them because cousins Erna and Siegfried had made the critical decision to flee Germany in 1937, coming to America well before Kristallnacht (The Night of Broken Glass, November 9-10, 1938), Pearl Harbor, and America's joining our European Allies in WWII. It was early enough that Erna and Siegfried were still allowed to bring very little money, (not enough to start a new life, according to their daughter, Judi), clothing, and furniture to America with them! Jeffrey and I still have their Secretary desk and their "kleiderschrank" in our home (German for "wardrobe", a very large wood stand-alone closet with room for hanging clothes as well as several shelves, made sturdily with interlocking pieces of wood – no screws or bolts!). Erna and Siegfried's only child, our cousin Judi, offered these to us when she and her husband Bernie moved long ago. I must say, neither piece matches my decorating style, but back when Judi offered them to us decades ago, I couldn't bear to say "no thanks" – because I knew the history of the furniture and its family owners, and it was important to me to keep those pieces and the memories (and perhaps Erna and Siegfried) alive within the family.

Unbeknownst to us previously, in just this one email – Oliver told us something new and astounding that we didn't know about "quiet reserved" cousin Erwin (who we knew as "Irvin" here in America): that he had escaped to Baltimore via Lisbon in 1941. Later in 2014, through Oliver's ongoing research, we discovered that Erwin had hidden and moved from country to country across Europe to escape the Nazi regime and certain death, looking for work so he could eat and survive, leaving hastily whenever the Gestapo got too close. He finally escaped after two years of running and hiding – somehow obtaining passage on a boat from Lisbon, Portugal to Baltimore. We had no idea! Of course, like many Survivors of the Holocaust, he never talked about it.

So we learned within several more emails from Oliver and Ira that Oliver had been assigned by Rolf to find any living relatives of Erwin, his sister Erna and her husband Siegfried, so that Gail could hopefully help them in Germany to find any descendants of those three. The "association of volunteers based in Meinerzhagen, Germany" wanted to invite those descendants to a Stolpersteine-laying Ceremony for "their" relatives, to be held in Germany later that year (2014). "Their" relatives would be memorialized with the laying of a "stone" – a "Stolperstein", a "stumbling block". "Their" relatives turned out to be "our" relatives. "Those descendants" turned out to be us!

As Gail began sending family pictures to our Significant 4, Ira would ask in her email, "Can you tell me who is sitting/standing beside (so and so) in this picture? Were they friends or relatives?" As emails and photographs began flying across the ocean at the speed of light, we couldn't wait to get home from work to check our emails to see what new information they'd sent that day.

As our email relationships began to develop quickly, and Gail began identifying the individuals in our family pictures, it took only a short time before we three American Jews and these four Germans who are not Jewish realized that the Julius Stern for whom they were seeking descendants was not "our" Julius Stern who was Dad's father. The Julius Stern they were seeking was actually Erna and Erwin's father Julius Stern, our cousin Judi's maternal Grandfather! We'd known for a long time from Dad that two of the Weil Sisters – Cilly and Auguste – both had married men named Julius Stern, who were actually not related! Stern was a very common German surname. These four Germans weren't even looking for us! They were actually looking for Judi (Erna and Siegfried's only child, first-generation American, granddaughter of the Julius Stern for whom these four Germans were seeking descendants.). Thus, Gail helped these four Germans find the people they were actually looking for, who also happened to be our cousins, and in addition – these four Germans got a "bonus" in meeting us along the way. This opened another whole avenue of exploration which could now include Dad's parents and younger sister!

Tragically, Julius and Cilly Weil Stern (Erna and Erwin's parents, Judi's maternal grandparents, and Cilly was one of Auguste's sisters), Aunt Jenny Weil (another sister of Auguste, and Dad's maternal aunt), Uncle Wilhelm Weil (Auguste's brother, and Dad's maternal

Nine Weil/Stern/ other family members, pre- Holocaust: Every one of them was murdered by the Nazis.

uncle), Julius and Auguste and Margot Stern (Dad's parents and younger sister), Selma Weil Meyer who married Max (Auguste's sister, and Dad's maternal aunt and uncle), Susanne Meyer (sister of Max; sister-in-law of Selma Weil Meyer), and of course millions of others – Jews and non-Jews, were exterminated – gassed – shot – incinerated – tortured – inhumanely experimented on – murdered – and massacred – during the Holocaust, the Shoah.

So back to the email. Let me make something clear right out of the gate: both my husband Jeffrey and I independently thought this self-described German Historian Oliver's email was a scam, although to be fair – no one was asking for money. That would've clinched the scam theory for us. Also, let me make it clear that Gail never thought that! She believed the email immediately and never thought anything was fishy! Jeffrey was not particularly interested in pursuing this email or responding. He's generally a skeptic. I, on the other hand, was embedded with "Polyanna" genes at birth – because I am one of the most trusting (and to be honest – gullible) persons I know. Yet because I have always been that way, but have also seen too much in the world to show complete trust, and have also been "had" a time or two, and because I trust Jeffrey's opinions based on his extensive knowledge about lots of things and his street-savvy, I, too, on my own, was skeptical immediately.

Jeffrey and I talked about it with Gail, shared our views, and Gail said she was writing back to them. She asked if we wanted her to share our email addresses with "Oliver, the German Historian living in Paris, France" or not. My curiosity and interest was sparked enough to say "yes" without hesitation. Jeffrey immediately followed suit, both of us figuring there wasn't any significant danger in just sharing our email addresses with this Oliver person to find out more.

Thus began our incredible journey. At the beginning of 2014, I could never have imagined, nor could any of us, the paths we would travel before-during-and since that August 2014 trip to Germany – geographically, physically, emotionally, and spiritually. Thus began our developing "email relationships" with four significant individuals from Germany, significant because they changed our lives individually, as a family, and as part of the history – past-present-and future – of the Jewish people.

Chapter 2

STOLPERSTEINE

In order to understand the significance of Stolpersteine (the plural of one Stolperstein), here's an introduction from the extensive Stolpersteine website as of 4/8/2021: www.stolpersteine.eu/en.

The artist Gunter Demnig remembers the victims of National Socialism by installing commemorative brass plaques in the pavement in front of their last address of choice.

There are now STOLPERSTEINE [1] in at least 1200 places in Germany, as well as in Austria, Belgium, Croatia, the Czech Republic,

---

1   Lit. "stumbling stones or blocks".

Finland, France, Germany, Greece, Italy, Hungary, Lithuania, Luxembourg, Moldova, the Netherlands, Norway, Poland, Romania, Russia, Slovakia, Slovenia, Spain, Switzerland and Ukraine.

Gunter Demnig cites the Talmud saying that "a person is only forgotten when his or her name is forgotten". The Stolpersteine in front of the buildings bring back to memory the people who once lived here. Almost every "stone" begins with HERE LIVED... One "stone". One name. One person.

For 120 euros, anybody can sponsor a stone, its manufacture and its installation. ... The 75,000th STOLPERSTEIN was placed in December 2019, and they now exist in some 2,000 places in Europe. There are also already more than 25 Stolperschwellen.

From Gunter Demnig on the website:

Considering all the effort that goes into making and laying a Stolperstein, the number of stones is limited. The sculptor Michael Friedrichs-Friedlaender makes each one by hand. This is a conscious decision that counters the Nazis' mass extermination policies, turning numbers back into names.

Therefore, this commemorative art project will always remain symbolic. This makes it all the more important for each individual to be commemorated in a way that is befitting. Often there is close cooperation between family members, neighbors, the inhabitants of the buildings in front of which Stolpersteine are laid, as well as local associations, schools and educational institutions...

We consider that one of the pillars of our democracy in Germany is to remember the crimes of National Socialism. We have unbounded esteem for all forms of commemoration and advocate diversity when it comes to Germany's 'memory culture'. We cooperate with other commemorative projects all over the world. Therefore, we appeal for respect for the original idea behind the Stolperstein and for the protection of the art project's form. Thank you and best wishes, Gunter Demnig and the Stolperstein team ...

Please note: Unfortunately, Gunter Demnig's timetable for the next months is already full – we cannot organize any more Stolperstein-laying ceremonies before 2022.

Stolpersteine and the novel coronavirus (Covid-19)
Update: 19th March 2021

As a result of the increasing number of COVID-19 cases and new measures introduced by the authorities in Germany, we regret to announce that we once again have to cancel Gunter Demnig's Stolperstein installations. ... We don't want either Gunter Demnig or anybody else to risk contracting the virus. We hope that you understand. We will continue to follow advice from the World Health Organization and local health authorities and inform you of any changes. ...

Sources of information for research about inscriptions or addresses:
- *the International Tracing Service (https://www.its-arolsen. org/english/)*
- *the Federal Archives of Germany (http://www.bundesarchiv. de/index.html.en)*
- *the Memorial Book (http://www.bundesarchiv.de/ gedenkbuch/directory.html)*

NB: We consider this a reliable source. Inscriptions for Stolpersteine should tally with the information found in the Memorial Book. If your information does not tally, please inform the Federal Archives. They will do their best to amend their information even if this might not occur immediately.

- *Yad Vashem (http://www.yadvashem.org)*
- *local archives and historical societies*
- *the Union of Persecutees of the Nazi Regime (VPN)*
- *trade unions*
- *churches*
- *groups and associations for Sinti and Roma*
- *groups and associations for homosexuals*
- *groups and associations for Jehovah's Witnesses*
- *hospitals can provide information on the Nazis' euthanasia programs.* [2]

---

2 www.stolpersteine.eu/en; with written permission of Gunter Demnig, April 29, 2021.

Our Significant 4 in Germany taught us that the three criteria for a person to "qualify" to have a Stolperstein placed are:

- The person was forced by the Nazi government into a ghetto and/or concentration camp; this includes those who survived as well as those who died.

- The person was forced to flee and/or hide in order to escape their horrific outcome if arrested by the Nazis.

- The person committed suicide, choosing the time & method of his/her own death, thereby "cheating" (this author's interpretation) the Nazis of their glory in arresting, torturing, dehumanizing, and killing them.

We also learned that Stolpersteine are purposely placed directly into the pavement, flush with the level of the sidewalk. Besides the obvious safety factor of not wanting to create an actual fall risk if the stones are raised, which may or may not have even been considered, there is a lot of symbolism in the placement and size of the stones.

First, they are placed at the last known *freely-chosen* residence of the victims, which is one reason why accurate research is critical prior to each Stolperstein's installation. This means the last place the victims chose to live in – on their own, of their own free will, before they were abducted by the Gestapo, had their homes seized and their livelihoods taken from them by Nazi bans which made it against the law for any other Germans to employ them or frequent their businesses.

Second, the Stolpersteine are placed in the ground, causing people to *bow down* in order to read the inscriptions. Third, they are smaller than some of the larger memorials to victims of National Socialism so that they are more readily called to a person's attention as they walk by or on the shiny plaques in the ground. Therefore, while the Stolpersteine Art Project is meant to keep alive the memory of the individual victims as well as the memory of what happened to them, the smaller Stolpersteine placed into pavements of neighborhood streets may elicit a deeper intrusion of memory into everyday life, according to Demnig. Furthermore, the stones emphasize that every victim's life was significant, not just a statistic, and that each victim lived "here", in this neighborhood (*Hier wohnte* – Here lived...) – not in some unknown place. As well, noted previously, the German word Stolpersteine literally means stumbling stones or blocks. Even before the Holocaust, it was common in Germany to say when someone tripped or stumbled that "There must be a Jew buried there." An anti-semitic "warning"? Finally, here is my symbolic interpretation of Stolpersteine: either these stones may be "stumbled upon" and noticed by people walking down the street, thereby causing people to look at them and "remember" the significance of that person's life as well as what happened to them, or perhaps it means that each victim's life was "interrupted" by the Shoah – thereby creating a "stumbling block" that interfered with, and usually ended, their life. Perhaps both apply simultaneously.

During our days in Germany, we were appalled and upset to learn that when Jewish cemeteries were destroyed throughout Nazi Germany, the gravestones were often stolen, vandalized, destroyed, and/or recycled as sidewalk paving stones. Those actions represent desecration of the memories of the dead. When people walk on the recycled sidewalk pavements, they are therefore walking on the gravestones of the dead. In addition, over time the Stolpersteine brass plaques become dirty, dusty, blurred, and blackened from repeated footsteps, making it difficult to read the individuals' inscriptions. These factors led to opposition to Stolpersteine by some of Munich's Jewish community, who have since implemented an alternative method of commemoration since July 2018. Their alternative method of commemoration consists of wider memorial plaques, made out of a different material, placed on the walls outside the last known home or workplace of the victim. Munich, known as the home of the Nazi movement, remains the only major German city to ban Stolpersteine in public places, though there are some Stolpersteine installed there on private property. Thus, the "new" memorial plaques on Munich's public buildings now co-exist with the Stolpersteine in pavements on private property. To clarify, those Munich Jewish citizens in opposition to Stolpersteine very much supported the idea of some form of commemoration for victims of the Holocaust. They just opposed the specific method of Stolpersteine being placed in the pavement, which method is ongoing today throughout Europe since the first Stolperstein installation in Cologne, Germany by Gunter Demnig in 1992.

Once the research about a particular person is completed, individual Stolperstein are manufactured by hand. In this process, the person's name, dates and locations of birth, deportation, and death, if known, are engraved into the brass plaque. Besides the words *Hier wohnte...* ("Here lived...") engraved on most of these plaques, many also have the word "*Ermordet*": German for "murdered".

Finally, during a public ceremony with the town's citizens in attendance, and sometimes with the descendants of the victims present, Stolpersteine are then inserted, delicately and reverently like a fragile plant, into the pavement at the individual's last known freely-chosen residence or workplace. Often there are several Stolpersteine placed at the same "address". This is because Hitler ordered the victims to move from place to place, allowing them to bring only minimal clothing and possessions with them while they were awaiting deportation. Often, as in our family's case, they were forced to move in with other family members who'd also been "downsized", creating cramped living quarters with little if any privacy, no control over what was happening to them, nor any power to change their circumstances because they would risk death and worse forms of imprisonment.

My family and I have had the bittersweet privilege of watching Gunter Demnig silently carve out the existing pavement where each Stolperstein will be laid, insert the stone into its carved-out resting place, and then dust off and shine each laid Stolperstein, leaving it polished, bright, and easy to read for the details of the individual victim commemorated. As the ceremony concludes, there is a final poignant gesture of compassion, kindness, and respect for the significance of each victim's life, which my family and I have also been privileged to observe: young students from the town place roses around the Stolpersteine.

Stolpersteine commemorate. Stolpersteine memorialize. Stolpersteine "remember" each victim as someone who mattered, so that they will never be forgotten. Those individuals were marginalized, traumatized, and victimized by the Nazi regime because they were labeled by Hitler and his Nazis as "different", "other", a "burden" to German society, not the "perfect Aryan" (Sound familiar?). Without any trials, due process, or evidence, they were blamed and shamed falsely, tortured and exterminated, for practically everything negative that befell Germany and Europe long before Hitler and his Nazi party came into power – and beyond. Remember: Besides being Jewish and non-Jewish, those individuals targeted by the Nazi regime for systematic persecution and mass murder were loving family members, neighbors and friends, babies, children, unborn children, parents, grandparents, cousins, aunts and uncles, nieces and nephews, brothers and sisters, sons and daughters. Some of them were our family, on Jeffrey and Gail's side. Some of them were my biological family, recently discovered maternal ancestor victims, and quite likely there are victims that we do not know about from my paternal ancestors as well. Were some of them your family?

While there were indeed Sheroes and Heroes in many countries including Germany during those tragic years (HIAS, England's Kindertransport, and the Jewish Resistance), despite the very real obstacles and dangers, there were still far too many citizens and world leaders in Germany, Europe, and even the United States whose response was silence and not allowing immigrants fleeing from persecution and certain death to seek refuge and asylum in their own countries (Sound familiar?), rather than taking emergency humane actions to stop the genocide and save lives. As well, you may recall that British Soldiers refused entry to Palestine, as it was called at that time, to a number of ships with Jewish refugees seeking asylum from Nazi persecution, including the "Exodus". The true story of those Jewish refugees on that ship is portrayed in a well-known movie by the same name.

In Germany, silence persisted amidst the evidence of smoke and ashes from the crematoriums blowing into their backyards as their own children played, amidst Kristallnacht's November 9-10, 1938's vandalism of Jewish neighborhoods and businesses and the burning of Synagogues, amidst watching Jews being forced by Nazi laws to step off the sidewalk into the streets when any German was walking by, amidst seeing Jews and other victims being publicly humiliated – Rabbis' beards being publicly shaved off in the streets, being marched through town with their yellow Jude star badges, amidst watching neighbors being falsely arrested, forcibly removed from their homes by the Gestapo, and then "disappearing", amidst some's self-perceptions of being "privileged" – according to a definition I recall from one of the female speakers at the January 21, 2017 first National Womens March in Washington, DC: "The definition of privilege is not being concerned about an issue or taking action to create positive change... because it doesn't affect you personally." That was a huge personal bucket of ice in my face when I heard that, and along with Martin Niemöller's quotation "First they came" – it continues to inspire me to take ongoing actions for social justice for every group of people – for we are all brothers and sisters, we are all human beings part of the same family of Humanity – Mishpacha.

Our Significant 4 told us that it was only much later during the Holocaust, not in the early years, when it became a risk to one's own life – the risk of being arrested, imprisoned in the camps, or killed themselves – if they were caught trying to help the victims. And yet, even that didn't stop those neighbors, friends, and strangers who did secretly hide Jewish people, bring them food, create counterfeit visas and names for them, help them escape, or take in persecuted victims' Jewish babies and children to raise them in their own non-Jewish religion to save those children's lives. Those responding with silence and prohibiting persecuted victims from entering their own safer country contributed to the mass suffering and loss of so many more lives... unnecessarily, and for a longer period of time.

If **I and we** choose to stick our heads in the sand, turn a blind eye or a deaf ear, or respond with nothing but a mute voice...

If **I and we** choose not to pay attention to local and global news, not to learn from history, not to take any action amidst the persistent 2021 domestic and global acts of violence, hate crimes, mass shootings, and the caste system and systemic racism that persists in our own country ... **I and we** are no better than the too-many others who did the same in the past, who **I and we** continue to pass judgment on today, **I and we** are doomed to repeat history – and in fact we are already doing so with regard to the five current ongoing international genocides (mentioned in a future chapter). Tragically, we know how history turned out. If **I and we** continue to say nothing, do nothing, the only thing that will happen is that more of our brothers and sisters will continue to suffer and die unnecessarily. If that happens, shame on us and our leaders.

Chapter 3

WHO IS CONSIDERED A HOLOCAUST SURVIVOR?

The Holocaust was the genocide of six million European Jews and millions of non-Jews during World War II.

Of note, when I was googling 3/2/21 to check the accuracy of "The Final Solution" phrase, another link to click on was: "Best Holocaust documentaries." I know that means which documentaries best portray the truth of the Holocaust in all its horror and man's inhumanity to man, but the way it's written implies that the two words "best" and "Holocaust" belong not only in the same phrase, but also next to each other – which they clearly do not. What a chilling oxymoron!

"Who" is considered a Holocaust "Survivor" differs amongst Holocaust researchers, prominent relevant organizations, as well as "Survivors" themselves. As well, my research revealed that the criteria for who's considered a Survivor has also changed over the past 76 years since the war and the Holocaust ended.

The US Holocaust Memorial Museum acknowledges as Jewish Holocaust survivors those who were displaced, persecuted, or discriminated against due to the racial, religious, ethnic, social, and political policies of the Nazis and their collaborators between 1933 and 1945. In addition to former inmates of concentration camps, ghettos, and prisons, this includes, among others, people who were refugees or were in hiding. Roma and Sinti, Poles and other Slavic peoples, Soviet prisoners of war, persons with disabilities, political prisoners, trade union leaders, "subversive" artists, those Catholic and Lutheran clergy who were seen as opponents of the regime, resisters, Jehovah's Witnesses, male homosexuals, and criminal offenders, among others were also victims of Nazi persecution. [1]

Yad Vashem, the World Holocaust Remembrance Center

---

1   www.ushmm.org/remember/holocaust-survivors

in Israel, defined a Holocaust Survivor as follows when I first researched it several years ago: "It is difficult to define the term Survivor." [2] That's it, nothing more, nothing less. Their definition has changed over time, as noted in an article by Emanuella Grinberg in Smithsonian Magazine:

Philosophically, one might say that all Jews, anywhere in the world, who were still alive by the end of 1945, survived the Nazi genocidal intention, yet this is too broad a definition, as it lacks the distinction between those who suffered the tyrannical Nazi "boot on their neck," and those who might have, had the war against Nazism been lost. At Yad Vashem, we define Shoah survivors as Jews who lived for any amount of time under Nazi domination, direct or indirect, and survived. This includes French, Bulgarian and Romanian Jews who spent the entire war under anti-Jewish terror regimes but were not all deported, as well as Jews who forcefully left Germany in the late 1930s. From a larger perspective, other destitute Jewish refugees who escaped their countries fleeing the invading German army, including those who spent years and in many cases died deep in the Soviet Union, may also be considered Holocaust survivors. No historical definition can be completely satisfactory. [3]

As well, Grinberg writes in her article: "No single authority determines whether or not a person is considered a Holocaust survivor." Of glaring absence to me in Yad Vashem's definition above are all the other millions of victims who were not Jewish! I don't know if there is more to the definition that might include non-Jews that isn't included in the article above, if the omission of non-Jews was accidental or purposeful, or what might be the reason for that.

Unexpectedly, I discovered a Social Security Administration definition of a Holocaust Survivor, likely used for determination of benefits.

---

2   www.yadvashem.org

3   Smithsonianmag.com/history/what-and-who-defines-being-holocaust-survivor-180972076/"How the Definition of Holocaust Survivor Has Changed Since the End of World War II", Emanuella Grinberg, May 1, 2019.

Program Operations Manual System (POMS) – Social Security
Effective Dates: 12/21/1999 – Present
GN 00302.327 Definition of Holocaust Survivor

A. General: This policy applies to survivors of the Holocaust. However, not everyone who was caught up in the events preceding and during World War II qualifies to use these procedures. Only those who meet the definition below may have their DB established under the special procedures.

B. Definition:

For purposes of this policy, individuals who meet the following requirements qualify as survivors for whom the special rules of evidence apply.

If the individual was a:

- *Member of a group of people who were systematically persecuted and exterminated by the Nazis: examples: Jews, Gypsies, Jehovah's Witnesses, Blacks, Asian or Pacific Islanders,* ***and*** *...*
- *Misstated his/her age to avoid: Persecution by the Nazis, or Confinement in concentration camps, or Extermination in concentration camps, or Other threats to life by the Nazis,* ***and also*** *...*
- *Presented acceptable evidence of survivor status,* ***then*** *... The individual is a Holocaust survivor and the special rules of evidence in GN 00302.330 will apply.* [4]

More recently in 2016, Dr. Rebecca Clifford wrote in the British Academy blog:

These days, we take a broad view when we discuss the concept of a 'survivor' in this context: all those who, because of their Jewish origins, faced the prospect of murder by the Nazis or their collaborators during the Second World War – but lived – are now seen as survivors. This includes those who lived through the horror of the concentration camps, but also those who survived in ghettos, in hiding, by passing as non-Jews, by joining the partisans – our current understanding of a 'survivor' is widely, and rightly, anyone

---

4   https://secure.ssa.gov/apps10/poms.nsf/lnx/ 0200302327

who escaped murder by whatever means possible. [5]

A visit to the Kindertransport Association website reveals their definition:

A Holocaust survivor is a person who was displaced, persecuted, and/or discriminated against by the racial, religious, ethnic, and political policies of the Nazis and their allies. The Kindertransport children are child Holocaust survivors. [6]

What I've personally gleaned from the literature is that the definitions of "Holocaust Survivor" have changed over the years to become more inclusive of identified victims, including many more individuals in addition to those who were imprisoned in concentration camps, for example, "flight survivors" – those who fled, those who were saved by Kindertransports, those who were partisans/resisters and fought back, those who hid, and others impacted by the Holocaust. As well, Holocaust literature appears to include two common themes in varying degrees: suffering and loss, which has sometimes been a bone of contention even amongst Holocaust Survivors, i.e. who suffered more and who lost more.

Therefore, depending on which of these experts' criterion you accept, Erna, Siegfried, and Erwin, along with my father-in-law Ralph – were all Holocaust-Shoah Survivors. Yet my father-in-law never considered himself one – saying he believed that only those who'd survived Nazi Concentration Camps, who had numbers tattooed on their arms, were Holocaust Survivors. Immediately after WWII for some time, that was the definition of a Holocaust Survivor.

From my childhood and throughout my life, I learned my information about the Shoah from textbooks, Sunday School, non-fiction books, fiction novels, and movies. [7] Once married to Jeffrey for years, I learned some more information from the bits and pieces that my father-in-law shared (He shared little, and

---

5   https://www.thebritishacademy.ac.uk/blog/who-holocaust-survivor/ Who is a Holocaust Survivor? by Dr. Rebecca Clifford, Jan 27, 2016.

6   www.kindertransport.org/history09_FAQ.htm#1

7   "Exodus"; "Life is Beautiful"; "Sophie's Choice"; "Schindler's List"

only if we asked.), attending Yom Hashoah remembrance events in the Baltimore community with him, as well as without him after he died. Of course, we continue to learn even more from our Significant 4 in Germany, beginning with Oliver's "finding" us in 2014.

With the plethora of evidence available, including well-kept documentation by the Nazis themselves, I cannot understand how anyone can continue to cling to their false belief that the Holocaust is "made up, fictional, or wasn't that bad". I cannot understand how anyone can choose to accept such a falsehood and deny with such conviction that the Holocaust ever occurred.

As hurtful, tragic, and unacceptable as anti-Semitism and Holocaust denial is for Jewish people, they are not the only "peoples" throughout history and ongoing to be marginalized, isolated, and scapegoated with false blame for causing events throughout millennia that created suffering for others. Jewish people have been falsely blamed for killing Jesus, causing the Black Plague, being responsible for hard economic times, and being responsible for Germany's losing WWI, to name a few. Sadly, there are more "antis". You know them... all the "antis" you "bear witness" to on the daily news.

Similarities between the Caste System and the Holocaust

In her 2020 best-selling book "Caste: The Origins of Our Discontents", Isabel Wilkerson discusses three caste systems, naming these three groups of chronically marginalized scapegoats throughout history and tragically ongoing in 2021:

- The Untouchables – the lowest caste in India;
- People of color – back to generations of slavery in America;
- Jews – most chillingly during the Nazi regime in Germany and Europe. (Author's note: And let's not forget the Roman Era and the Spanish Inquisition.)

Until I read her book, I was only aware of one caste system

– India's. I am grateful to her for expanding my horizons, enlightening me with facts, history, and her perspectives, and for enriching and continuing to transform me into the person I am still becoming.

As you read the following select excerpts [8] from her book "Caste: The Origins of Our Discontents", I encourage you to think not only about this chapter's definitions of Holocaust Survivors and victims, not only about the other groups of people impacted by caste systems she writes about, but most importantly – think about your own beliefs and values, and keep an open mind.

Wilkerson writes:

A caste system is an artificial construction, a fixed and embedded ranking of human value that sets the presumed supremacy of one group against the presumed inferiority of other groups on the basis of ancestry and often immutable traits, traits that would be neutral in the abstract but are ascribed life-and-death meaning in a hierarchy favoring the dominant caste whose forebears designed it. A caste system uses rigid, often arbitrary boundaries to keep the ranked groupings apart, distinct from one another and in their assigned places.

Throughout human history, three caste systems have stood out. The tragically accelerated, chilling, and officially vanquished caste system of Nazi Germany. The lingering, millennia-long caste system of India. And the shape-shifting, unspoken, race-based caste pyramid in the United States. Each version relied on stigmatizing those deemed inferior to justify the dehumanization necessary to keep the lowest-ranked people at the bottom and to rationalize the protocols of enforcement. A caste system endures because it is often justified as divine will, originating from sacred text or the presumed laws of nature, reinforced throughout the culture and passed down through the generations. [9]

... In the years leading to this moment (author's note: the 2016 US elections), it had begun to spread on talk radio and cable television that the white share of the population was shrinking.

---

8   Publisher's written permission granted to include these excerpts.
9   Wilkerson, Isabel. "Caste: The Origins of Our Discontents", New York, Random House, 2020: 17.

In the summer of 2008, the U.S. Census Bureau announced its projection that, by 2042, for the first time in American history, whites would no longer be the majority in a country that had known of no other configuration, no other way to be.

Then, that fall, in the midst of what seemed a cataclysmic financial crisis and as if to announce a potential slide from preeminence for the caste that had long been dominant, an African-American, a man from what was historically the lowest caste, was elected president of the United States. His ascension incited both premature declarations of a post-racial world and an entire movement whose sole purpose was to prove that he had not been born in the United States, a campaign led by the billionaire who was now in 2016 running for president himself. [10]

After the 2016 American presidential election,

What had happened to America? What could account for tens of millions of voters choosing to veer from all custom and to put the country and thus the world in the hands of an untested celebrity, one who had never served in either war or public office, unlike every man before him, and one whose rhetoric seemed a homing device for extremists? [11]

... How could so many people, ordinary working folks, who needed healthcare and education for their children, protection of the water they drink and the wages they depended upon, 'vote against their own interests', as many progressives were heard to say in the fog of that turning point in political history? ...

... The earth had shifted overnight, or so it appeared. ...

... Only recently have geophysicists had technology sensitive enough to detect the unseen stirrings deeper in the earth's core. They are called silent earthquakes. And only recently have circumstances forced us, in this current era of human rupture, to search for the unseen stirrings of the human heart, to discover the origins of our discontents. [12]

Wilkerson states that in researching her book, she looked *... into the world's most recognized caste system, India's, and*

---

10 Ibid., 6.
11 Ibid., 10.
12 Ibid., 11.

examin(ed) the parallels, overlaps, and contrasts between the one that prevailed in my own country and the original. I also sought to comprehend the molecular, concentrated evil that had produced the caste system imposed in Nazi Germany and found startling, unsettling connections between the United States and Germany in the decades leading to the Third Reich. [13]

.... The Nazis had been especially taken with the militant race theories of two widely known American eugenicists, Lothrop Stoddard and Madison Grant. Both were men of privilege, born and raised in the North and educated in the Ivy League. Both built their now discredited reputations on hate ideology ... and advocated for the exclusion and elimination of 'races' they deemed threats to Nordic racial purity, foremost among them Jews and 'Negroes'. [14]

A racial slur that the Nazis adopted in their campaign to dehumanize Jews and other Non-Aryans – the word Untermensch, meaning "subhuman" – came to them from the New England-born eugenicist Lothrop Stoddard. ... [15]

Hitler had studied America from afar, both envying and admiring it, and attributed its achievement to its Aryan stock. He praised the country's near genocide of Native Americans and the exiling to reservations of those who had survived.... The Nazis were impressed by the American custom of lynching its subordinate caste of African-Americans, having become aware of the ritual torture and mutilations that typically accompanied them. Hitler especially marveled at the American 'knack for maintaining an air of robust innocence in the wake of mass death'.

By the time that Hitler rose to power, the United States 'was not just a country with racism,' Whitman, the Yale legal scholar, wrote. 'It was the leading racist jurisdiction – so much so that even Nazi Germany looked to America for inspiration'. The Nazis recognized the parallels even if many Americans did not. [16] *...*

In their search for prototypes, the Nazis had looked into white-dominated countries such as Australia and South Africa, but 'there

---

13   Ibid., 28.
14   Ibid., 79-80.
15   Ibid., 80.
16   Ibid., 81.

were no other models for miscegenation [17] law that the Nazis could find in the world,' Whitman wrote. Their overwhelming interest was in the 'classic example', the United States of America. [18]

... Hitler had made it to the chancellery in a brokered deal that conservative elites agreed to only because they were convinced they could hold him in check and make use of him for their own political aims. They underestimated his cunning and overestimated his base of support, which had been the very reason they had felt they needed him in the first place. ... The old guard did not foresee, or chose not to see, that his actual mission was 'to exploit the methods of democracy to destroy democracy.'

By the time they recognized their fatal miscalculation, it was too late. Hitler had risen as an outside agitator, a cult figure enamored of pageantry and rallies with parades of people carrying torches that an observer said looked like 'rivers of fire.' Hitler saw himself as the voice of the Volk, [19] of their grievances and fears, especially those in the rural districts, as a G-d-chosen savior, running on instinct. He had never held elected office before. [20]

As soon as he was sworn in as chancellor, the Nazis unfurled their swastikas, a Sanskrit symbol linking them to their Aryan 'roots', and began to close in on the Jews. They stoked ancient resentments that dated back to the Middle Ages but that rose again when the Jews were made the scapegoats for Germany's loss and humiliation at the end of World War I. Seen as dominant in banking and finance, Jews were blamed for the insufficient financial support of the war effort, although historians now widely acknowledge that Germany lost on the battlefield and not solely for lack of funds. [21] ...

---

17 Miscegenation: See https://www.merriam-webster.com/ dictionary/miscegenation – a mixture of races especially: marriage, cohabitation, or sexual intercourse between a white person and a member of another race. The word miscegenation is associated especially with historical laws against interracial marriage. In the United States, such laws were declared unconstitutional in 1967.

18 "Caste", 82.

19 Volk: See https://www.merriam-webster.com/ dictionary/ Volk – German phrase: one people, one realm, one leader – motto of Nazi Germany.

20 "Caste", 82.

21 Ibid., 82-83.

What the Nazis could not understand, however, was why, in America, 'the Jews, who are also of interest to us, are not reckoned among the coloreds,' when it was so obvious to the Nazis that Jews were a separate 'race' and when America had already shown some aversion by imposing quotas on Jewish immigration. [22] *...*

In September 1935, Hitler summoned the Reichstag to the annual Nazi rally in Nuremberg to announce new legislation that had been incubating since the Nazi takeover. By then, Hitler had either imprisoned or killed many of his political opponents, including the murders of twelve members of the Reichstag and of his longtime friend Ernst Rohm, the head of a Nazi paramilitary unit, the S.A. All of this rendered the Reichstag a puppet arm of the government, having been intimidated into submission. [23] *...*

That legislation, the Nuremberg Laws, defined who was a Jew, *... banned marriage and intercourse outside of marriage between Jews and Germans, and it forbade German women under forty-five to work in a Jewish household.*

Thus began a campaign of ever-tightening restrictions. Jews were henceforth stripped of citizenship, prohibited from displaying the German flag, denied passports. With that announcement, 'Germany became a full-fledged racist regime,' the historian George M. Fredrickson wrote. 'American laws were the main foreign precedents for such legislation.' [24]

Comparing the subjugation of Jews, African-Americans, and the Untouchables of India, Wilkerson writes:

Held hostage in labor camps in different centuries and an ocean apart, both Jews and African-Americans were subjected to a program of purposeful dehumanization. Upon their arrival at the concentration camps, Jews were stripped of the clothing and accoutrements of their former lives, of everything they had owned. Their heads were shaved, their distinguishing features of sideburns or mustaches or the crowns of lush hair, were deleted from them. They were no longer individuals, they were no longer personalities to consider, to engage with, to take into account.

---

22 Ibid., 85.
23 Ibid., 86.
24 Ibid., 87.

During the morning and evening roll calls, they were forced to stand sometimes for hours into the night as the SS officers counted the thousands of them to check for any escapees. They stood in the freezing cold or summer heat in the same striped uniforms, with the same shorn heads, same sunken cheeks. They became a single mass of self-same bodies, purposely easier for SS officers to distance themselves from, to feel no human connection with. Loving fathers, headstrong nephews, beloved physicians, dedicated watchmakers, rabbis, and piano tuners, all merged into a single mass of undifferentiated bodies that were no longer seen as humans deserving of empathy but as objects over whom they could exert total control and do whatever they wanted to. They were no longer people, they were numbers, a means to an end.

Upon their arrival at the auction blocks and labor camps of the American South, Africans were stripped of their given names and forced to respond to new ones, as would a dog to a new owner, often mocking names like Caesar or Samson or Dred. They were stripped of their past lives and identities as Yoruba or Asante or Igbo, as the son of a fisherman, nephew of the village priest, or daughter of a midwife. Decades afterward, Jews were stripped of their given and surnames and forced to memorize the prison numbers assigned them in the concentration camps. Millennia ago, the Untouchables of India were assigned surnames that identified them by the lowly work they performed, forcing them to announce their degradation every time they introduced themselves, while the Brahmins, many quite literally, carried the names of the g-ds. [25] ...

At the depths of their dehumanization, both Jews and African-Americans were subjected to gruesome medical experimentation at the hands of dominant-cast physicians. [26] ...

(S)cholar David Livingstone Smith, who specializes in the study of dehumanization, wrote: 'Dehumanization is a joint creation of biology, culture and the architecture of the human mind.'... 'The human story is filled with pain and tragedy, but among the horrors that we have perpetrated on one another, the persecution and attempted extermination of the Jewish people, the brutal enslavement of Africans, and the destruction of Native American

25   Ibid., 142-143.
26   Ibid., 147.

civilizations in many respects are unparalleled.' [27]

In America, (a) certain kind of violence was part of an unspoken curriculum for generations of children in the dominant caste. 'White culture desensitized children to racial violence,' wrote the historian Kristina DuRocher, 'so they could perpetuate it themselves one day.'" [28]

Ms. Wilkerson further shared how the 2020 COVID pandemic has exposed the disparities in available healthcare and deaths in the US.

'To a watching world,' wrote 'The Guardian', 'the absence of a fair, affordable US healthcare system, the cut-throat contest between American states for scarce medical supplies, the disproportionate death toll among ethnic minorities, chaotic social distancing rules, and a lack of centralized coordination are reminiscent of a poor, developing country, not the most powerful, influential nation on earth.'

The pandemic, and the country's fitful, often self-centered lack of readiness, exposed 'a failure of character unparalleled in US history,' in the words of Stephen Walt, a professor of international relations at Harvard University. [29] ...

Ms. Wilkerson describes her trip to Germany while researching her book, "Caste". ... *Nigel Dunkley, a former British officer and now a historian of Nazi Germany,* [30] was her Guide there at selected sites of historical import.

'We have a memorial to everyone victimized by the Nazis,' Dunkley said. 'There is a memorial to homosexuals who perished. There is a memorial to the Sinti and Roma right outside the Reichstag. We have lesser memorials to lesser groups. And then we have the stumbling stones.'

These are the micro-memorials of discreet brass squares the size of one's palm inscribed with the names of Holocaust victims and placed throughout the city. More than seventy thousand of these

---

27   Ibid., 149.
28   Ibid., 150.
29   Ibid., 357.
30   Ibid., 343.

stumbling stones, known as Stolpersteine, have been forged and installed in cities across Europe. They are embedded among the cobblestones in front of houses and apartment buildings where the victims whose names are inscribed on them are known to have last lived before being abducted by the Gestapo. 'Here lived Hildegard Blumenthal, born 1897, deported 1943, died in Auschwitz,' reads a stumbling stone clustered among others outside an apartment building in western Berlin. Nearby are the stones for Rosa Gross and Arthur Benjamin, who were deported in 1942 and who perished in Riga.

The stumbling stones force the viewer to pause and squint to read the inscription, force the viewer to regard the entry doors the people walked through, the steps they climbed with their groceries and toddlers, the streets they strolled that were the everyday life of real people rather than abstractions of incomprehensible millions. Each one is a personal headstone that gives a momentary connection to a single individual. Leaning over to read the names on the stumbling stones forces you to bow in respect. [31]

Wilkerson further describes the stark contrast between the Germans' sense of duty and humanity to the Nazi victims after the Shoah versus America's homage to the Confederates after the Civil War. Mr. Dunkley took her to the site of Hitler's hideout, *... built thirty feet underground and protected by two meters of reinforced concrete ... where he shot himself in the head after biting into a cyanide pill, and where his hours-long wife (Eva Braun) had bitten into a cyanide pill just before him, on April 30, 1945. His body was unceremoniously dragged to a nearby lot and set afire.*

In America, the men who mounted a bloody war against the United States to keep the right to enslave humans for generations went on to live out their retirement in comfort. .... When they (Confederate president Jefferson Davis and Robert E. Lee) died, they were both granted state funerals with military honors and were revered with statues and monuments.

An American author living in Berlin, who happens to be Jewish and to have been raised in the South, often gets asked about Germany's memorials to its Nazi past. 'To which I respond: There

---

31   Ibid., 344.

aren't any,' Susan Neiman, author of *Learning from the Germans: Race and the Memory of Evil*, has written. 'Germany has no monuments that celebrate the Nazi armed forces, however many grandfathers fought or fell for them.'

Rather than honor supremacists with statues and pedestals, Germany, after decades of silence and soul-searching, chose to erect memorials to the victims of its aggressions and to the courageous people who resisted the men who inflicted atrocities on human beings.

They built a range of museums to preserve the story of the country's descent into madness. They converted the infamous villa at Wannsee, where fifteen men worked out the details of the Final Solution to kill the Jews of Europe, into a museum examining the consequences of that fateful decision. The country converted the Gestapo headquarters into a museum called the Topography of Terror, a deep dive into the founding of the Third Reich. [32]

As for the man who oversaw these atrocities, Germany chose quite literally to pave over the Fuhrer's gravesite. There could be no more pedestrian resolution than that.

In Germany, displaying the swastika is a crime punishable by up to three years in prison. In the United States, the rebel flag is incorporated into the official state flag of Mississippi. It can be seen on the backs of pickup trucks north and south, fluttering along highways in Georgia and the other former Confederate states. A Confederate flag the size of a bedsheet flapped in the wind off an interstate in Virginia around the time of the Charlottesville rally.

In Germany, there is no death penalty. 'We can't be trusted to kill people after what happened in World War II,' a German woman once told me. In America, the states that recorded the highest number of lynchings, among them the former Confederate States of America, all currently have the death penalty.

In Germany, few people will proudly admit to having been related to Nazis or will openly defend the Nazi cause. 'Not even members of Germany's right-wing Alternative for Germany party,' wrote Neiman, 'would suggest glorifying that part of the past.' ...

In Germany, some of the Nazis who did not kill themselves were

---

32   Author's note: We explored this museum with our Significant 4 when we were in Germany.

tracked down and forced to stand trial. Many were hanged at the hands of the Allies for their crimes against humanity. The people who kidnapped and held hostage millions of people during slavery, condemning them to slow death, were not called to account and did not stand trial.

In Germany, restitution has rightly been paid, and continues to be paid, to survivors of the Holocaust. In America, it was the slaveholders who got restitution, not the people whose lives and wages were stolen from them for twelve generations. Those who instilled terror on the lowest caste over the following century after the formal end of slavery, those who tortured and killed humans before thousands of onlookers or who aided and abetted those lynchings or who looked the other way, well into the twentieth century, not only went free but rose to become leading figures – southern governors, senators, sheriffs, businessmen, mayors. [33] *...*

(At the) Wittenbergplatz subway station [34] *off Kurfursten-damm, ... the Fifth Avenue of Berlin ... It was through these station doors that thousands of Jews took their last look at their beloved Berlin before being forced onto trains that would carry them to their deaths. This fact, this history, is built into the consciousness of Berliners as they go about their everyday lives. It is not something that anyone, Jew or Gentile, resident or visitor, is expected to put behind them or to just get over. They do not run from it. It has become a part of who they are because it is a part of what they have been. They incorporate it into their identity because it is, in fact, them.*

It is a mandatory part of every school curriculum, even for grade school students, and it is never far from view for any citizen. This is not to say that everyone is in agreement as to the lengths to which the country goes to reinforce this history. What seems not in contention is the necessity of remembering. [35] *...*

---

33 "Caste", 345-347.

34 Ibid., 348. There is a sign at the station, in German, translated here: "Places of Horror That We Should Never Forget. Then it lists the places never to be forgotten: Auschwitz, Dachau, Bergen-Belsen, Treblinka, Buchenwald, Sachsenhausen, and half a dozen other concentration camps."

35 Ibid., 347-348.

When Dunkley takes German students on tours of the history of the Third Reich, he asks them their reaction to what they have seen. 'Do you as Germans feel any guilt for what the Germans did?' he will ask them.

They will go off into groups and have heated discussions among themselves, and then come back to him with their thoughts.

'Yes, we are Germans, and Germans perpetrated this,' some students once told him, echoing what others have said. 'And though it wasn't just Germans, it is the older Germans who were here who should feel guilt. We were not here. We ourselves did not do this. But we do feel that, as the younger generation, we should acknowledge and accept the responsibility. And for the generations that come after us, we should be the guardians of the truth.' [36]

'This is a civilization searching for its humanity,' Gary Michael Tartakov, an American scholar of caste, said of this country (America). 'It dehumanized others to build its civilization. Now it needs to find its own.' [37]

Frightening. Shocking. Too many similarities between Nazi Germany and the United States. Quiet your mind ... think about this: Does any of it sound familiar to America's repeated and ongoing stains of history of White Supremacists and others marginalizing those perceived as "others?"

Here in America, some Americans have perpetrated stealing Native American lands and forcing the people to live on reservations, slavery, eugenics, lynchings, separate water fountains and restrooms for whites and "coloreds/Negroes," FDR's turning away Jews who were fleeing from Nazi persecution in the '30s, Jim Crow laws, "redlining" in communities, recent prior American Administration policies, language, and actions between January 20, 2017 at noon – January 20, 2021 at noon, publicly calling Mexicans "bad hombres, drug dealers, criminals, and rapists", closing America's borders, establishing laws to prevent immigration of anyone perceived as "other," and turning away those seeking asylum in our country to flee violence in their own, Georgia's governor signing voter-suppression laws in

36   Ibid., 349.
37   Ibid., 357.

March 2021 (and a number of other states introducing the same), politicians lying and supporting their leader – relying on him and his large base of supporters to attain their own political goals, the insurrection at our US Capitol in Washington, DC on January 6, 2021 that cost lives and so much more, the torch-carrying men of Charlottesville Virginia on August 11-12, 2017 shouting "Jews will not replace us," multiple deaths of people of color at the hands of police (mostly men), "I can't breathe," attacking peaceful protesters, political divisions, and intimidation and bullying of opponents who disagree.

As well, there are too-numerous-to-count mass shootings in the US (and elsewhere), almost always by disturbed white males: Oklahoma, the Charleston church murders, the New Zealand mosque two consecutive mass murders March 15, 2019, the Pittsburgh Synagogue murders, Sandy Hook Elementary School in Connecticut, Marjory Stoneman Douglas High School in Parkland, Florida, Columbine. Tragically, this is not an all-inclusive list.

While WWII and the Holocaust occurred during Hitler's Reich regime between 1933-1945, "caste" has existed here in the USA and globally in India for centuries: anti-these, anti-them, pick the group. There seems to be an "anti" for basically every "group name" these days. While they're too numerous to count, here are a few: LGBTQ, Latino, Muslims, Mexicans, immigrants, AAPI (Asian Americans and Pacific Islanders), "illegals", anti-Palestine, anti-Israel, anti-guns, anti-2nd amendment, and now we're hearing some new ones since 2020 related to COVID: anti-maskers, anti-half-maskers (those who wear a mask covering only their mouth, and exposing their nose), anti-vax'ers, anti-science. For every group name, you can be sure there's an "anti" group who hates them – which always leads to suffering in many forms, too often from acts of violence, hate crimes, and mass shootings. As these "antis" continue to persist and increase, they demonstrate all the stark undisguised ugliness of the human race.

> *"Those who cannot remember the past are*
> *condemned to repeat it."*
> Reason in Common Sense,
> George Santayana, 1905

This is why we must remain vigilant, because while many people frequently recite the well-known slogan borne of the Holocaust: "Never again", those words and other popularized slogans are meaningless unless we continue to take actions to ensure that these and similar tragedies never happen again.

When will we learn from our past? How much is enough? What is our Tipping Point? When will we stop practicing and bearing witness to "man's **in**humanities to man"? And when, when – will we finally begin to consistently practice and bear witness to "man's **humanities** to man"?!

Of relevance, I recall hearing a recent 2021 hopeful news report that mentioned the possibility of the US beginning to pay people of color, descendants of ancestors who were slaves, some form and amount of reparation similar to the German government's Wiedergutmachung (restitution, reparation). I googled it, and found that Evanston, Illinois is our first US city to do so. As I, too, feel shame for this prolonged dark period of American history of man's inhumanities to man, I strongly support this first US historical reparation for slavery. While I realize that we can never "repay" enough for the pain and trauma, or restore those ancestors' dignity and sense of worth – what we can do here in the US – just as Germany continues to do – is provide some form of financial reparation to individuals and families impacted. As well, we can treat every person of color the exact way we wish to be treated, because the words of our founding fathers in the Declaration of Independence should be more than words on paper. We must act on those words consistently to treat every human being as truly equal with the same equal rights that were endowed to all of us:

"We hold these truths to be self-evident, that all men are created equal, that they are endowed by their Creator with certain unalienable Rights, that among these are Life, Liberty and the pursuit of Happiness."

It's The Golden Rule, people – do it for every human being. If it's not already an ongoing daily practice, make it one.

Chapter 4

DEVELOPING EMAIL RELATIONSHIPS
January 2014 – August 2014

Throughout the eight months following Oliver's initial email in January 2014, we developed unique "email relationships" with Ira, Oliver, Rolf and his wife Christina. They all spoke English, but Rolf wrote to us in German, and his wife Christina would translate it underneath in English for us. All four are proficient in English, which was a good thing for us since we do not know the German language.

So now, let me begin to introduce you to each of our "Significant 4". There are many other German people we met who are also significant to us and our experiences. However, in 2014, we became the closest to these Significant 4, because we spent six days and evenings with them when they chose to do the research and become our personal guides for our Family Heritage journey that we'd requested. We came to "know" each other through our communicated words in our emails, as well as through our unspoken words. Each time they found new information, they asked us if we wanted them to send it to us, for it was always sad tragic news. We always said "yes" nonetheless.

Within that first month of January, Gail responded to them: "Thank you again for opening this avenue for us. My heart has sang and cried every day since I received your first email." Ira recognized the need to ask us even before we arrived if we'd need any special accommodations such as kosher food. You will learn how special these Significant 4 have become to us through the rest of the chapters, as their genuine essence will be revealed by the many stories that follow. As you continue to read, you too will realize that they are indeed Mensches. You too will realize that we came to "know" each other ...through our hearts.

Ira is a German Archivist in Meinerzhagen who contacted us shortly after Oliver did, in that first month of January 2014, seeking information we might have to clarify who's who and where their descendants might be – to see if we knew them. Ira explained that a 1989 North Rhine-Westphalia state law mandated that every town have an archive of important documents. Later in the 80s, public citizens began to research WWII and the Holocaust in Meinerzhagen, according to Ira. In fact, even before then, other groups in other towns began to research related documents as well. Sometime later in January, Ira sent us a newspaper article from her town describing a program she'd given related to WWII and the Shoah, and the article included a picture of her. It wasn't until then that we realized that Ira is a woman! Of course, being American, we thought SHE was a HE, and that HIS name was pronounced "eye-ra". Apparently, I'd forgotten about that early picture she'd sent identifying her as a woman. So much later, weeks prior to leaving for Germany in August 2014, when I asked for a picture so we could recognize Ira and Oliver at the Frankfurt Airport when we arrived – SHE sent a picture of herself with her two adult sons; SHE has long blonde hair!

Oliver is a German historian who was born in Germany, but has been living in Paris with his wife and young son since the early 2000's; his Mom still lives in Meinerzhagen, so he and his family visit Germany often. He's particularly interested in WWII and the Holocaust era. For us here in America, it sounds like a very long trip to travel from one country to another. However, from Paris to Meinerzhagen by car is less than a 6-hour drive depending on traffic! Oliver is particularly fluent in English, as if it is his first language (which it is not), and he speaks several languages. He took it upon himself at each and every event to automatically interpret what the speakers were saying in German, without us even asking. And even when our new friends began talking amongst themselves in German, he would interpret for us immediately afterward. This was but one of the many kindnesses Oliver and the others showed us.

Rolf was retired already, an active member and the Leader of the Meinerzhagen chapter of the Stolpersteine Initiative organization, which we'd never heard of before Oliver's email. Rolf had devoted a part of his life to studying forced labor and laborers, which brought him to study the Holocaust. I was acutely aware upon first seeing his name in an email that my father-in-law "Ralph" was originally named "Rolf" at birth by his parents in Germany. Sometime after coming to America, he Americanized his name to Ralph. I immediately felt "connected" to Rolf because of this, long before I ever met him in person. Rolf, 72 years old at that time – the oldest of these "Significant 4" and all of us – had more energy than all of us put together! Seriously, he put me to shame. I was huffing and puffing when we went for a "leisurely walk" around the lake in the woods one day, but Rolf didn't break a sweat or have any difficulty continuing to walk and talk at the same time! Two phrases he repeated often during our entire journey were: "Come, come, we go!", because we all were slower and often had trouble keeping up with his vitality and brisk pace. He also repeated, "We must NEVER forget!" (about the horrors and the lessons of the Shoah / the Holocaust); he always spoke this with great passion.

Rolf's wife Christina traveled the journey with him and with us, and Rolf always deferred to her for translating his emails into English for us. She became much more than her husband's interpreter. In the beginning, we didn't know much about any of these four, although within a very short time we could clearly sense their integrity and kindness.

As well, you'll be seeing Herbert on many of the emails. Herbert is also significant as a member of the Meinerzhagen Stolpersteine Initiative: he was the Founder of that chapter years ago, and he requested to please have the honor of driving us back to the Frankfurt airport at the end of our journey – which he did. The Stolpersteine Initiative is made up of volunteers who contribute to the Mission of the Initiative, choosing to join together with like-minded Germans to "repair" the injuries and atrocities the German Nazis perpetrated, doing their best to right the wrongs, right the past. This includes their advocating with neighbors and local government officials for the placement of Stolpersteine to honor the memories and significance of the lives of those murdered during the Shoah, those forced to flee, and those who chose to commit suicide because of their untenable circumstances. Those three categories of people were persecuted, tortured, and murdered – simply because of their religious, political, and/or gender preferences, because they were not "perfect Aryans" according to Hitler, and because Hitler used them as scapegoats for the negative circumstances befalling Germany. Other "righting the wrongs" by this organization include paying for the Stolpersteine, as it is not allowed for Survivors, descendants of Survivors, or descendants of those murdered in the concentration camps to pay for these special memorial stones, these "stumbling blocks".

Years after our first journey to Germany (August 2014), Dietmar and "his" Christina also became significant in our lives as the new Leaders of the Meinerzhagen Stolpersteine chapter. Gail and I spent more time with them and we got to know each other better during our Spring 2018 return. During our initial visit in August 2014, we met them only briefly at the Meinerzhagen Stolpersteine Dinner Ceremony the night before the laying of our family's Stolpersteine, where they sang and implemented the evening's program. As well, they and their daughter provided music and singing during the Stolpersteine-laying ceremonies on August 29, 2014. You'll also see Barbara and Heinz from Rexingen mentioned, and their personal museum of Holocaust history, as well as Gudrun – a special member of the Meinerzhagen chapter of the Stolpersteine Initiative who touched my soul.

Shortly after Gail's budding relationship with our Significant 4 (Ira, Oliver, Rolf, and his wife Christina) began in January 2014, she sent Oliver the last letter Dad had written to his parents, which she asked Oliver to please translate from German for us. Dad was able to continue communicating with his parents by letters from his arrival in the US in September 1938 up until the Fall of 1941, when his last letter (written by Dad on December 7, 1941) was returned to him stamped "Service suspended. Return to Sender". So although physically separated by miles and ocean, WWII, and the Holocaust, we know that Julius, Auguste, and Margot did know that Dad had indeed arrived safely in the United States and made it to Ohio to live with cousin Bella and her family (who'd emigrated from Germany much earlier, before Dad was even born). By this time in December 1941, Dad had not heard back from his parents for a month. Keep in mind that by December 1941, Kristallnacht had already occurred (November 9-10, 1938, The Night of Broken Glass), emigration was forbidden, German soldiers were being conscripted into the army, and life was even

Dad's last letter to his parents, 12/7/41; envelope returned to sender unopened.

more difficult for victimized persecuted Jews in Germany and throughout Europe.

In a January 8, 2014 email from Oliver, in which he attached the below English translation of the last letter written by Dad to his family, Oliver wrote:

"In the attachment, you will find a translation of the letter written by Ralph Stern in 1941. It is a very personal and touching document and I hope I translated the numerous idiomatic and colloquial expressions well enough (it is not so easy to translate into a foreign language). In this letter he asks whether his sister Margot is still in Rheydt. This is a city not far from Dusseldorf, and today it belongs to the city of Monchengladbach. There are plaques (Author's note: Stolpersteine) in Monchengladbach, but I have not found her name on the website of the plaque project there. In Bonn and in Bad Godesberg, there have been commemorative plaques for more than ten years now, I think. As the plaque project is not finished, it is of course possible to set a plaque for Margot Stern. The second document in German is a little bit trickier because it is in old German script and has to be transcribed first. Best regards, Oliver"

As you read Dad's last letter to his parents and sister below, keep in mind these contexts: As a young teenager in Germany, Dad had already "lived" many of Hitler's persecutory orders against the Jews together with his family before he fled Germany:

– He was banned from public school and only allowed to go to a 1-room school with one teacher for all Jewish children of that town from kindergarten through high school.

– He lost his family home in Hohenlimburg, was forced to move to a different town, Meckenheim, and moved with his sister and parents into another relative's crowded apartment there – none of this of their own free will or choice.

– He'd likely heard stories, and worse – perhaps even observed Jews being harassed and arrested in the streets. (Beards and sideburns were publicly shaven off of Rabbis and other Orthodox Jews to humiliate and dehumanize them.) According to historical references, wearing the Jewish armband badge did not begin in Germany until 1939, after Dad had arrived in the US. However, it's probable that his parents, sister, and other relatives were forced to do so.

The few times Dad did talk about his life in Germany before emigrating to the US, he told us that in the years even before the war that food was rationed. "You needed a wheelbarrow full of cash to stand in line to buy a loaf of bread, and Jewish children were no longer allowed to play outside with their non-Jewish friends, per Hitler's orders." I remember Dad saying: "It changed overnight. Our friends were not allowed to play with us anymore. My father's customers were not allowed to do business with him. A few of my father's friends came to his back door once it was dark outside so they wouldn't be seen, to apologize to him that they couldn't be seen together anymore or support his business. It was like on Monday, I went to school and played with my friends. On Tuesday, I couldn't do that anymore."

Furthermore, he and his German relatives in Ohio (and later Maryland) likely read American newspapers and listened to the news on the radio, so they must have had some idea of the worsening situation in Germany and Europe (although the Holocaust did not become publicly "known" and validated for some time). In the three years since his arrival in America at 15 years old, he'd learned how to correctly use American currency, how to speak English fluently, how to drive a car, and he had a job. From the ages of 15-18 and beyond, he was always working on a plan to rescue his family and bring them to America, but he was unable to gather the exorbitant amount of money to do so as Hitler continued persecuting and murdering Jews and other "others." Can you imagine how that must have eaten away at him, not being able to rescue his parents and sister from such harm, feeling so powerless?

Dad never continued his formal education once here in the US. I'm not clear why, though it's likely he needed or chose to work and contribute money to the household expenditures. This was one of Dad's regrets, that he never finished school, never received a high school diploma. All his life, he inaccurately perceived himself as "uneducated" because of that, when in fact he read the newspaper and listened to multiple news shows daily ("60 Minutes", a favorite over the decades), and he was more educated about current events locally, nationally, and globally than me.

It's unknown what his parents and sister may have written to him from Fall of 1938 to the Fall of 1941, as we do not have any letters from them directly to him. Jeffrey recalls that these were in a lock-box that was stolen when their home was burglarized decades ago. From the light positive tone of Dad's letter at the end of 1941, it appears quite likely that his parents were not telling him what was happening to them and other Jews. I can only speculate that either his parents were trying to protect him from the horrors of their life that he could do nothing about, or perhaps their letters were being read by the SS before they were sent – so they were worried about punishment or death if that were discovered, or the Nazis did not allow them to even send any letters to others after a certain point in time. We only have the one letter from his Mother, which she'd written to a German neighbor in 1942 (not to Dad), interpreted by Oliver as well in January. That letter's interpretation will follow in this chapter.

Here is Dad's letter (kindly interpreted by Oliver only a week or so after his initial email "finding" Gail in January 2014), the contents of which had remained a mystery to us because it was written in German to his family back home, packed away with his other painful memories in his home for 73 years at that time. This included pictures of what he "bore witness" to when he helped liberate Dachau on April 29th, 1945 as a US Army soldier. Yes, the very pictures you've likely seen in history books, newsreels, and Holocaust Museums – the mounds of confiscated shoes no longer needed by the deceased, the dead naked broken skeletal bodies in piles on the ground, gaunt adults and children wearing striped prisoners' uniforms. By the time of this letter, Dad had moved to Baltimore, Maryland to be with other relatives and get a job, and he was 18 years old (just two months shy of turning 19).

•••

Baltimore, Maryland
930 Chauncey Ave
December 7, 1941

Dear Parents,

Although I have not received any letter from you for more than four weeks, I will not make a fuss and I do not want to let you wait. Unfortunately, I forgot to wish you pleasant holidays in my last letter, and therefore, I would like to do that now. Unfortunately, I do not have any joyful message for you, like I got visas via Cuba for you, for instance. It costs more than $1500.00 per person. No one easily lends such an enormous sum. I would love to have you here, but so far I have not managed to find the money. I wish I could write you something different, but... Dear Siegfried, (Author's note: This is his cousin Erna Stern Schwarz's husband. Shortly after they'd married in Germany, they emigrated to the US because of the increasing dangers for Jews in Germany.) who has so many rich relatives here, could not even find enough money for his own parents. (According to Judi, Siegfried's family did not have rich relatives – although that was Dad's perception.). Unfortunately, the A. (Oliver's note: Americans?) are not so generous when it comes to lending money although they could easily do with a few thousand dollars less. Thus, as you, dear Mum, always write in your letters, we will have to trust in G-d and hope that everything will turn out for the best.

With every new day, I like Baltimore a little bit more. The job is just what I need and I learn quite a lot there. Although I am working in the department that deals with the (Oliver's note: spare?) parts I get to know everything nevertheless. I hope I will have learned enough soon to take a position as a motor mechanic. Then I could easily earn between $25 and $30 per week.

What is dear Margot doing? Is she still in Rheydt (Author's note: a German city)? If she got a professional training and came to the US she could easily find a very good position because there is a great demand for trained professionals here.

What news do you have? I could not tell you much about what is going on here. We are all in good health, except for uncle Jack, who has the thing with his nerves again. However, in his case, you cannot say any longer that he is ill, because he has it most of the time.

I wish you all the best for the New Year and I hope to G-d that next year I will not have to write any letters but will be able to present you my wishes personally.

Unfortunately, there is nothing else of interest I could tell you about. Please write me as soon as possible. I have been waiting for a letter from you every day and I have always been deeply disappointed.

Many greetings to everyone, in particular to Uncle Wilhelm!

Many greetings and kisses from your son...Ralph

Many greetings to Margot

Gail wrote this back to Oliver: "Oliver, thank you so much for your interpreting the last letter my Dad sent to his parents. It is truly heartbreaking, but also helps me understand my dad even more. Words cannot express my gratitude to you."

Gail forwarded us everything, and shortly after the initial email trail began, I also wrote to them. Moving forward in January, our Significant 4 began emailing all three of us together (Gail, Jeffrey, and me) so we all received the same information at the same time.

Such innocence, naivety, faith, trust, and hope at 18 years old. Of course, Dad could not have known when he wrote that letter on December 7, 1941, that:

- On that very same day, America would be unexpectedly attacked by Japan at Pearl Harbor, followed days later by Germany and Italy declaring war on the United States. Once again, America would be at war.

- Sometime after, he would volunteer along with many other patriotic citizens to join the US Army and defend America against her enemies. Those enemies now included his own German neighbors in his own Deutschland from which he'd just escaped from persecution for being Jewish several years before! Joining the US Army was how he became naturalized as a United States citizen before shipping off to Germany to join in the US and allies' war efforts to stop Hitler, the Nazis, and the Holocaust.

Just stop to think about that for a minute. German-born, he was a German citizen whose father fought loyally and valiantly for his country alongside his German neighbors in WWI, and was awarded the Iron Cross Medal for his Service by his German government. Julius Stern, Dad's father, received that German Military Medal more than two decades prior to Dad's joining the US Army in the early 1940s. German-born, he was a German citizen forced to flee his homeland at the age of 15 because of the Holocaust, because he was Jewish, because he, his family, and millions of others were being persecuted, losing all of their rights simply because of their religion, political views, and/or health status, due to a zealous German Nationalist in power as Chancellor (and later, Fuhrer) of the German Reich.

Dad had traveled by train and then ship, alone, from Meckenheim, Germany, to France where he met up as planned with HIAS [1] workers and other children fleeing to the US, to NY, without understanding or speaking any English, with little money in his pocket, leaving everything and everyone he loves behind, and hoping his parents' and sister's plans to join him in the US as soon as possible would happen.

German-born, he became a US Citizen November 19, 1943, (according to HIAS records) once he'd voluntarily joined the US Army to help in the war efforts. German-born, now fighting as a

---

1   HIAS — Hebrew Immigrant Aid Society: "Founded as the Hebrew Immigrant Aid Society in 1881 to assist Jews fleeing pogroms in Russia and Eastern Europe, HIAS has touched the life of nearly every Jewish family in America and now welcomes all who have fled persecution." www.hias.org

US Citizen for America against his country of birth Germany, it would be three years and four months after Pearl Harbor, on April 29, 1945, when he and his 42nd Rainbow Division Army brothers would liberate the Dachau Concentration Camp Survivors in Germany.

After WWII, he also returned to Germany as a US Army Intelligence Officer to assist with identifying Nazi war criminals. He was well-equipped to do so since he spoke fluent German as his first language. As well, he would be granted six months of

Dad, (Left, holding the dog), and an army buddy stationed in Germany during 1940s.

"compassionate leave" while still a US Army soldier in uniform, to return to his hometown in Germany – accompanied by a fellow US Army soldier in uniform, in order to try to find out what happened to his parents, sister, and other family members. Because the two of them were in American military uniforms, people in Germany were afraid to talk to them about anything they might have known about his family. Therefore, despite these attempts and his further contacts with the Red Cross once back home in the US, he was never able to find out what had happened to his family – other than that they were presumed dead and had likely suffered the same fate as other Jews all across Europe.

On December 7, 1941, he could not have known that this would be his final letter to his parents and sister, and that it would be returned to him sometime later – unopened and unread. And finally, on December 7, 1941, he could not yet have known that September 7, 1938 – the day his parents most assuredly desperately hugged and kissed him goodbye as they watched him get on the train from Meckenheim to Hamburg for his eventual destination in America – would be the last time he ever saw his parents, sister, and other family members again.

Also on January 8, 2014, Ira answered in her email one of Gail's recent questions wondering about the outcomes of "our" Julius Stern, his wife Auguste, and Dad's sister Margot who was four years younger than him. Up until then, all we sort of "knew" (but rather "assumed", from history) was that they were "obviously" killed in the concentration camps, because Dad was unable to find them or find out anything about them after the war, and they had never communicated with Dad since before his December 7, 1941 letter was returned to him unopened. Since Dad never knew the actual details of his parents' or sister's outcomes, nor the dates of their deaths (whose deaths were presumed), he chose the most solemn days of the Jewish High Holidays – Rosh Hashanah – when we ask G-d to inscribe us in The Book of Life for another year – as the date for their three Yahrtzeits (the Jewish anniversary of their deaths). On that day, every year, he would light Yahrtzeit candles and go to synagogue to say prayers for them in community with others. As we grew into adulthood, we continued the same.

On January 8, 2014, with the latest data Ira knew at that time, she responded with this about "our" Julius/Auguste/and Margot Stern's apparent demise:

"The 'memorial book' Bundesarchiv says that Julius, Auguste and Margot were deported to Minsk Ghetto. I can ask from where (which source) they know this. In the list of the deportations is mentioned that they were transported to Minsk, Maly Trostenets. Many people were shot there. I have no other information."

From: Rolf
To: Gail, Ira, Oliver, Jeffrey, Judi, Sheri, Herbert
Date: January 9, 2014 at 11:45 AM
Subject: AW: Son of _____ (brother of Julius Stern, born Meinerzhagen) and Ilse, San Francisco

Dear Gail,
Probably in the fall of 2014 the "Initiative Stolpersteine Meinerzhagen" wishes to lay six memorial "stumbling blocks" in front of the former house Hauptstrasse 6 in Meinerzhagen (on the right side of Café and restaurant Pollmann), where the family Julius Stern once lived (Author's note: Judi's grandfather). You will find the text enclosed that will be engraved upon the blocks to be laid for the members of the family. You will get more information under: www.stolpersteine-meinerzhagen.de. For more details about the laying of these, until now more than 40 thousand memorial 'stumbling blocks', please see under www.stolpersteine.eu. If a person lived in several places (so Jenny Weil) you can lay "stumbling blocks" in every town, as well in Meinerzhagen, Hohenlimburg or in Bad Godesberg. The headline on the blocks is "Hier wohnte" (Here lived). The members of the Initiative and citizens will give money to pay (for) the "stumbling blocks".

We would like to invite the descendants of the victims to come to Meinerzhagen to attend the ceremony. Therefore we ask you to send us the postal address of the descendants. More information I will give you later.

My wife Christina tried to translate my letter.

With kind regards from Germany to USA, Initiative Stolpersteine Meinerzhagen. ... Rolf

On January 10, 2014, Gail wrote back with more thanks and more questions, concluding with: "I am so sorry for all my many questions. We just want to know everything, and all of you have been so kind to us. I hope we get to meet you."

Within that first month of January 2014, Gail, Jeffrey and I had already discussed the probability of our taking a trip to visit Hohenlimburg, Meckenheim, Rexingen and Bad Godesberg. Gail and I were enthusiastically looking forward to this adventure, and Jeffrey remained noncommittal. Gail and I intuitively knew that this was not only a once-in-a-lifetime opportunity that could never be re-created, but was also expected to be a life-changer for all of us. Gail had already given Ira permission (which Ira had requested from her) to send Gail's previous letters/pictures/and information to any others who might be able to supply critical family information from archives, books, museums, and other reliable resources, "and to anyone else who might learn from it or who might be able to help (us)."

In that same email to our new friends (our Significant 4), Gail recounted a trip we'd taken with Dad and cousins Erna (mother of Judi) and Alma (daughter of Bella) and her husband, to the Washington DC US Holocaust Museum shortly after it opened. Gail described it as "a wonderful and painful experience", describing the glass wall there with the names of all the towns in Europe where Jews had lived before the Holocaust, and how Dad, Erna and Alma pointed out all the names of the towns where they and other cousins had lived. And Gail wrote: "And now you, through your work and the work of others, are bringing these towns alive for me. Thank you. We so want plaques for all of our family placed in the appropriate places. In the US, in certain cemeteries, there is a tradition of engraving on the back of headstones, the names of loved ones killed in the Holocaust. On the back of my parents' stone, we engraved the names of Julius, Auguste and Margot, but would love to have a forever marker for them where they last lived. Who should I contact? I eagerly await more information."

Here is Rolf's note (January 19, 2014), written to the appropriate person in Germany, pertaining to our request for all four of our family – both parents and both children – to have Stolpersteine laid for them so that they can be "united, together at last" at the site of their last freely-chosen home, in Hohenlimburg. At some point, we learned that "our" Julius, Auguste, and Margot, as well as Aunt Jenny Weil already had Stolpersteine placed for them at other sites throughout Germany – but all of those sites were ones they were forced to move to by Hitler and the Nazis, not a "freely-chosen home". You may recall from chapter 2 on Stolpersteine, that the original intent for the location of the Stolpersteine as stated on the stolpersteine.eu website is (repeated here): "at the individual's last known place of *freely-chosen* residence or work".

All three of us felt very strongly about this, for although the four would clearly not be there physically, ever again – we wanted, or rather **needed** to have all four of them at their Hohenlimburg home together again, united spiritually, as the healthy productive loving family they once were ... for all eternity ... at their last home before they were forced to move – where they were last happy, together, so that they could rest in Peace, together ... finally.

This particular note from Rolf, for whatever reason, either did not come translated in English or I couldn't find the translation amidst my emails or printed papers, so I asked my dear Sister of My Heart – Beate, in Germany (my Skype pal; we met during an online course training to become Certified Peace Ambassadors, and immediately connected.) – if she would please translate the letter for me into English (Feb 2019), which of course she did. Shortly thereafter, I did find the original English translation from Christina, Rolf's wife.

From: Rolf
To: Herr _____,
Date: January 19, 2014 6:37:56 AM EST
Subject: Obstacles to the family Julius and Auguste Stern, born Weil, formerly living in Hohenlimburg, Wessel Bachstraße 4

Dear Mr. ___,
I refer to our telephone conversation of 01.14.2014 and inform you the facts discussed together again. The "Initiative stumbling blocks Meinerzhagen" plans include the installation of six stumbling blocks in front of the house Zur Alten Post 8 (formerly Main Street 6) in Meinerzhagen in the fall of 2014 in accordance with Appendix.

It should also (include) Jenny Weil, born on 14.08.1892 in Rexingen, sister of Cecily Stern (Author's note: Cilly), born Weil. Jenny Weil moved on 25/11/1933 in Bad Godesberg (Alte Bahnhofstrasse 8) Meinerzhagen, main road 6 and on 04/03/1935 to the family of her sister Auguste in the Wessel Bachstraße (4) to Hohenlimburg.

And thus to the family star in Hohenlimburg in Wessel Bachstraße (4) according to data from the Federal Archives, the city of Meckenheim and Gail Stern:

Julius Stern, born on 02.02.1886 in Hohenlimburg, deported on 20/07/1942 from Cologne to Minsk, murdered (in your dashboard so far not listed)

Wife Auguste Stern, born Weil was born on 14/06/1887 in Rexingen, deported on 20/07/1942 from Cologne to Minsk, murdered (in overview) (Julius Stern and Auguste became married in 1921 in Meinerzhagen.)

Son Rolf Stern, born on 07.02.1923 (in Hohenlimburg), fled in 1938 from Meckenheim to the United States (15 years old on a Kindertransport), the sole survivor of his family, a father of Gail Stern (in Overview not included).

Daughter Margot Stern, born on 15.01.1927 in Hohenlimburg, deported on 20/07/1942 from Cologne to Minsk, murdered (in overview included).

Sister in law, sister and aunt Jenny Weil, born on 14.08.1892 in Rexingen, deported in 1942, unknown place of deportation (presumably 15.06.1942 Izbica and Sobibor) killed (in their review has not yet included).

The family of five star / Weil moved in May 1938 from Hohenlimburg to sister Selma, nee Weil, born on 01.07.1889 in Rexingen, Meckenheim, High Street 15. There has relocated the city Meckenheim to the Murdered Jewish citizens stumbling blocks.

For the listed five victims of Nazism have yet been laid no stumbling blocks in Hohenlimburg. With an installation outside the house Wessel Bachstraße (4) would this family be together symbolically. Obviously plan the descendants of stumbling block laying in Meinerzhagen to come to Germany. Therefore, I would like to see a coordinated laying in Meinerzhagen and Hohenlimburg. I would also be willing to come to preliminary talks to your board meeting. However, we are of 28.02. until 21.03.2014 in Israel. The time taken from your prospective board meeting on 25.03.2014 will appear given the necessary lead time (Demnig etc.) relatively late. First, we should call on short notice.

So much for today.

Friendly greetings from the Sauerland to Hagen

Stumbling blocks Meinerzhagen Initiative, Rolf

This total stranger, just two weeks after initially "finding us", was clearly advocating strongly for something we'd just recently expressed our wish for, something we "needed", something "symbolic" and spiritual, something that would cost money paid by German members of the local Stolpersteine Initiative chapter and other German citizens. In addition, our request and Rolf's request was something that would involve city government officials' time, efforts, organization, and collaboration with the Meinerzhagen Stolpersteine Initiative Leadership.

Whoever heard of such a thing?! Especially for something that happened so long ago? Especially for something that was so heinous and tragic? Especially for something that a number of people (some Germans and non-Germans alike, some still to this day) would either like to sweep under the carpet, minimize, or completely deny its occurrence? Especially ...for total strangers across the Atlantic Ocean?!

Not once did I ever think: Well it won't bring them back! What's the point? It's 72 years later, too late to do this now! Why are these people doing this? Did their fathers, grandfathers, brothers, and uncles become Nazis willingly, or were they conscripted by Hitler into the Army – forced to become Nazis later in the war? I always sensed that these people believed it was simply "the right thing to do", as Rolf was quick to tell us repeatedly during our time with him in Germany: "We must NEVER forget!", and that this was their way of making sure the World's collective "we" would NEVER forget (in addition to all of the blatant documented evidence in pictures, words, and videotaped testimonies). Quite the opposite, I continue to believe that our Significant 4, other Stolpersteine Initiative members, and any number of other Germans are "Mensches" – who know that what happened in their country was wrong, feel great shame about it, and feel a deep humane desire to do anything possible to:

- Tell the truth (Remember that there are both Survivors as well as other "Witnesses" to the horror of the Shoah, though they are elderly and many have died.),
- Memorialize, and
- Recall the significance of the lives of all of our loved ones, recognizing that each was somebody's son, daughter, brother or sister, aunt or uncle, parent, or grandparent – who led productive lives as loyal German citizens and fought bravely for their country during World War I.

And finally – I believe that "they" do this in order to be a part of the World's Solution, to take action rather than to remain silent as many of their predecessors did, to do whatever they possibly can to prevent this from happening again, anywhere, any time, to any human being.

Within a week or so of Oliver's initial email in January 2014, Gail had also sent our Significant 4 another letter we had from Dad's collection of papers, written clearly in a sharp-angled handwriting, in German. Gail had wondered if it was a letter from Dad's father Julius to Dad. She sent the letter requesting their translation into English. We'd had the letter for decades, but since it was written in German, we had no idea who'd written it, to whom, the date, nor what it said. The letter did appear to be written on printed stationary from "our" Julius Stern's scrap metal shop (which shop and livelihood was taken from him by the Nazis and their new "laws").

Over several emails, Oliver and Ira translated and transcribed it. Here is the letter from Dad's mother Auguste to one of their neighbors. Though there was no visible date on the letter, Oliver determined that it must've been during the time that they were "living" in the convent in Bonn-Endenich in the summer of 1942 with many other Jewish families.

Part 1 of 2 pages – Auguste's letter:

Dear family (Author's note: neighbor), I hope you are well. For 14 days, since my brothers and sisters left, I have become unsettled, I do not feel well in general and I have a lot of work since Margot has arrived here and has been going to the "Wandplatten Wessel" factory, so I have to share the few things which are left as well, but life is just so useless, and nevertheless, I have to stay strong and must not leave my poor husband alone, now that there is no one left. What news have you received from (other), how are (other) and (other)? I really thought, dear Ms. (neighbor), I would hear from you or you would show up at the gate, I would be called ...

Oliver noted with the letter's attachment: "The Wandplatten Wessel factory mentioned in the text was a factory in Bonn not far from Endenich where Jews from Bonn were detained in a former convent before being deported."

Gail wrote back to them on January 10th: "Oliver, Thank you so much for the translation of the first page of Auguste's letter. Attached is the second page. Life was clearly painful at the time. Gail"

From: Ira
To: All of us
Sent: Sunday, January 19, 2014 3:50 pm
Subject: AW: family Stern / Weil / Schwarz

Dear Judi, dear Gail,
Thank you very much for your information. I never thought that we can recognize the persons on the picture. Sorry for the delayed response. (Author's note: Ira never thought they'd be able to **identify** the people in some of the pictures, as she and the others did not know any descendants before they "found" us – even accidentally! So you see, even in the first few weeks of getting to know each other, there are reciprocal relationships already developing between these four Germans and we three American Jews, between the "Teachers" and the "Learners" – and already, those definitions are blurred, for we are each both

Teachers and Learners in these developing relationships.) ...

Mrs (name) is the daughter of Walter, born 1913 in Meinerzhagen. He escaped to Palestine in 1937. His sister escaped to Great Britain in 1939. Their parents lived in Meinerzhagen, Hauptstrasse 15 close to Julius and Cilly (cousin Judi's maternal grandparents) living in Meinerzhagen, Hauptstrasse 6. In 1935, Julius Stern (Judi's grandfather) could not pay any more the rent for his shop. He moved the shop in a room of an apartment in the house Hauptstrasse 15. I think it was a room in the apartment of Max. It was a short time after Max had to close his shop and the others moved to other cities, so I think there were empty rooms in the apartment of Max. In 1938, (name) died. Her sister moved to Meinerzhagen and was living in the apartment of her brother-in-law Max. In 1939 (two people) moved to Cologne (like Julius and Cilly) and came back to Meinerzhagen, Kirchstrasse 5 (house of {name}). They lived there together (Julius, Cilly, (Author's note: and four others)). Julius, Cilly, (and the others) had to move to the house in Werlsiepen, outside of Meinerzhagen und (and) were deported to Zamosc (with others) on 28.April 1942 together, maybe to Sobibor on 27.May 1942. There is a book about this deportation (Ralf Piorr, editor, "Without coming back, the deportation to Zamosc in April 1942," Essen 2012).

You are related, but it is long time ago (he married her, 1844, sister of a Stern. He was the father of Julius Stern (Author's entry: Judi's maternal grandfather)). Judi (our cousin in Baltimore, Erna and Siegfried's only child), the sister of your grand-grandfather married (name). They lived very close together, they were in the same synagogue, I am sure they feted their family celebrations together and they suffered the same fate up to the end together.

You asked for Rexingen. Mrs. Barbara and Mr. Heinz are doing this work. They founded an association for restoring the synagogue in Rexingen and searching the Jewish history in Rexingen (today 170 members). They have a memorial book and there are some "Stolpersteine": http://www.ehemalige-synagoge-rexingen. So it is different from town to town./ aktivitaeten/stolpersteine-gedenbuch (click the letters). I translated the memorial documents about (two names). Round about 37% of the citizens of Rexingen were Jewish in ca. 1850. The Jewish and the Christian school were in the same building.

There is a picture from 1928. The synagogue in Rexingen was destroyed in 1938. Since 1952 it is a protestant church. All Jewish things were restored since 1997 and it is now a house of learning and a museum. (Author's note: In August of 2014, we met Barbara and Heinz, thanked them for their dedication and ongoing work, and visited this restored synagogue / museum!) ...

In some towns they lay the plaques only for murdered victims. I don't know how it is in Hohenlimburg, Bonn or Rexingen. Mr. Rolf is working on it. In Meinerzhagen there are plaques for all members of a family. For those who could escape, too. They should be together. We think they were all victims of holocaust. But it is a little bit complicated. Every city council has to decide. The plaques lay in the sidewalk and the town is the owner of the ground of the sidewalk (normally). So it is different from town to town.

Are there any descendants of Erwin Stern?

Best greetings, Ira

Also on January 19, 2014, Oliver emailed us: "Thanks a lot for the scan of the note! ... please scan and send me the back of the note so that I can translate it. Hopefully, it contains a signature and the date when it was written, which will help us put it into context.

In the meantime, I have sent emails to various archives in Germany to find out about Margot Stern's stay in Rheydt referred to in Ralph Stern's letter, liquidation or so-called "aryanization" of property in Hohenlimburg, Bad Godesberg, Meckenheim and Rexingen as well as restitution claims after the war and finally the pogrom in 1938 in these places. Apparently, there are eye-witness accounts of the pogrom in Rexingen and in Hohenlimburg, but I do not know these testimonies yet.

I checked my notes and I found the reference of a file in the Munster State Archives concerning Julius Stern's (Author's note: Judi's grandfather) mobile property in Meinerzhagen (bank account, furniture etc.) from the 1950s. The file deals with the trial 'Julius Stern (represented by the Jewish Trust Corporation) vs the German state'. I will order it next time in Munster (probably in February). Hopefully the State Archives in Munster will have answered my email in the meantime concerning restitution claims in Hohenlimburg. It is of course possible to contact them in English. I would suggest waiting for their reply to my request, because I think the archives will send references to files dealing with your family's property in Hohenlimburg. With these references, it would be possible to order copies.

The address Wesselbachstr. 4 perfectly fits into what we already know. It is very close to the synagogue, however, it is not clear whether the house still exists because Wesselbachstr. 6 and 7 have been demolished, for instance. I tried to check the names from Ralph Stern's (Author's note: Dad's) phone-book. ...

You wanted to know about my background. I am a trained historian specialized in contemporary history (I finished my Ph.D. at Dusseldorf University on a topic from the 19th century.) and have been living in Paris for ten years now. I think for any German historian one crucial question is: How were Hitler and the Nazis possible and why in Germany? I am currently preparing a new project (second book) on antisemitism in the 19th and 20th century and will hopefully be able to raise funds this year. I would like to study the "Rothschild" stereotypes (including "banker" and "stock exchange" stereotypes) in the late 19th and 20th century from an international perspective (France, Germany/Austria, UK/US). Apart from that, I am also interested in the local history of Meinerzhagen, particularly during the Weimar Republic and the Nazi period, because this period has been neglected by our local historians so far. Among others, I have been doing research on the history of the perpetrators during the Nazi regime (a topic which has not been studied so far) and I started collecting material on the local SS unit some time ago.

I will keep you informed once I have got new information. Best regards, Oliver"

Oliver's email to us, 1/20/14:

"Ira sent me a file which shows that unfortunately your grandparents' house must have been demolished as well (see attachment). However, the synagogue still exists and can be visited. I think I found other photographs from that area (Wesselbachstr. 6 and 7 demolished in 1969 and another house which could be Wesselbachstr. 4)."....

Gail's January 20, 2014 email to Oliver, Jeffrey, me, and cousin Judi:

"Sad, but amazing information. (This) photo in the Yad Vashem photo archives is of the last Jews in Hohenlimburg lining up on April 23, 1942, in front of the synagogue for deportation. ... The synagogue was reopened as a memorial site in 1986. I so wish we had known that when my dad was alive. It was, of course, where he had his Bar Mitzvah. Apparently about 400 Jews now live in Hagen...interesting. I cannot wait to go there.

Thank you again for opening this avenue for us. My heart has sang and cried every day since I received your first email. Gail"

Gail wrote back about Ira's comment above: "We think they were all victims of holocaust.", asking her to explain who the "We" are. She also asked if they knew anyone who could help us plan a "family heritage trip" while we'd be in Germany for the Stolpersteine Ceremonies. Ira emailed back on January 21, 2014, mentioning that she'd speak with Rolf and the other members of the Stolpersteine Initiative about how they could help us plan a family "heritage trip" to Germany, saying "It will work. We hope also that it will be possible to lay 'Stolpersteine' in several towns at the same time."

On January 21, 2014, Ira wrote:

"You asked: who are the 'we'? There are some people in Meinerzhagen working on all related with the victims of National Socialism: first the Jewish victims in our town, but also political victims (communists; 4 were shot in March 1945.), members of social democratic party, people in resistance to the system (members of the resistance in the churches), so called "gypsies", forced workers or euthanasia victims. The Nazis killed people with mental handicaps. Homosexual people came also in concentration camps. In 1939 Meinerzhagen had 4735 (1944: 5207) inhabitants and 1700 forced workers. Most of them had to work in a great factory (production of weapons). In relation with the German reunification there was a program for restitution the forced workers from Russia, Ukraine, Poland and so on. In this time I got contact to some forced workers and I asked them for their experience. They told me how it was as a 16 or 17 year old young girl, captivated on the street and brought to Germany for work. It was a racist system: the forced workers of the Netherlands (not real so called Aryans, but near by) got a little bit more bread than the forced workers of France, the Ukrainians a little bit more than Russians. 26 of them died in Meinerzhagen, many of them little children. They were buried in the Jewish cemetery (they were not Jewish). ...

The people working on it (Author's insert: our family's Stolpersteine) are Rolf and the members of the 'Stolpersteine Initiative' ... All members decided that there should be 'Stolpersteine' for all victims.

There are also historians, like Oliver (coming from Meinerzhagen) and me searching for the whole history of Meinerzhagen, not only the victims but also the offenders, the local Nazis. Meinerzhagen was growing very fast by admitting so many German refugees from the east after the war. (There were 12 million of German refugees escaping or being expelled from the eastern part of Germany, today Poland, after the war.) But it is still a small town (20,000 inhabitants today). Everyone knows everyone. ... It is known (Author's insert for grammatical reasons) the names of the local Nazi leaders, the names of the people who bought the Jewish houses very cheaply (so called Aryanization), the people who bought the furniture, the clothes and all things the deported Jews had to leave behind. All people who profit from this. They were reputable (sometimes mighty) citizens in town and their descendants are reputable citizens in town. They want to forget these old things. ...

Concerning the reaction of the descendants of the offenders: there are two groups. One group says: forget it, don't talk about it, few defend their grandfathers (It was a hard time for Germans too, they obeyed orders only, something had to be done, because the Jews were too rich, too mighty and so on.). There is anti-Semitism in German society today too and not only in circles of some neo-Nazis. There is a picture of 'the Jew' in some heads and it works without any real living Jew (like in the past: neighbor is a good Jew, because he is not so 'Jewish'). This anti-Semitism is a minority and in society it is a taboo to talk about. (Author's note, added Spring, 2021: When "zooming" with Ira, she remarked sadly that it is no longer a taboo for Germans to talk about being anti-Semites, per the current environment in Germany.). In Germany, living Jews always have to defend Israeli policy – although they are Germans, not Israelis. For some Germans it is something like 'easing the burden' to say: 'look what the Jews (Israelis) are doing to the Palestinian people'.

The second group of descendants of the offenders want to know. Young people are coming in my archive and asking: I want to know what my grandfather was doing, no one is talking about that in my family. Or they ask: How could it be, that a member of 'SS-Leibstandarte Adolf-Hitler' and SS-Division 'Das Reich' was mayor in Meinerzhagen in the 1960s ...

Some of the buyers of Jewish property were at that time so called 'Jewish friends'. I don't know their motive. (A) family lived in the second part of the house in Werlsiepen (after the first deportation on 28.April 1942) and they helped the three Jewish women living in the other part up to the second deportation on 27.July 1942 to Theresienstadt. They had a close contact. The three women were 'baby sitters' to the (family's) children, that was forbidden. They gave food and helped, what they could do. They bought Jewish property – I think after the first deportation and before the second deportation. Maybe to save it? In some cases I don't know. Most of the buyers just made a good deal. ...

There is also a problem with the 'Stolpersteine'. Some owners of former Jewish houses don't want 'Stolpersteine' because they think: everyone seeing the 'Stolpersteine' is thinking: they profit of the fate of others. There is one thinking like this. He bought a 'former Jewish' house in 1976. He and his family ha(d) nothing to do with 'Aryanization'. Others are supporter(s) of the 'Stolperstein-Initiative'. The 'Stolperstein-Initiative' and I gave information about the fate of the Jewish people in presentations, in schools, in the newspaper before the first 'Stolpersteine' were laid and now there is a great – not only acceptability, but also supporting. It was a great 'event' in town when the first 'Stolpersteine' were laid in June 2013.

There is a tradition in doing this. In the 1970s and 1980s

there was an association called 'Christians and Jews'. They searched, they filed a petition for laying the memorial-stone for the deported Jews of Meinerzhagen and they organized the visit of the former citizens in 1982. In that time the resistance in town was much greater (old Nazis were still living).

To my personal view: I feel not guilty about this, because I think to be guilty is something individual. Everyone has to do in his one life. I am born 1961. But as a German I am responsible what to do with history today and we all have our own family history. My father was much older than my mother is, so he was adult in 1933. He came from Vienna to a town near Meinerzhagen in 1929 and he was anti-Semitic and racist his whole life. He died in the age of 95 in 1997. He was a well educated and multilingual man. He studied economy and languages in Vienna, became member of the NSDAP in March 1939 (that was relative late – all people, who want to profit from the Nazi system wanted to be a member very early). I don't know exactly what he did in that time. He was a manager of a great factory building machines (metal industry) and he was a translator. At 'Austria-American-Institute' in Vienna he translated Sigmund Freud to American students in the 1920s. He was responsible for the forced workers in that factory because he could speak a little bit Russian ('they were treated very well' ?). But he was very nationalistic, anti-democratic (monarchist), very elitist in his thinking (social-Darwinism) and a dominant character. In some things he was not close to the Nazis. He thought that most of the Nazis were uneducated, proletarian bullies. But he believed in the Aryan race as 'the crown of the creation'. And he had the typical Vienna anti-Semitism. It was (and is) very common in Vienna. I think it has much to do with envy. 'The whole upper-schools and universities were full of Jews'. The Jews in Germany and Austria rose from an overacted (most poor) minority to respected well situated citizens and that aroused envy. There was a time the Jews rose more quickly (in a social way) than the others because they were better at school. In their status as a minority they had more ambition.

I never had a chance in discussions with my father – one reason to study history. But it had nothing to do with knowing facts or not.... Best greetings, Ira"

Gail's email January 22, 2014 back to Ira and all:

Dear Ira,

Thank you for your wonderful letter, and your willingness to answer all of my questions. Already I have learned much from you, and have much more to think about. I have been 3 times to Germany, and have never felt entirely comfortable. Your writing provides a different perspective. I so look forward to meeting all of my new friends (you, Rolf, Oliver, and Christina), and to sharing not only our facts, but also more of our feelings... Gail.

On 2/5/14, Ira passed on this email to us, which she translated. Ms Ingrid Sonnert at the Meckenheim archives had sent it to her earlier. It includes some research from Ms Sonnert's book, cited below:

Per orders from the Gestapo in 1942, Jews were relocated to assembly camps where they awaited eventual deportation. The handful of Jews still living in Meckenheim got the order to move to Endenich, into the monastery "Zur ewigen Anbetung". (Author's note: the convent; including our six family members): Selma Weil, widow of Max; Susanne, Selma's sister-in-law/ Max's sister; Julius Stern (Author's note: "our" Julius Stern), his wife Auguste Weil Stern, and their daughter Margot Stern; and Jenny Weil, sister of Selma and Auguste). The Stern-Weil family had moved from Hohenlimburg in 1938 to live with Selma and Susanne in their Meckenheim house, Hauptstr. 15. The Stern's son ROLF had escaped to America in 1938. (Author's note: This is Dad, who escaped several years before this 1942 order.)

As well, Ira added that Uncle Wilhelm Weil was also "living" in the monastery while awaiting deportation.

Those Jews stayed in the Endenich monastery for only a brief time, and were transported from there in June and July 1942 per the Cologne Gestapo to the Koln-Deutzer-Messehallen (per Ira: the Cologne trade fair hall). They were allowed to take food for 8 days, 50 Reichsmark of money, dishes, and one suitcase with bedding, clothes, and shoes. On 15 June, Jenny Weil, Susanne and Selma left the monastery, were brought to the Cologne hall, and from there probably to Lodz (Author's note: Ira corrected this in her email per her research, stating there was no transport to Lodz, but there was one to Sobibor via Cologne and one to Theresienstadt from Cologne on that day.). Family Stern was deported on 20.July probably to Minsk. The last that is written down and the last sign of life is: "moved – unknown to which place". .... Selma, Susanne, and the family Stern-Weil were deported from Bonn-Endenich 1942 to Lodz (see Ira's correction above) and Minsk and were killed there. ... No one came back. [2]

Email January 20, 2014, from Gail to: Oliver, Significant 4, Herbert, Jeff/ me, and cousin Judi:

"Oliver, ... Now I have sent you the second page of the letter (Author's note: Auguste's letter; page 1 was interpreted by Oliver earlier this month.). I think that the words at the bottom of the page were written by my father. I am very anxious / nervous to read the second page. My grandmother sounds so sad in the first page. I also wonder who Mrs. (name) was... perhaps a non-Jew who my grandmother thought might help them? In handwritten notes by my father on a Claim for Restitution form, the question as to who might know the whereabouts of missing personal property the answer was "(name)", with an address in Meckenheim, where my grandparents and aunt (Margot) were living until moved to Bonn and then Minsk...."

From: Oliver
To: Gail, Judi, Jeffrey, Sheri
CC: Ira, Rolf, Herbert
Date: January 22, 2014 at 7:13 PM
Subject: Translation of the note / references on Nazi Germany

... Please find enclosed the translation of the second page of the note. Ira had transcribed it yesterday, and she thinks it was written in late June 1942 (due to the remark on the brothers

2 Ingrid Sönnert, Dietmar Pertz, Ihre Namen werden bleiben! Dokumentation zur Geschichte der Meckenheimer und Rheinbacher Juden und ihrer Friedhöfe, Zeugnisse jüdischer Kultur im Rhein-Sieg-Kreis, Band 5, Siegburg 2013, page 31 and 32.

and sisters already deported two weeks before). The "gate" mentioned on page 1 probably refers to the former convent in Kapellenstrasse 6 in Bonn-Endenich where they were detained.

I think the (two families) were friends of your grandparents who kept some of their belongings at their home for them (e.g. the reference to the suitcase). There were similar cases in other places. However, the fact that Mrs (neighbor) had not shown up at the gate also reveals the complete segregation of the remaining German Jewish population in the late 1930s and early 1940s. ...

... There are also quite a few fine studies by German historians, but many of them have not been translated into English, unfortunately. For instance, there is Peter Longerich's "Davon haben wir nichts gewusst ..." ("We did not know anything about that ...") (See here: http://www. amazon.de/ Davon-haben-nichts-gewusst-Judenverfolgung/dp/ 3570550419/ref=cm_cr_pr_ product_top) which analyzes what Germans (many of whom would say after the war "We did not know anything about it") actually knew and how German society responded to the anti-Jewish policy of the regime since 1933 and its increasing violence (discrimination, seizure of property, pogrom in 1938, deportations to death camps).

Best regards, Oliver

Part 2 of 2 pages – Auguste's Letter:

"Hmm anyway we will have to muddle through somehow. G-d will protect us even in the middle of nowhere. You probably had many cherries and gooseberries, we do not have such things here any more. I would like to ask you dear Mr (name), to fetch my husband's woolen gilet, (Author's note: a warm vest/ waistcoat) which is in our suitcase, and to send it with the key to the (name)(?) family where my husband will get it, as you are a man of honour. I would like to thank you very much, because if we should have to leave and get out there into misery, he could at least keep warm in the gilet. May you all stay in good health and best wishes. Yours truly, Mrs Stern".

Again, not for the first or last time – I cry. So many emotions

– sadness, grief, anger, terror, horror, helplessness, humiliation, injustice, powerlessness, loss of control, depression, shame at man's inhumanity to man, loss of family, loss of life and happiness, productivity, citizenship, and safety, feeling like the world has suddenly turned upside down, separation, and abandonment (Clearly felt by Auguste, surely by their son – my father-in-law Ralph here in America, and felt by me – even in 2019-2021, still, sparked yet again when writing and editing this book). It asks loudly of me, "What would I do today, if this was happening to my family?", and just as loudly – "What WILL I do today, what HAVE I done today, when this (or some other injustice, intolerance, fear-sparked "anti" action) happens to someone else's family, families, communities?" Will I stand up and speak out, or will I remain silent because of fear, inertia, thinking "someone else will do it"? Auguste's translated letter summons up every picture I've ever seen in the DC Holocaust Museum and in Yad Vashem (the Holocaust Museum / Remembrance Center in Israel), every Kaddish Prayer I've ever recited when a loved one has died, or for a "stranger" who is Jewish and may no longer have anyone left to recite Kaddish for them. Auguste's letter summons ...perhaps every loss I've ever experienced.

From: Oliver
To: All
Date: February 5, 2014
Subject: Mail from Hagen and Bonn

Dear All,

I hope you are fine. I am sorry for the delay but I had been waiting for news from the archives I contacted.

I finally received a letter from Hagen City Hall with information on your family's addresses in Hohenlimburg. The letter says that Julius, Auguste, Rolf and Margot Stern moved to Wesselbachstr. 4 on April 1, 1930 where they stayed until May 17, 1938, the day they moved to Meckenheim, Hauptstr. 15 (thus, they left Hohenlimburg about six months before the pogrom in November 1938).

Before April 1, 1930, they had been living in Hohenlimburg,

Egge 14 (unfortunately, the documents do not say since when). I found a street "An der Egge", which lies further west, but I am not sure this is the same street as there is also an area not far from Hohenlimburg castle (and the Wesselbach Valley) called "Egge". I will try to check it with someone from Hohenlimburg and maybe the names of the streets have changed since then. ...

Furthermore, I received an email from the city archives in Bonn, which sounds quite interesting (documents concerning the pogrom in November 1938, seizure of property and restitution claims after the war). I think these documents will have to be analyzed with the corresponding files kept in the Rhineland State Archives (which are currently being transferred from Dusseldorf to a new site and which will be accessible again in May this year).

By the way and since you asked, I intend to be in Meinerzhagen in autumn when the plaques are laid. Luckily enough, Paris is not that far away. (I usually travel by car.)

Best regards from France, Oliver

Ira wrote on February 6, 2014:

... cemetery Bonn tombstone Berthold and Sophie Weil, parents of Auguste, Cilly, Wilhelm, Simon, Jenny and so on.

There was an old picture in the shop window in Meckenheim. It is the house next to Max and Selma. In former times it was a shop: upholsterer "Freischem". Today in both houses (old Freischem and Max and Selma's) is a shop "Freischem". These are the last photos for today.

Best greetings, Ira

From: Ira
To: All
Date: February 6, 2014
Subject: Meckenheim III Endenich

On the stone on the Jewish cemetery Meckenheim is written: cemetery of the Jewish community / parish Meckenheim, in memorial to the dead 1933-1945.

Monastery Endenich: After expelling the Benedictine-nuns

out of the monastery by the nazi regime this house was used in 1941 and 1942 as an assembly camp for 474 Jews from Bonn and Bonn surroundings (Author's note: This is where "our" Julius, Auguste, and Margot were interned briefly, as three of those 474 Jews, from Spring 1942 until their deportation to Minsk on July 20, 1942.). From this place they were transported to the extermination camps. Only seven survivors are testified.

Mit freundlichen Gruessen, Ira

From: Sheri Stern
To: Ira, family, others of Significant 4
Date: February 8, 2014
Subject: Re: Bonn

As always, Ira and all – amazing. "Seeing, hearing & feeling" such details/puzzle pieces of our loved ones' lives – is a life-altering experience for us all.

As always, we thank you for your ongoing dedication to your Missions, and for sharing so much with us. Please know the difference you are making in our lives, especially touching our Neshama (Soul) by acknowledging with respect and dignity the significance of the lives of our loved ones. There is power in our ability to heal one another.

We look forward to meeting all of you in Meinerzhagen in the Fall. Take care, Sheri

From: Ira
To: Sheri (and family, and others of Significant4):
Date: February 21, 2014
Subject: AW: Bonn

Dear Sheri, dear Gail, dear Judi,
Thank you very much for your touching words.
There are some pictures house Wesselbachstr. 4, Hohenlimburg. There is one picture from Israel and one from Argentina, (and two people) in the garden of Julius Stern (Author's note: "our" Julius Stern).
Best greetings, Ira

Wesselbachstr. 4: Childhood Germany home (boxed) of Dad, Margot, and parents Julius and Auguste Stern, at #4 Wesselbach Strasse (street).

From: Ira
To: Gail, family, Herbert, and rest of Significant 4
Date: February 22, 2014
Subject: deportation

Dear all, There is a book about the deportation from Cologne trade fair (Messe Koln Deutz). First part is in German, second part (the same text) is in English. It describes the last way of your family. First part is a general introduction. Second part (next mail) is about the deportation to Minsk. Third part is about the deportation to Lublin / Sobibor on 15.06.1942. Up to now it is not exactly known to which camp Wilhelm, Selma, Jenny and Susanne were deported from internment camp Bonn-Endenich (monastery). Probably it was the train to Lublin.

Sorry, that I am not able to find the appropriate words for this. Best wishes, Ira

Same day, February 22, 2014, from Ira:

"Dear all, Here is the text about the deportation to Minsk. Julius, Auguste and Margot are mentioned. [3] ...

In Bonn is a Memorial Center for all victims of the National Socialist regime. There is a audio and a video document from (name) Weil, son of Wilhelm, living in Bonn again since 1976. I think he is talking about his life, his experience in the Nazi-time, his family and so on. I could not hear or see it yet, but Mrs. (name) (Memorial Center Bonn) will make a copy. There is a wall with all names and pictures (if there are some) of all who were deported from Bonn (also monastery Bonn-Endenich) in that Memorial Center. There are the names of Julius, Auguste, Margot, Selma, Wilhelm, Jenny and Susanne – so I know. Mrs. (name) (Memorial Center Bonn) asks if she can take your pictures for this wall (Author's note: Gail had previously sent Dad's family pictures to our Significant 4). ...

Rolf asked the artist Mr. Demnig for a date between 20.August and 02.October 2014 for the Commemoration Ceremony ('Stolpersteine'). Before and after these dates there are school holidays here and we want to involve the pupils. There is a first answer. Maybe it is at the end of August. There will be an exact date soon.

We will see soon. Best wishes, Ira"

This email about the deportation that we received in February 2014 pierced my heart. It contained the actual deportation list including the names of my father-in-law Rolf/Ralph's mother Auguste Weil Stern, father Julius Stern, and sister Margot Stern. There were their three names, in black and white, all typed and neatly listed together as a family – with their dates and places of birth and their dates and places of deportation. Above their names were other groupings of someone else's beloved family members, and so on and so forth. It struck me that this deportation list was as concrete, and impersonal, as a grocery list. It could've

---

3   Corbach, D., 1999. Chapter VI. Transport: Minsk 20.7.1942. In Departure: 6.00 a.m. Messe Köln-Deutz — Deportations 1938-1945, Cologne, p. 545. Scriba-Verlag Publishing House.

Stern, Arthur I.
von Niederbardenberg
* 23. 2.1896 Allendorf
vh.

Stern, Nanny S. (Rosenbaum)
* 1. 9.1905 Baumbach
vh.

Stern, Ilse S.
* 30. 5.1931 Neukirchen
led.

Stern, Walter I.
* 13. 3.1925 Neukirchen
led.

Stern, Johanna S.
* 22.11.1898 Meersen
led.

Steinhardt, Siegmund I.
von Niederbardenberg
* 12. 6.1915 M.-Gladbach
led.

Strauss, Bernh.I.
von Bonn
* 7. 9.1860 Zorn
verw.

1049. Stein, Hanna S.
von Köln, Horst-Wessel-Platz
* 21. 7.1911 Köln
vh.

1050. Stein, Helene S.
* 22.12.1931
led.

1051. Stein, Susanna S.
* 23. 3.1933
led.

1052. Stein, Sulamith S.
* 6. 8.1934
led.

1053. Stein, Beruria S.
* 19. 5.1936
led.

1054. Steinmann, Karl I.
von Niederbardenberg
* 26. 4.1896 Burgsteinfurt
vh.

1055. Steinmann, Rehe S. (Cohen)
* 2. 6.1899 Bonn
vh.

1056. Steinmann, Hannelore S.
* 1. 6.1936 Burgsteinfurt
led.

1058. Steinert, Ernst I.
von Köln, Horst-Wessel-Platz
* 8.11.1886
vh.

1059. Steinert, Jakob I.
von Bonn
* 3. 3.1899 Heimersheim
vh.

1060. Steinhardt, Paula S. (Levy)
von Bonn
* 6.11.1895 Bonn
vh.

1061. Steinhardt, Irene S.
* 7. 3.1928 Bonn
led.

1062. Stern, Julius I.
von Bonn
* 2. 2.1886 Hohenlimburg
vh.

1063. Stern, Auguste S. (Weil)
* 14. 6.1887 Rexingen
vh.

1064. Stern, Margot S.
* 15. 1.1927 Hohenlimburg
led.

Deportation list to Minsk: Note last three names at bottom of page, Julius and Auguste – grandparents of Jeffrey and Gail; Margot – aunt of Jeffrey and Gail.

just as easily said "2 pounds of potatoes, 1 gallon of milk" for all the absence of emotion that was present. Except that these were human beings, who were being sent far away, often separated from their loved ones – to be tortured and murdered – simply because they were Jews (or Romas, homosexuals, mentally ill, political prisoners, or otherwise "others" according to Hitler's disturbed views of Aryan perfection).

Upon receiving their deportation list, for a long time I cannot speak. I cannot move. There are no words. Before seeing this list, and before Oliver's initial email, all I "knew" were the bare bones of what "likely" actually happened to them – and that was from history books, Hebrew School, novels, and the movies "Schindler's List" and "Sophie's Choice". But now, once again, I had our family's list in front of me – in black and white on my computer – and suddenly it's no longer unknown. The images this Deportation List conjures up for me, not just for our family, but for so many of our People and other human beings, is overwhelming. Suddenly, it's real. I cannot "unsee" it. I cannot forget it. Once again, I cry.

As well, Ira sent further relevant text attachments from Dieter Corbach's book: "Departure: 6.00 a.m. Messe Köln-Deutz – Deportations 1938-1945, Cologne." Below are portions of three of the many testimonies and documents in that chapter: one by a Survivor, one by a Nazi, and one by the book's author.

Author Dieter Corbach noted on page 734: "It is strange that we have quite detailed information about the course of the journey and about the dreadful end of the deportation train Da 219 to Minsk/Trostenez on 20 July 1942 which no one survived."

Testimonies from Corbach's pages 744-747: "(name), who came to Trostenez in October 1942, reports:

Document 53

A suitcase stood ready, into which we were to throw all valuables. Next to this suitcase lay a girl who had probably just been shot, who was still bleeding from her head wound. She was obviously dead. However, nobody said a word about it. It was as if all that was normal, it occurred calmly and naturally. However, everyone who saw this knew that this was no joking matter, and so one threw even one's last possessions into this suitcase. [4]

"Finally caravans drove up which the people boarded without making things difficult, believing that they were now being taken to work. ... In the preceding days Russian prisoners of war had been made to dig huge pits ... in the pine forest near Blagowtschina, about 4 km from the Trostenez camp, which could easily be sealed off and activities there could hardly be observed from a distance. The victims who were not killed in the gas lorries – because their capacities were often inadequate or the vehicles were defective – were driven alongside these pits and then shot in the neck with pistols by execution details and thrown into the pit. If there were any signs of life, submachine guns were fired into the masses of bodies until nothing moved anymore. By way of trial, however, the gas lorries were used from June 1942 on, in which up to 60 victims were locked up closely packed. These lorries drove up to the pits where a hose with the exhaust fumes of the running motors was attached, and one waited for about 15 minutes until the death struggle of the victims had ended. Then Jewish concentration camp inmates or Russian prisoners of war had to drag the bodies out of the lorries and throw them into the pit. They themselves were also murdered after this dreadful work. It can no longer be established exactly in what atrocious manner individual victims of the death train of 24 July 1942 were killed. However, at this time gas lorries were mostly used." [5]

Document 54

Statement by a member of Dept. IV of the KdS/BdS Minsk, Johann Paul Rumschewitsch, regarding the execution site Blagowtschina:

"As I recall, these executions took place in the summer of

---

4   Book footnote 122. Interview with Hans Münz on 19.10.1992. Sagel-Grande, Irene u. a.: *Justiz und NS-Verbrechen*, Band XIX, Amsterdam 1978. ("The Judiciary and Nazi Crimes").

5   Book footnote 123. Ibid, pp. 193-196. According to the files dated 21.5.1963 of a legal claim against W. Heuser and from reports by H. Münz dated 19.10.1992.

1942, probably in July. As far as I can remember, the staff of the department had to line up in the evening. We were informed that a Jewish operation would be carried out the next day. At this time tasks were assigned [...]. In the early morning of the next day, it may have been about 5.00 or 6.00 hrs, I rode on a lorry with others to the execution site near the Trostenez estate. Two pits had already been dug there. Shooting took place only at one pit during my presence. The second was still empty when I returned to quarters in the evening. ... Apart from other departmental staff, the members of the Latvian detachment, which consisted of about 40-60 men, rode with me to the execution site. A further assignment was made there and then by Dr. Heuser. Dr. Heuser was in charge of the execution, which I can still recall exactly. Along with other comrades, I was assigned first to the cordon. Not long after our arrival at the execution site the first lorries with Jews came along. They were ordered to undress and were then taken to the pit. A large number of the Jews went calmly to the pit, others had to be driven or dragged there. I guess that I was cordoning-off until about 11 hrs. Then I was assigned to the detail which supervised or carried out, respectively, the undressing of the Jews and leading them to the pit. I was relieved of this duty in the early afternoon. The relief took place as follows: So far Dr. Heuser had done the shooting, which I had seen myself. He now stepped up to me and said: 'Now you go to it, I have finished.' Then I went to the pit myself. At this time it was about half full of corpses.

The herding of the Jews no longer took place in an orderly fashion, at least at the time when I had to shoot. Some of the Jews who did not go willingly to the pit ran along its edge, others threw themselves into the pit immediately without having been hit. This caused disturbances of the execution. I was able to observe that some, who were already lying in the pit, were still moving. That prompted me, after having fired my pistol three or four times, to go to the issue point for ammunition in order to get my submachine gun. With it I continued shooting at those who were still moving in the pit. Then I no longer shot at the Jews which had been brought up. At first I fired aimed single rounds with the submachine gun. Then, however, I could no longer bear to watch it and fired the remainder of the magazine blindly into the pit. I left the pit and went to Heuser, who was standing near the undressing site, and said to him: 'I can't go on.' He replied: 'Get away.' I then busied myself at the undressing site. The execution lasted until evening. [...] These had been Russian Jews. Men and women and occasionally also children were shot on that day. I still remember that several adult Jews had taken a small child between them as they went to the pit. Approximately 20 staff members of the department, among them also Latvians, were assigned as marksmen. The Jews were brought to the pit in 3 minute intervals. Sometimes it also took 5 minutes. A pause in a form that would have stopped the execution never occurred. If someone wanted to eat something, he went to the lorry containing the ammunition, food and drink. I do not know of anyone who refused an order of this kind (to be assigned as marksman)." [6]

The chapter continues on to relate this: "However, even in these horrible mass graves the dead found no rest, because starting in the autumn of 1943 they got down to opening the mass graves, to cremate the corpses on huge pyres and to obliterate the pits in order to provide no evidence for the advancing Soviet troops. In the jargon of these monsters this was called 'disinterment' ....

By 15 December the last of the 34 pits was levelled and covered with branches. Goldapp held a friendly speech for the 45 workers and said good-bye to each individual with a handshake. He told them they would now leave for Minsk and could take a shower there. Everyone was given a bar of soap and a towel. They boarded the waiting lorry without suspecting that this was a gas lorry. After a quarter of an hour of desperate struggle everything was quiet. A detail of six to eight new prisoners had to drag the corpses out of the lorry and place them on the pyre. At the end they also had to lie down next to the corpses and were shot by policemen. Then these burned down the last pyre and afterwards they left for two weeks home leave to celebrate Christmas with their families." [7]

•••

---

6 Book footnote 124. Central Office of the State Justice Department, Ludwigsburg, 2-AR 73/61, pp. 579, 580 and 590, copied in Kohl, Paul: *Ich wundere mich, daß ich noch lebe*, Gütersloh 1990, pp. 230/231. ("I wonder That I Am Still Alive").

7 Book footnote 127. Ibid.

Speechless.

Overwhelmed with horror and grief. I could not then, nor now, read on.

In receiving and reviewing Ira's latest research, yet again, we now had more information than we had before, more tragic depressing information passed on to us from three credible sources – Ira, the Meckenheim Archives, as well as testimonies in a historical text. It was only February of 2014, but I was already beginning to wonder if I really wanted or needed more information. I mean, was I "better off" just knowing that they were murdered during the Holocaust, or knowing more details? Once again (in February 2014 when I receive and read this information), I wonder not only if I want any more information about our family, but also whether or not I even want to go to Germany at all and re-experience this renewed pain all over again. For I already feel the pain acutely from that information, more than 4,000 miles away and 72 years later. And yet – I also wondered how I could possibly stay home "safely" tucked away in the USA, and not participate in this once-in-a-lifetime opportunity. Once again, in the re-telling of this, and re-imagining it, my heart is racing, I'm short-winded, and nauseated (May 2019, while writing this book).

I believe that it was several years after our 2014 Germany trip that Ira's research led her to find the exact dates that "our" Julius, Auguste, and Margot were murdered by the Nazis: July 24, 1942, just four days after they were transferred from the Bonn-Endenich Convent with many other Jews to the large Cologne Exhibition Hall. From there, they were deported in uninhabitable cramped cattle cars to Minsk, alongside the excrement from every "passenger" as well as their own, and alongside those humans who died during the transport. Upon their arrival in Minsk, they were shot and murdered, falling into a mass grave (that presumably they themselves had likely been forced to help dig, or perhaps other Jewish prisoners or other prisoners of war dug). I can't even... I grieve yet again now that Ira's discovered this fact borne by documentation.

It's horrific enough to imagine any human being treated this way. Now how could I bear this "knowing", this pain – from finding out that this actually is how our family members' lives ended? How dehumanizing, humiliating, and petrifying to likely have been forced by male Nazi soldiers at gunpoint to strip naked, strangers seeing strangers naked, children seeing their parents, grandparents, and other family members and friends naked, knowing what was coming next? Parents likely trying to shield their children from the spraying bullets, husbands and wives likely clinging to each other in their final moments, the pain and agony of those who did not die immediately? How many must have recited the "Shema" prayer in their final moments, sanctifying the name of G-d? What were Julius, Auguste, and Margot's last words to each other in those frenzied last moments together, moments of despair and hopelessness from the knowledge that they were about to be murdered?

I was depressed, anxious, and angry for some time. I grieved, as if it had happened just yesterday. From the pain of this knowledge, Jeffrey, Gail, and I changed one of Dad's annual rituals – that of his selection of his own annual date, Rosh Hashanah, to recite the Kaddish Prayer for their Yahrtzeit (annual anniversary of their deaths). Once Ira discovered and notified us of the July 24, 1942 date of their deaths, all-three-together in a Minsk forest and buried in a mass grave, we changed the date of their Yahrtzeit to the Hebrew date for July 24, 1942, and forever more continue to recite Kaddish for the three of them on that date, remembering all the victims of the Shoah as well. Additionally, in 2021, Gail, Jeffrey and I are exploring the process of having Dad's tombstone re-engraved on the back with the actual date of Julius, Auguste, and Margot's deaths, now that we have that date. I wrote an email back to our Significant 4 with gratitude for this information, and how it has impacted us.

From: Oliver
To: our Family, Herbert, and rest of Significant 4
Date: Fri, Mar 14, 2014
Subject: Photos from Hoehenlimburg etc.

Dear All,
I hope everybody is fine.
In the attachment, you will find photographs from Hohenlimburg cemetery and of the synagogue. Unfortunately,

several tombstones are in a rather bad condition so that the names are not clearly readable. Rolf, who is in Israel right now, took more pictures and will probably send them once he is back.

The white house next to the synagogue is the former Jewish school. We also went to the street which was "Eggestrasse" when your grandparents were living there. Unfortunately, no. 14 no longer exists, and there is a parking lot today, but we will try to find old photographs showing no. 14. ... The garden belonging to your grandparents' house is clearly recognizable on these pictures, and on some of them, you can only see the synagogue but not the school which was built later.

Ira gave me a short text on Hohenlimburg from an encyclopedia on Jewish communities in German-speaking countries. It says the Jewish school next to the synagogue had to close in the 1920s already because there were not enough Jewish pupils. This would mean that your father Ralph Stern probably attended Wesselbach school, which was a public school. I will try to get information on this school and to find out whether there are any chronicles and photographs from the 1920s and 1930s.

Rolf and I also went around the synagogue and saw your grandparents' garden. There is a sort of stair made of concrete which leads into the garden, and a part of the old metal fence is still there....

In a book on the Nazi regime in the "Siebengebirge" area (mountains near Bonn on the right bank of the Rhine), I found information on the Mundt jam factory. This factory used forced labour (about 55 workers), and there are sources on forced labour kept in the district archives. Ira thinks that Julius Stern probably worked there; so he had the right to leave the former convent in Endenich (and go and fetch the woolen gilet from the suitcase, for instance), whereas your grandmother was confined there. Her very sad last note sounds like that and says it between the lines, I think. ...

In the letter written in late 1941 your father refers to his sister's stay in Rheydt. The files of the registry with the addresses and names of people moving in or leaving town definitely were destroyed during the war, so it is rather difficult or even impossible to find out where she stayed.

The State Archives in Munster have answered in the meantime as well. Their reply sounds very promising, but they asked me to apply for special permission to order the documents which are of interest (prosecutor's documents on Hohenlimburg in 1938, documents on seizure of property, restitution claims after the war etc.), and I will do that next week. ... Best regards from Europe, Oliver

From: Oliver
To: All
Date: Sat, Mar 15, 2014
Subject: Correction and additional information

Dear All,
It's me again.... Ira found evidence for the fact that the street names in the Wesselbach area in Hohenlimburg were different in the 1920s and 1930s. She found a newspaper article on a woman from Hohenlimburg who helped the (name) family in the Nazi period. This woman's family owned a bakery in Eggestrasse 16 (present-day An der Kehle 40). You will find a photograph of this house in the attached document as well, and Rolf and I saw it on our walk in Hohenlimburg recently. If the bakery was Eggestrasse 16 at that time then one of the two neighbouring houses must have been Eggestrasse 14, the house where your grandparents had been living until 1930. I remember that there were houses next to the bakery, but I do not remember whether they were old or new ones. I also found information saying that present-day "Boingstrasse" (a narrow street under the water tower) was also called "Eggestrasse" before. It should be possible to check this soon in the Hagen city archives with old address books and maps from the 1930s. Anyway, your grandparents moved just a few hundred meters from Eggestrasse into the other house in Wesselbachstrasse 4, and both places were very close to the synagogue.

I also checked the information on the Jewish school. According to one of Ira's references, it was closed in 1926/1927, thus just 20 years after it had opened (another article Ira gave me states that the school next to the synagogue existed since 1906).

Best regards, Oliver

From: Ira
To: All
Date: March 26, 2014
Subject: AW: Correction and additional information

Dear All,

It seems that the artist Gunter Demnig can come to Meinerzhagen on 29.August 2014. We wait for his official recognition. We are in contact. ... We think that it would be good to visit Meinerzhagen, Hohenlimburg, Bonn-Bad Godesberg and Rexingen before that date – if this would be possible from your side. How long do you want to stay in Germany?

There is something I want to tell you. (Name) Stern had an elder brother who was a cattle trader and he lived in Ludenscheid, a town nearby. In 1940 he was a widower, an old man and he rented an apartment in a house in Schutzenstr. 2 for a long time. The owner of this house was (name), an old and ill man. The son-in-law of (the owner) was member of the SA and he wanted that his father-in-law should give notice to quit this Jew. But (his father-in-law) did not. So, after some time of trouble, his son-in-law and another member of SA denounced him. A special-court in Dortmund judged him to 1 year and 2 months in prison for being a "friend of Jews" and hearing foreign radio stations. Three days after (the father-in-law) was arrested by the Gestapo (4.May 1940), the renter of the apartment, (the elder Stern brother), died (from) a heart attack at the age of 82. The owner of the house, who would not "kick out" the Jewish renter, was denounced by his son-in-law, and was imprisoned, was so ill that they let him free. But not so long time. From 8.March 1941 to 8.March 1942 he (the owner of the house) was arrested (again) in a hospital of the prison in Bochum. A man, who was not able to break the rules of humanity and who took the consequences. After the war he didn't want to denounce his son-in-law, who brought him to prison. He died in 1948 in the age of 78. ....

Dear Gail,

Concerning to the letter of your father. He wrote the letter to his parents on 07.December 1941. The letter came back to him.

He wanted to get the money for visa. But he had no chance. Even if he would have had all the money and the visa, he had definitely no chance to rescue them at that time. On 23.October 1941 Reichsfuhrer SS Heinrich Himmler gave the order that emigration of Jews is forbidden. [8] I have this order in the archive for several times. In Meinerzhagen I found not the date 23.October 1941, but a document with the date 4.November 1941 (attachment) and 6.January 1942. There was no chance to get out of Germany in a legal way after 23.October 1941. It was war. German troops had occupied all countries around (Netherlands, Belgium, France, Poland, Denmark, Norway and so on). Europe was under German occupation without Spain, Portugal, Sweden and Great Britain. There was no chance to cross a border illegal. I don't know whether your father had known this.

I wrote a summary of all what we know about your family yet. But – sorry – in German. I try to translate it. But I need some time. You asked for the camp. They were brought from Bonn to Cologne first. I think they were definitely in the train to Minsk on 20.July 1942. Julius, Auguste and Margot are mentioned in that list. Usually they brought the arriving people not to a camp or to Minsk Ghetto. They shot them immediately after arriving in a forest called Blagowtschina near the village Maly Trostenets. Some were killed in gas lorries there.

The SS counted all victims. ... Someone working in a "Centre for the Genealogical Inventory", got a copy of these lists with names in October 1941 and by accident it survived. These lists are in "Markisches Museum Witten" today. ... Today there are the only complete proof of the deportation from Cologne.

Sorry that this mail is very hard for you again.

How kind of Ira to make a point of commenting on Dad's ongoing attempts to rescue his parents and sister and bring them to the US. Clearly, she empathized with his agony over this. Clearly, she empathized with us, his remaining family, over the pain this caused us from knowing Dad's pain. Clearly, she

---

8   Permission granted by Ira at Meinerzhagen Archives: Emigration Ban 04.November.1941. Source: Archive of the city of Meinerzhagen, B 1.3 file 217b. Stadt Meinerzhagen, 58540 Meinerzhagen.

Abschrift!

Geheime Staatspolizei
Staatspolizeistelle Dortmund   Dortmund, den 4.11.1941.
IV B 4 136/41 g - 1066/Schr.
        Br.9605.   G e h e i m !

An die Herren Landräte des Bezirks pp.

Betrifft: Auswanderung von Juden.
Bezug: Ohne.

        Reichsführer SS und Chef der Deutschen Polizei hat
angeordnet, daß die Auswanderung von Juden mit sofortiger
Wirkung zu verhindern ist.
        Lediglich in ganz besonders gelagerten Einzelfällen,
z.B. beim Vorliegen eines positiven Reichsinteresses, kann nach
vorheriger Herbeiführung meiner Entscheidung der Auswanderung
einzelner Juden stattgegeben werden.

                                Im Auftrage:

                                gez. Bovensiepen.

Der Landrat
des Kreises Altena.   Altena, den 11. November 1941.

fgb.Nr.L.51 p.u.v.(g)

                An

        die Herren hauptamtlichen Bürgermeister des Kreises.

                Abschrift übersende ich zur Kenntnis und Beachtung.

Reichsfuhrer SS Heinrich Himmler's order banning emigration of Jews from Germany, 23.October 1941. The Mayor of Meinerzhagen received this order on 04. November 1941 (4.11.41).

empathized –because she is human, humane, and compassionate, a person of integrity and honor... a Mensch.

From: Rolf
To: All
Date: April 4, 2014
Subject: Stolpersteinverlegung am 29.08.2014 in Meinerzhagen und Hohenlimburg

Dear All,

Gunter Demnig's office confirmed August 29, 2014 as the day when the commemorative plaques are going to be laid in Meinerzhagen and in Hohenlimburg. The "Stolpersteine" association in Meinerzhagen will send you official invitations by mail.

I would like to give you some information right now so that it will be easier for you to plan your trip: ... (Author's note: details of distances between towns we'd be visiting and potential schedule) ...

We will be in Hohenlimburg with the artist Gunter Demnig on August 29, 2014. Of course, the detailed program of the trip depends on you and on how long you would like to stay in Germany.

Now, Oliver in Paris will just have to translate this. I cannot wait to meet you here.

All the best, Rolf (mit Hilfe von Ira und Oliver)

(Author's note/English translation: with help from Ira and Oliver)

Once we were given the date (Friday, August 29, 2014) of our Family's Stolpersteine Commemoration Ceremony from our Significant 4, Gail set about arranging air travel for the three of us to go to Germany. Jeffrey was still not certain he wanted to come at all, even though he'd come to believe that the Significant 4 and the Stolpersteine Initiative were real. It didn't seem to "call" to him in the ways that it called to Gail and me. He said he didn't want to go because he doesn't like long international flights (which is true, but he takes them anyway). I don't think he was still on the fence because he didn't want to know more, or because it was too sad, or because he was nervous about our safety as Jews in Germany. It could've been related to the cost of the trip, which was expensive – especially for two of us. It could've been that he thought it was particularly expensive to spend such a large amount of money to cross the Atlantic Ocean "just" to spend essentially one day in Germany for a few ceremonies that might take a total of 3-5 hours, including transportation between Ceremony sites. As well, it could've been that the Mission of the trip didn't grab ahold of his Soul or tug at his heartstrings, his curiosity, or his sense of Adventure the way it did for Gail and me. In any case, he ultimately did decide to join us. Perhaps part of his decision was that we'd both told him early on that the two of us were going anyway, even if he chose not to come.

From: Oliver
To: All
Subject: Suggestions for your trip to Germany
Date: May 5, 2014

Dear All, Thank you very much for your message!

Here are our thoughts and suggestions: (Author's note: details about booking flights, which airports, alternatives, accommodations, car rental booking from the US would be best if that's what we want to do, distances from airport to town). ... We (Ira and Oliver) would like to accompany you to Rexingen, and of course, we can offer you to pick you up at the airport in Frankfurt or Stuttgart and to take you to Rexingen. ... Rolf, Christina and Ira can accompany you on both tours (the convent in Bonn-Endenich and the Memorial Center). Oliver can take you from Rexingen to Bonn or Meinerzhagen and will join us again on August 28 and 29 in Meinerzhagen and Hohenlimburg.

In Meinerzhagen (August 28 at the latest) – Host families will be ready to accommodate you, if you want, or we can of course book a hotel for you. We are glad to show you around and introduce you to the town and region, which was your ancestors' home.

On August 29 at 10 a.m., the commemorative plaques for your family (Julius Stern (Author's note: the grandfather of cousin Judi), Cilly Stern, Erna and Siegfried Schwarz, Erwin Stern and Jenny Weil) will be laid in Meinerzhagen. "Stolpersteine" will also be laid for (a Stern) family at Kirchstr. 5. You are of course kindly invited to attend this ceremony as well.

After that, we are going to go from Meinerzhagen to Hohenlimburg (26 miles). At 1 p.m., "Stolpersteine" will be laid for your family (Julius Stern (Author's note: Now this is "our" Julius Stern, Dad's father), Auguste Stern, Rolf Stern and Margot Stern) at Wesselbachstr. 4. We can show you the town of Hohenlimburg, the synagogue and the Jewish cemetery. ....

If you want to travel to Paris (Author's note: Jeff and I had never been there, and were considering a side trip after Germany before returning to the US.) you can take a train from Meinerzhagen to Cologne and from there the high-speed train "Thalys" to Paris (Cologne-Paris: 3 hours 15 minutes). Oliver will travel back to Paris with his son by car on August 31 as well and would be able to pick up two persons. (Author's note: Oliver would be able to drive us to Paris since he was returning there with his son.)

Looking forward to meeting you soon. All the best, Rolf, Christina, Ira and Oliver

From: Rolf
To: Gail, Herbert, Ira and Oliver
Date: Tuesday, May 06, 2014

Hallo Gail,
Only to let you know: I send you enclosed the inscriptions of the stumbling plugs, which we want to lay down in Hohenlimburg, Wesselbachstrasse 4, August 29th, 2014 at 1 p.m.

I have a question: Do you allow me to send your pictures of Julius Stern (Author's note: "our" Julius Stern), Auguste Stern, nee Weil, Margot Stern, Selma, nee Weil, Susanne und Jenny Weil to the Memorial place / Gedenkstatte in Bonn? There are rooms in memorial of the victims of the Shoah. In one room there are only pictures on the four walls, but there is only one from your family, Wilhelm Weil. I would like to send the other pictures to

Bonn (Memorial Center), so we can find them when we visit this Memorial place together in August.

Please write only yes or no, so I can manage it.

We are looking forward to your coming.

Yours sincerely...

Mit freundlichen gruessen, Christina und Rolf

Inscriptions of the Stolpersteine to be laid in Hohenlimburg, Wesselbachstrasse 4, on 29. August, 2014

Hier Wohnte	Hier Wohnte	Hier Wohnte
JULIUS STERN	AUGUSTE STERN	JENNY WEIL
JG. 1886	Geb. Weil	JG. 1892
Deportiert 1942	JG. 1887	Deportiert 1942
Minsk	Deportiert 1942	Minsk
Ermordet	Minsk	Ermordet
	Ermordet	

Hier Wohnte	Hier Wohnte
ROLF STERN	MARGOT STERN
JG. 1923	JG. 1927
Kindertransport 1938	Deportiert 1942
USA	Minsk
	Ermordet

A Sunday May 11, 2014 email from Ira included a description of how we are related to the (name) family who live in the USA: "And yes, you are related but it is (a) long time ago and a little bit hard to explain. His grand grand grandmother Stern (mother of Julius, grandmother of {name} married {female} in 1887. She was a daughter of a Stern. His brother had a son, Julius Stern. Julius Stern married Cilly (Weil). Cilly's sister Auguste (Weil) married Julius Stern in Hohenlimburg, your grandparents. It is better to paint it."

From: Gail
To: All
Date: Fri, May 30, 2014
Subject: Stern Family

Thank you so much for your invitation to Meinerzhagen on August 29 for the laying of the Stolpersteine. My brother Jeff, his wife Sheri and I will be there. We are still working on the details of our trips, and will be in touch soon. This really means so much to us, and we very much look forward to meeting you, and to seeing Meinerzhagen. Many thanks, Gail

From: Oliver
To: all
Date: Sat, May 31, 2014
Subject: Picture from Hohenlimburg
Attachments: Julius Stern company eggestr. 14 hohenlimburg.jpg

Dear All, I hope everything is fine and travel arrangements are progressing well! We are also looking forward to meeting you in Germany in August!

A few weeks ago, Ira sent me an interesting email she had received from a specialist in Hohenlimburg's history. (He is also the editor-in-chief of a review on local history.) He had some information on the house Eggestrasse 14, which still exists. You'll find the photograph in the attachment. (The bakery mentioned in one of my previous emails is the house with the dark front next to it.) Rolf and I even passed by when we were in Hohenlimburg, but as the name of the street and the house numbers have changed since the 1930s we did not realize that the house we were looking for was there. The specialist from Hohenlimburg also wrote that Julius Stern (Author's note: "our" Julius Stern) ran a scrap trade (is that the right term for a trade with discarded metals?) and that his business was in Eggestr. 14 until 1933, when the family had already moved to Wesselbachstr. 4. The house on the picture is near the synagogue, the former Jewish school and the house in Wesselbachstr., and everything is within walking distance. Best regards, Oliver

From: Ira
To: All
Date: Saturday, June 7, 2014
Subject: AW: Stern Family

Dear All,

Thank you very much for your message. If there are any questions concerning your trip, please ask!

Dear Judi, dear Bernie! If there are any questions concerning your family – maybe I am able to answer. The book about the Jewish community in Meinerzhagen is growing – many parts are finished. There will be one part describing history of the Jewish community since 1810 and another part about the fate of every family – maybe something like a memory book. Most documents are part of the written material of the administration. I would wish I could find more – not written about them, but written by themselves. The written material of the "Synagogengemeinde Meinerzhagen" was confiscated (not destroyed) during Chrystalnight (Author's note: Kristallnacht, the Night of Broken Glass), but was destroyed some days before American troops were coming to Meinerzhagen (10.April 1945) for liberation. Also many many papers concerning the responsible local Nazis were destroyed. But some they forgot to destroy. I don't think that the book will be finished in August. But you will get all, what I have. Sorry, only some parts are in English also. Maybe later I am able to translate more – or someone better speaking/writing English can do it.

(Name) told me one story I want to tell you. There were a group of women, all neighbours of "Derschlagerstrasse" in Meinerzhagen. They met and they made a picture. Mrs (name) was part of this neighbourhood and part of that picture. Some times later a very bad article with that picture was in the newspaper "Sturmer" (who was the traitor?). This hate sheet was in a glass box – public for everyone. Mrs (name) went to the glass box, destroyed it and took the "Sturmer" away. She was arrested – not so long. Only, because it was a short time before they could rescue to USA in September 1938 and they had the papers for their rescue. It is astonishing that there were no more consequences. She was very, very courageous. It was absolutely dangerous what she did, – but why? The only sense of what she did (without reasonable anger) is to protect her neighbours – maybe the names were in that article, or you could recognize this "Jewish friends" with that picture. A very old woman from Meinerzhagen, … knew this story also (she was 11 or 12 years old at that time) and she has the picture of that group of women. I am searching for this article, but it is not so easy without knowing the date. You have to read some years. Parts of the "Sturmer" are online, but not complete. It is only hate and malice. It is a torture reading this. I did not find the article yet, but I will try.

We very much look forward to meeting you.

See you soon. Ira

On June 12, in an email I sent to our Significant 4 asking questions about travel details, I wrote: "PS – In case no one's notified any of you, we have received the lovely invitations to the Commemorations. Thank you. Your kindness, support, and "digging" into our family's history are most appreciated and touching. We are looking forward to this trip in a bittersweet way, and especially to meeting all of you who have been accompanying us on this incredible Journey of Remembrance, Commemoration, and Healing."

Initiative Stolpersteine Meinerzhagen   Stadt Meinerzhagen
                                            Meinerzhagen,
                                            06.05.2014

Jeff and Sheri Stern, USA

Dear Family Stern,

In knowledge of the fate of those who were murdered, expelled, or driven to suicide during the period of National Socialism, the town of Meinerzhagen has for decades taken extremely seriously the consideration and remembrance of the harm that was done to your Jewish ancestors. During this time, contacts with the bereaved families and their kin have been continuously fostered.

In that same spirit of concern, the "Initiative Stolpersteine Meinerzhagen" wishes to lay memorial "stumbling blocks" at the addresses of those Jewish families who once had their homes in Meinerzhagen. The purpose of this initiative is both to memorialize the fate of these families and individuals, and to admonish the living never to let such a system of injustice come again into existence. For more details about the laying of these memorial "stumbling blocks", please see the leaflet enclosed with this letter.

Supported by the decision of the district council of Meinerzhagen the first stumbling blocks were layed in June 2013 in the city of Meinerzhagen. The next – concerning your family, will follow on 29 of August 2014 in the city of Meinerzhagen.

The "Initiative Stolpersteine Meinerzhagen", along with the city of Meinerzhagen, kindly invite you to attend this ceremony. We would be greatly honored by the presence of members of your family on this occasion. In the enclosed leaflet, please find the text that will be engraved upon the blocks to be laid for your ancestors. A brochure is being prepared which will contain a biographical documentation for each block pertaining to the family or individual thereby remembered.

If you plan to attend, we would of course offer to pick you up at your destination airport (Cologne, Dusseldorf, Frankfurt) to prevent any further costs during your stay in Germany. Once in Meinerzhagen, host families will be ready to accommodate you, if you so wish. These hosts would be glad to show you around and introduce you to the town and region that your ancestors called home.

If you have any questions or suggestions concerning this invitation, please feel free to ask the "Initiative Stolpersteine Meinerzhagen" – (email of Herbert). We would be most honored by your acceptance of this invitation. For the rest, we refer to the contacts existing since January, 2014 with the preparation of your visit in Germany.

Mit herzlichen Gruessen (Warm greetings),

Herbert, "Initiative Stolpersteine Meinerzhagen"

From: Ira
To: Sheri
Date: Wednesday, July 16, 2014
Subject: AW: Stern Germany Plans

(Author's note: I asked Ira if the ancient Worms "mikwe" was what American Jews call a "mikveh", and whether it was functional or historical, as I was considering utilizing it.)

Dear Sheri,

The mikveh in Worms is only for historical/touring purposes. I saw it. There was water in it, but the mikveh and the whole area normally is public. Everyone can run around. There is no women's bathing cubicle. There is no Jewish parish in Worms today. Some few Jews are living there and they belong to the Jewish community in Mainz. The synagogue sometimes is "working". On Jewish holidays is a service in the synagogue Worms and the whole area is closed for others. ... There are round about 300,000 Jews living in Germany now, most of them coming from Russia in the 1990s (and many without knowledge about their roots). More than 100,000 are members of a Jewish community, which exists in greater cities only. Unfortunately a high standard of security for the Jewish Community buildings is necessary – not because of some Neo-Nazis, it's because of the possibilities of some radical Islamists – only for prudence. You must not be in fear. There exists a modern "working" Mikveh in Munich, in the Jewish Center. (She gave details and contact info if I wanted to schedule a Mikveh visit. I contacted them, but ultimately decided not to pack it into my already filled days, and honestly – because I was nervous about going there at night which is the only time they operate.)

There is a kosher restaurant also. It belongs to the Community Center too. What is about eating during your visit? Real kosher eating will be a problem in most places you will stay. What can we do? ... (Author's note: I'd asked how to pronounce her name) My name is pronounced: Ear–rah.

Greetings, Ira

From: Rolf
To: Gail
Date: Monday, July 28, 2014
Subject: Dokumentation der Lebensgeschichte von Ralph (Rolf) Stern

Dear Gail,

During the ceremony when Mr. Gunter Demnig puts down the stones in Hohenlimburg on August 29th, 2014 we want to tell something about the life of your father Rolf. Now I am studying the documents, but I never found a notice about his death. When did he die and where was he buried? Please can you write me these things, also about your mother Shirley? I am not quite clear with Rolf's profession? Is it correct to say he was a merchant and trader dealing with supplies for horses? Thank you for answering. I am looking forward to meeting you in Bad Godesberg on August 26th, 2014.

Best Greetings,
Christina und Rolf Janssen

Gail responded the same day:

"Hi Rolf, My dad died November 27, 2009, the day after Thanksgiving, peacefully in his home from heart failure. I was with him, and the whole family spent Thanksgiving day with him. Yes, he was a merchant trading in horse supplies. My mother was a nurse, with a Master's degree in Public Health. She died about 15 years before my dad, and he never took off his wedding ring. After family, the most important thing to my dad was education. Even though he never graduated from high school, he made sure that his family had all of the advantages of education. While my brother and I were in college, my mother went back to school and got her college degree, and then her Master's while I was in law school. Some men would not have been comfortable with their wife having more education than them, but he was different. … he was so proud of all of us, and so happy that his hard work made it all possible. The third thing that was important to my dad was charity. … He supported many charitable organizations, and taught my brother and me from an early age the importance of giving to others.

Thank you for asking. I very much look forward to meeting you. Gail"

In an August 1, 2014 email from me to Ira, I responded with joy about her sharing that her oldest son was going to be an exchange student for the upcoming semester in the US. I offered that if he was coming to a college near us in Maryland, we'd be happy to have him join us for a family dinner and show him some sights if he was interested and had time. I also wrote: "It's hard to believe we'll be on our way to meet you just 3 weeks from today (and Jeffrey's and my first trip ever to your country; Gail has been several times.)! We are very much looking forward to meeting you, Oliver, and Rolf and Christina, learning more about our family's history/and seeing where they lived and loved and experienced, and learning about your country and culture. It will clearly be an emotional trip for all of us, and I anticipate it will bring some emotional closure to a significantly impactful chapter of our and our family's history that has shaped us along with every other human being that was touched by that history. Please know how much we appreciate all your and the others' time and efforts and detailed plans leading up to this, and the fact that you all have chosen to personally accompany us on our Family Heritage Journey – using your personal time to do so. Looking forward, Sheri"

Ira wrote back on August 4, 2014, sending us their wonderfully detailed daily itinerary for us from August 25 – August 31, including all four of their work and private addresses and phone numbers (For G-d's sake, what stopped me from asking them for their blood types?!), and thanking us for our friendly offer to their son (but he would be studying in a state far from us). She also shared her "mother/parent" concerns, which I imagine most mothers/parents (including me!) all over the world, no matter their skin color, religion, or language share: "It is a greater problem for us (parents) than for him, that he will be so far away. I know, he is old enough." I empathized with her, sharing my same feelings when our kids went off to college – even though ours studied in our own state and country less than a two-hour drive from our home! At the end she wrote: "We will meet you in just 3 weeks and I am glad to accompany you on your way to the roots of your family. Looking forward, Ira".

Nothing in those particular exchanges about religion, ethnicity, or the history of trauma and tragedies that had brought us together in the first place. Just two women, both mothers, across the ocean, newly corresponding only by emails for the past seven months, sharing their concerns and joys, their common humanity and vulnerabilities, and looking forward to meeting each other. Normal.

This is how we three Jewish Americans and these four Germans had already evolved over the past seven months – together, across the ocean, without ever having "met". Four-zillion emails later – (from that first email from Oliver on January 3, 2014 through our journey to Germany in August 2014, and still ongoing today), we'd already developed significant relationships with Ira, Oliver, Rolf and Christina – all of whom thankfully for us communicated in English, and even translated (at our request) some of our family's heart-wrenching letters for us for the first time since the 1940s when they were originally written (one by Dad, one by his mother). Each time they had "new" information to share with us about our family, they respectfully and compassionately asked with exquisite sensitivity if we wanted to receive the information, advising us that it was often very sad. While they were exquisitely sensitive to our emotions, they were brutally honest about the facts/the realities – without sugar-coating anything or making any excuses for what Hitler and the Nazis and some German citizens did or did not do. Each time we said "yes, send it" (new information). Each time we received and read it, we cried and our hearts ached, but we yearned for more. We yearned for more information because they were able to fill in so many puzzle pieces of our family's lives for which we'd never before had any source, much less such reliable sources, for information. They were giving us back our family, our Mishpacha, with the details of our family's lives. One particularly touching email from Ira included this passage: "You may ask: how could this happen? We do not know. It was a time when the world went mad."

You'll note I say "our family" throughout the book. Although this is not the biological family into which I was born, they had become my family too, my second family, "our family" – decades ago. Jeffrey and I met when we were 16, high school sweethearts; we went "steady" in the 70s and I wore his school ring (with lots of tape around it!). We married at 21, and shared many wonderful memories of family holidays and grandchildren together, as well as the expected and unexpected difficult life events. I called my in-laws "Mom" and "Dad" because they truly were my second parents. There were never any mother-in-law jokes between us! In the process of writing this book, I've also sadly learned of biological family ancestors who were Holocaust victims. Besides personal family, "our family" also means to me our family of the Jewish people, and our family of Humanity.

Here are some additional facts I found about Dad's history through a 2003 interview that our cousin Jeremy conducted with Dad during one of our Family Reunions. Included here are some salient portions from Jeremy's post.

Ralph's family had been trying for some time to emigrate to America because of the active aggression against Jews in Germany since 1933. They were hoping to come to America through Auguste's sister Bella (nee Weil) Sanders who lived in Delphus, Ohio. Bella had come to the US in the late 20s or early 30s before Hitler's regime. Because Bella didn't have sufficient money to sponsor her sister Auguste, Julius, and both their children Rolf and Margot, Rolf/Ralph's parents made the decision that Ralph would be the one to escape from Hitler (Author's note: I can't even imagine needing to "choose" which one of my children to save, can you?!). When he was 15 years old, Ralph's parents gave him 500 marks (about $125 US dollars) and arranged for him to go to his aunt in Ohio (Author's note: via HIAS). At that time, there was no actual fighting in Germany yet.

On about September 7, 1938, just weeks before Kristallnacht, Ralph took a train from Meckenheim to Hamburg where he met other children from all over Germany who were going to America via HIAS. They traveled together by train from Hamburg to the town Aachen at the border of Germany and Belgium. Once at the border, Ralph learned that it was illegal to leave Germany with more than 10 marks, so he filled out a form to have his remaining 490 marks sent back to his family. Unfortunately, he made a mistake in filling out the form the first time. Instead of throwing out the form, he stuffed it into his suitcase. When he tried to pass through the border, a German guard found it in his luggage and suspected him of attempting to smuggle money out of Germany. Somehow, Ralph managed to convince the guard that he wasn't smuggling money, and he was allowed to pass through Belgium, eventually arriving at Lahavre, France, where he and the other children boarded a ship to America.

The sea journey to America took about eight days. During the journey, Ralph was given cornflakes for breakfast. As he'd never had them before, he ate them from a bowl without milk or sugar. An American woman aboard, who spoke a little German, noticed this and politely told him: "If you add sugar and milk, it tastes even better." (Author's note: When our children, Dad's grandchildren, were very young, and they learned of this – it became one of their most loved stories about their "Pop-Pop".)

... Ralph attended school for six months in Delphus, but had to quit at age 16 because he had to work to support himself. ...

In 1943, he joined the US Army, served in the medical corps, and was stationed in Germany. After the end of the war, and towards the end of his service, he served in the military government helping to translate. He was stationed as the Chief of Police in a small town in Austria, Zell Am See near Salzburg. In June or July 1945, immediately after the end of WWII, Ralph visited the town of Berchtesgarden, the site of Hitler's vacation home. When he arrived, the officer in charge declared that only those who ranked as officers or higher were allowed to use the elevator in the house. Shortly after, General Patton – head of the Third US Army – arrived and learned of this, after which the rules were changed so that any soldier, whether a General or an enlisted soldier, could ride the elevator depending on who was waiting for it first. [9]

Interesting significant details that shaped the man, the Mensch who Dad was, always.

---

9   http://www.flickr.com/photos/smoovej/6032862381/in/photostream

And so it was that our Significant 4 joined us at our family's Stolpersteine Ceremonies, and chose to become our private tour guides for our Family Heritage Trip to Germany. They chose to take time off from work to do so, and furthermore, Oliver left his home in Paris to drive to Germany to join us in these endeavors! So you can see, through our multiple emails, that we already cared about these people, and "knew" in our Souls that they cared about us and our family, before we ever met in person. Eight months of ricocheting emails was more than enough time to create the consistent feelings of warmth, empathy, trust, compassion, generosity, and kindness between us. They researched, learned, and shared so much about our family. There was never any mention of money or any way to compensate them for all of their time, personalized research, the actual Stolpersteine plaques for our family members, or our guided family journey. This was clearly no scam. And so, after all of that – there was every reason to go to Germany to meet our new friends, embrace and thank them, and attend the Stolpersteine Commemorative Ceremonies for our family members on August 29, 2014.

Chapter 5

PARANOIA SETS IN

July 2014 – August 2014

About six weeks prior to our trip, I suddenly became non-clinically paranoid. One day, when all the plans had been finalized and it was still too early to busy myself with packing, I suppose the significance of what we were about to do really hit me. And my unbidden unexpected response was ... paranoia and conspiracy theory.

Since Oliver's first email in January of 2014, I'd been completely caught up in our family's history and that of the Holocaust, the kindnesses which the Significant 4 had shown us, their compassion and generosity, how they treated us, and how they treated our deceased loved ones – showing great respect for the significance of their lives, as well as empathy and horror for the Nazis' inhumane atrocities. These Significant 4 – individually and in concert – gave the consistent impression over the previous months that they genuinely seemed to care about us and our family, both those living as well as those deceased – the few who were able to escape, and the too-many who weren't.

What's more is that I absolutely, irrevocably, undeniably wanted to go on this trip. Within weeks of Oliver's first email, I already "knew" this would not be "just" a trip, would not be a "vacation", but would be a true once-in-a-Lifetime Journey – emotionally and spiritually, besides geographically and culturally. I "knew" in my Soul that this journey would be life-altering, an adventure that could never be replicated, could never have a "re-do". Once I realized this was "real" and not a scam (perhaps in February 2014, though Gail knew it immediately upon receiving Oliver's first email!), both Gail and I knew that we'd change any plans we might've had in order to accommodate whatever date was set by the Meinerzhagen Stolpersteine Initiative for the Stolpersteine Commemorative Ceremonies, and that we wanted to do a Family Heritage Journey – to follow in the footsteps of Dad and his family, and hopefully learn some answers to the many questions we'd had for decades, but felt we couldn't ask Dad.

As further "evidence" that everything was "kosher" with these Significant 4 and the proposed Stolpersteine Ceremony, by now I'd looked up the Stolpersteine Initiative online and found a wealth of information that seemed to confirm their "real" existence as an organization. Their website talked about the artist who developed the project – Gunter Demnig – and had "real" contact information with emails as well as telephone numbers. Not to mention the fact that months prior – Ira, Oliver, Rolf and Christina had offered to be our personal guides on our custom-designed (by them, with our input and requests) Family Heritage Journey for four days prior to our family's Stolpersteine Ceremonies. Furthermore, they each made it clear that no money was expected from us, and that they would not accept any money for their time and efforts, though we offered several times even before making the journey.

So it may seem rather odd, after all that I've written above to convince you, the reader (and myself, back in the summer of 2014), that these are good people and the Stolpersteine organization is real ... that instead of all this making me feel better and safe about the trip – it actually translated into the opposite for me: paranoia and conspiracy theory! And that, from a woman who is usually Polyanna and trusts pretty much everyone!

It went like this in my head: Hmmm, why **are** these TOTAL strangers being so kind to us? Why **are** they so interested in we three Jews coming to Germany for this Stolpersteine Ceremony? What if these Significant 4 are in cahoots with some other Germans, and they want to do us harm? After all, they weren't asking us for money, and they wouldn't let us pay for anything. Why else was it so important to them that we come to Germany, unless ...?

Oh, though they never asked us for our credit card numbers, bank accounts, or Social Security numbers (or our zillions of computer passwords) – they *did* now have our home addresses, email addresses, AND our cellphone numbers. And of course, they can find out ANYthing about us on Google! AND, they clearly already know that we're Jewish. (It's time now for you, the reader, to imagine Alfred Hitchcock movie music playing in the background as my train of thought continues, and runs amok.)

OK, Sheri, get a grip. So what if they have that information about us? What can they actually **do** with it, and more importantly – what **will** they do with it? Well, for one – they can find us (and what, hunt us down?). Why **would** they want to do us harm? Because we're Jewish, and their neighbors and possibly their ancestors killed our family members and so many others? What if this is an elaborate conspiracy scheme to get three American Jews – descendants of other Jews – to come to Germany to ... WHAT? To continue to pursue "The Final Solution"? Because they want to finish the job that the Allies stopped Hitler from completing in 1945? To imprison us, take away our cellphones and passports so we couldn't have any contact with our family who wouldn't know where we were or what happened to us, no contact with the outside world, to starve and/or torture us or to perform inhumane experiments on us, to conscript us into forced labor, to march us through the frozen tundra to our deaths, to take us out in some distant forest to dig our own graves and then shoot us and bury us in an unmarked area that may or may not be discovered 50-70 years from now, to ....

And on and on I went, alarmingly easily and briskly, imagining every possible horrific fate that "could" happen to **us**, at the hands of these "Significant 4" (and possibly others they might be in cahoots with) – just like the fates that really happened to our family members, "real" fates which I'd been indoctrinated with in school, in history books and novels, and in movies and old newsreels for decades, and fates which I knew so many family members, my "People" of the Jewish Tribe, and others really experienced during the Shoah.

I actually feel sad and nauseous right now, embarrassed, guilty, and very ashamed of myself. Nonetheless, I'm keeping my thoughts in this book because they belong here, to show the negative spiraling thoughts that can come from a normally sane well-adjusted person, as an example to show how some "regular" people can develop and maintain harmful negative stereotypes because of what they're "taught". And then for some people, they group together with other like-minded people to take action on these negative stereotypes – especially if "they" feel threatened in any way (those who have lynched other human beings, segregated people onto reservations after stealing their land, segregated people into separate schools/restrooms/water fountains, isolated people and taken away their rights, murdered, gassed, incinerated, tortured, starved... and the list of man's inhumanities to man goes on. I'm crying right now as I write this [2/20/19; and again 5/12/21, as I review it for publication], knowing what I know now, and how I now personally "know":

Ira, the pragmatic and empathetic Archivist who searched and searched for more detailed information about our family. She has the skills, patience, compassion, willingness, and motivation to do so. And now I know *her* family, whose hospitality I enjoyed when I stayed in their home for several days during my return trip in May 2018: her husband, who enjoys learning American colloquialisms, and their two sons, both having graduated college now, who I enjoyed getting to know during that stay.

Oliver (and his wife, son, and a newborn daughter in 2021. Although we've not yet met his wife and son, he's shared pictures with us. We did have the pleasure of meeting his baby daughter during one of our international mishpacha zooms in June 2021. We all put her to sleep with the cacophony of our voices.). This soft-spoken Historian was able to share multiple references for historical facts at "New York" speed right off the top of his head. He knows his WWII / Holocaust history!

He demonstrated compassion when interpreting family letters written in German, always came to us and whispered the English translation of whatever was being spoken in German before we even had a chance to ask him to do so, both at events as well as restaurants – translating menus (VERY important!), and we've met up with him twice in the USA – when he came for conferences in DC and Philadelphia. We were thrilled to welcome him as our honored guest in our homes when he came to DC.

Rolf, the energetic passionate Leader of the Meinerzhagen chapter of the Stolpersteine Initiative, then in his early 70s when we first met in 2014, who we had difficulty keeping up with when climbing hills and steps! Passionate and compassionate about the Stolpersteine Mission, he advocated for us and our family early on in January to try to get Stolpersteine laid for Dad, his sister Margot, and his parents Julius and Auguste, to "reunite" them together at their Hohenlimburg home – the last place they'd lived and loved together as a family, before Hitler came into power and irrevocably altered their lives and so many others'. Organized and goal-oriented, he was not afraid to challenge the status quo with his local government officials to "make things right" for both the living descendants of victims of the Holocaust (us) as well as the deceased victims in our family. He frequently said, "We must NEVER forget!" And I will never forget how he held our faces gently, and kissed me and Gail on our foreheads every night when he took us back to our hotel, and called us "Liebe" (Dear, Love).

Christina, Rolf's wife, who clearly supported Rolf's and the Stolpersteine Initiative's Mission, and patiently translated for us the many emails that Rolf sent to us. She compassionately followed me into a Memorial Center bathroom when she sensed I needed some support. During our 2018 trip – she brought gardening tools and plants for all of us to plant together with them at our great-grandparents' gravesites during our 2018 trip – a loving moving ritual.

Old habits die hard, "they" say. And often, we're not even aware (I wasn't!) that we harbor such bigoted racist thoughts, such prejudice, such negative stereotypes with which we were indoctrinated. To be fair, I don't recall being taught that "all" German people were Nazis. However, that was my only knowledge about German people, never having met any before. We must always add reason and rational thought to what we are taught. Just because a large group of people (Nazis) perpetrated such atrocities of inhumanity upon so many others (including Jewish people) at one time in history, and because there remains today in Germany, Europe, America, and elsewhere groups of individuals with "neo"-Nazi ideology, intolerance, and hatred towards anyone who's "different" or "other" – does not mean that all Germans are Nazis today or even back in the 30s and 40s during the Shoah, nor that all Germans want and/or wanted to do us (Jewish and other people) harm. It was like a visceral knee-jerk reaction for me, related to my brain's hardwiring from my life experiences and teachings, summoned by my dark side, by my fears, by my sense of feeling unsafe because of "the unknown", by my unconscious ignorance.

By now, Jeffrey had "cut bait" months ago by choosing to come with me and Gail. We'd paid for our roundtrip airfare tickets, had reservations for several hotels, had paid for trip travel insurance, and had decided at Gail's recommendation to begin the Journey with three days in Munich first – just the three of us, before we met up with our Stolpersteine Friends – because Jeffrey and I had never been anywhere in Germany. And besides, Jeffrey and Gail didn't seem concerned or worried at all!

That said, the reality and the paranoia (that I'd artificially created) surrounding what we were about to do set in – for me! I began to think: Wait a minute. You mean we're travelling more than 4000 miles across the Atlantic Ocean (one-way; and back, hopefully!) to meet four people we've never met, to arrive in a foreign airport where we don't speak their German language, and meet up with two of those four people and GET IN THEIR CARS, NO QUESTIONS ASKED, NO WORRIES, AND GO WHEREVER THEY DECIDE TO TAKE US? Seriously?! Of course, we'll have no idea if they're actually taking us to where they say they're taking us, because we've never been there before, and we certainly don't know the area or the directions, and we can't even read their road signs BECAUSE THEY'RE IN GERMAN AND WE DON'T KNOW THAT LANGUAGE!

I mean, what IF ...this whole past eight months of emailing has been "a scheme"? A scheme for what, Sheri? They had not only never asked us for money, they actually told us that we were not allowed to pay for the Stolpersteine for our family (as evidenced by documentation on the www.stolpersteine.eu/en website that I'd checked), and that they would not accept money from us for being our Family Heritage Guides. Yes, but... what if these four were in cahoots with this "real?" organization on the internet ("It's on the Internet ..., it must be true!"), The Stolpersteine Initiative, that "reportedly" existed in multiple European countries – those that Hitler had conquered, usurped power, and killed their Jews/Romas-Sintis/anyone who disagreed with him and his policies/etc? What if together they were planning to torture and kill us, separate us and place us in concentration camps? For what purpose, Sheri? You're being ridiculous, you're being paranoid, you're really losing it!

And then, time and again, I would regain enough of my previous long-term sanity as if I'd never lost it. And then, I'd tell myself rationally that my "thinking" was over-thinking, distorted, irrational and paranoid – none of it based in reality, just short-term, "fixed false beliefs" (which by the way, is the clinical definition of "delusions", one type of psychotic symptom, a break with reality). And then, I'd feel better, even if just for awhile, as if that "bucket of ice" I'd just thrown in my face snapped me out of my paranoid tirade ... back into reality. And I could go on feeling better for a few hours, realizing how absurd my thinking and behaviors were: considering canceling our trip, losing money from plans already made and paid for, having Gail and Jeffrey (and likely others) laugh at me for how far my paranoid ideation had taken me, and possibly missing out on a once-in-a-Lifetime Journey. I could hear it now: "What? Are you kidding me? Seriously, you think there's a very real possibility that these four Germans have conspired with other Germans to get you all to trust them enough to come to their country on some ruse of a kind commemorative gesture, to do terrible things to you as their Nazi countrymen did to your family and so many others decades ago? Get a grip, Sheri!"

On the other hand ... was it worth some teasing and their considering having me committed to an institution, to save our lives? Notice, I didn't say to "possibly" save our lives!

I was so torn – wanting to go, wanting to think kindly and positively of these four people whom we'd never met, and wanting to trust them. I mean, genetically and historically, remember – I am Polyanna. And I do truly believe in the inherent goodness of Humanity (most of Humanity, anyway). And really, in my sane moments, I thought: "Come on, Sheri. What's in it for them to bring us all the way to Germany to harm us? And surely, they'd be caught if they harmed us ... I mean, wouldn't they? Surely, our children would report us missing ... I mean, wouldn't they? And the US Embassy and the FBI and CIA would become involved, and there would be an international search for us, right? Yea, but what if they never found us, or found us so late that we were damaged or ill beyond redemption, or dead? You mean, "damaged" like YOU are thinking right now, Sheri?! Hello?! I know, but ...

And on and on it went. "They" didn't need to bring me to Germany to torture or kill me. *I* was doing one hell of a job of self-induced-torture right in my **own** home, in my **own** mind, in my ***own*** country! My mind was traveling to places unknown, although I never left my couch or earned any Frequent Flyer miles. How many of us shackle ourselves, imprison our own minds with irrational thoughts that cause us anxiety and distress time and time again, when we could live more fully and rationally by simply turning the key in those shackles and slipping them off. For "we" are the ones who hold the keys. And clearly, I'm "hiding" behind the "we" now, when in full disclosure – you know that I'm clearly talking about "me". Ahhh – an active creative imagination can be such a Blessing ... ***and*** a Curse.

So when I reached my first threshold of agonizing repetitive self-torture after a couple of weeks, now four weeks pre-trip, I decided to take positive action. I tried to look two of the Significant 4 up online, Ira and Oliver, since they were the ones we would first encounter at the Frankfurt airport. While I'd already found www.stolpersteine.eu online and reviewed it some time ago, I now decided to go back to their website and see if there actually ***was*** an actual Stolpersteine Ceremony scheduled for Friday August 29, 2014 in Meinerzhagen, Germany, as well as whether any of the Significant 4's names were on the website.

Indeed, the website ***did*** show the date of August 29, 2014 in Meinerzhagen as one of the dates for the laying of Stolpersteine. This was the date that the Significant 4 had given us for ***our*** family's ceremonies. Okay ... that's good, that helped a lot. However, I did not find any of their four names on that website (not realizing at that time that our Significant 4 were working with a ***local*** Stolpersteine Initiative chapter, in Meinerzhagen, so that's why their names were not on the ***national*** European Stolpersteine website), which caused me further concerns.

So maybe they really weren't who they claimed to be; maybe they didn't really work where they said they did. Even though they sounded genuinely compassionate and knowledgeable throughout their emails, maybe that was part of the ruse to get us to trust them enough to bring us to Germany. So then, my more logical left brain took over (finally!), and led me to check LinkedIn to see if they were really who they said they were. Unfortunately, I was not tech-savvy enough to navigate that site at that time, and found no information on any of them.

So ... I did what any technologically-challenged adult would do: I stopped trying, stopped investigating, and told myself that I was being ridiculous (and paranoid). After all, neither Gail nor Jeffrey – who are both very level-headed and logical – had ever brought any worries up, and they'd just laugh at me anyway. So I went along like that – keeping my worries to myself, without mentioning a word about my doubts to Jeffrey or Gail. And, I was feeling "okay" about going to Germany after all, though I still didn't feel "complete" because I hadn't researched them or the whole concept thoroughly enough. I didn't feel comfortable that I'd done all my homework, but if Jeffrey and Gail were okay with it – I certainly trusted both of them enough to follow their lead.

Well, that only lasted another couple weeks, until two weeks pre-trip – when I finally decided I had to say my fears out loud to Jeffrey. I figured I'd rather have him laugh at me and tell Gail and our friends how paranoid I was, than possibly be harmed or killed. (Notice I now said "possibly"! That's progress, right?!)

So did Jeffrey qualm my fears, did he say I was being paranoid, did he roll around on the floor laughing at me? NO – he increased my fears with his response: "Yea, I know – I've been thinking that we really don't know much about them, too." Oy vey, if Jeffrey was worried too, we were in deep trouble! I told him I'd tried to look all four of them up on LinkedIn, with no success. Then out of the blue, it suddenly dawned on me that I could Google each of them, as well as their work addresses (some of which we already had as their "signature lines" on their emails), to see if their names were mentioned there and/or if their work addresses identified the type of work that was done in that office. That would help.

So between me looking that stuff up, and Jeffrey effectively accessing LinkedIn, we did indeed find the information we were seeking about Ira and Oliver, the two who were picking us up at the Frankfurt airport in their cars and taking us to our first stops and our hotel. Believe it or not, boys and girls, Ira and Oliver were **both** exactly who they said they were! I felt so much better, as did Jeffrey, but I decided on one more bit of "research" (I realize I'm stretching to call this "research"!) to clinch the deal and feel safe – once and for all.

So I emailed Ira, and asked for a picture of both her and Oliver, "so we can recognize you at the airport when you pick us up." (I'd forgotten that she'd already sent us a picture of herself from

a German newspaper article back in that first month of January.)
And I asked Ira to let us know how to pronounce her name, so we
could get it right. Finally, I asked again for their work addresses
and phone numbers, as well as their personal mobile numbers
(because there'd been so many emails back and forth, that I
wasn't sure which one had which information in it, so this would
save me "time" from looking back over hundreds of emails – I
explained to them.). Also, I explained that we wanted to have their
work numbers and addresses "in case there were any mix-ups"
with our plans to meet. As well, I guess I was pretty transparent
when I said I wanted to leave their contact information for our
adult children – "just in case." I guess I "explained" too much!
I was too worried about hurting their feelings to ask for their
personal home addresses, thinking that would "give us away"
about our (my) doubts about them.

Ingenious of me, don't you think? No one could identify any
suspicions I had from those simple requests, right? Ha! Our plan
was that Jeffrey and I would compare the pictures and work
addresses they sent us with the ones he'd found on LinkedIn – to
assure they were one and the same, and that all was "kosher," so
we could go to Germany in peace, knowing that we'd "done our
homework, our due diligence" (and to negate my paranoia and
distrust, and prevent me from being psychiatrically hospitalized
– unless it was absolutely necessary! I'm sure some of you now
are thinking, "Hmm, that ship has already sailed, girl.").

Well clearly, Ira read between the lines! She sent us all
Significant 4's work and home addresses, all 4 of their work and
mobile numbers, as well as a picture of herself – with her two
adult sons! Furthermore, she explained why her husband was
not in the picture with them ... because he was taking the picture!
I figured that no shady axe murderer would send a picture of
herself with her two sons! As well, she sent a picture of Oliver,
and her car. As well, Oliver sent a picture of his car, which even
happened to show his license tag number clearly! The Oliver
picture that Ira sent us was the exact picture of him on LinkedIn.
Imagine that!

Here is what I emailed back to Ira on August 10, 2014: "Thank
you for sharing pictures of you and your two sons with us. With
our mutual exchanges of pictures and other details, it is like

families sharing families across the miles. Appreciate the picture of your car as well. (Oliver sent us a picture of his previously.)" Did I ask them for a picture of their cars? I don't even remember. It's not like we were meeting them in a parking lot or garage! They were coming directly into the terminal at baggage claim to "claim" us! Most likely, they'd figured out that I was anxious by reading between the lines of my email (or even more likely, it was blatantly obvious in my email that I didn't trust them!).

One would think that I'd finally be at peace, and I was – as far as meeting the Significant 4. But the piece that I still did not feel peaceful about was the fact that we were three Jews traveling to Germany, the seat of the Holocaust/the Shoah, which is in Europe – from which we'd heard about much continuing anti-Semitism. Thankfully, I have never personally experienced anti-Semitism in America; I don't know about Jeffrey or Gail. Some (mostly Jewish) friends and acquaintances said they couldn't believe we were going, they wouldn't go if it was them, how could we ever "set foot" on German soil where they killed our People, weren't we afraid, and cautioned us that we shouldn't wear anything in public (or even hidden under our shirts) that identified us as Jews (i.e. Star of David jewelry, Chai jewelry – a Hebrew letter representing the number 18 and long life, a kippah/yarmulke – skullcap worn by Orthodox Jews, or a Tallit – a prayer shawl worn by Jewish men and some women.).

My initial response was: "What? Not wear my beautiful Star of David that I'd gotten a couple of years ago when I was in Israel? Not wear my Chai necklace that my father gave me when I was hospitalized for a collapsed lung years ago? Not wear my beautiful kippah for when we'd visit a Synagogue? Jeffrey should not bring and wear his kippah that our son had brought him as a gift from Israel? I was MAD, angry that others were telling me this! Angry that there might be some truth to this, not solely based in fear. Ever since we began to plan this trip, I'd felt a strong urge and need to "announce" my Judaism while sojourning in Germany – the land that had grown Nazis and killed our family, our People. I wanted to "show" Germans in a very public way, to prove to them everywhere I went in their country, that "We are STILL here! AND, we're PROUD of being Jewish."

Then I was angry at Jeffrey, who quickly agreed that we

shouldn't bring or wear anything that identified us publicly or privately as Jewish. For the first time ever, in our almost-50 years together, I thought my brave strong husband – who has always publicly and proudly identified as a Jew – was acting cowardly. For the first time ever, I thought my brave strong husband was taking the path of least resistance. For the first time ever, I thought my brave strong husband was thinking only with his heart instead of his brain. For the hundredth (millionth?) time, my brave strong husband and I disagreed.

It took me awhile to process this issue, especially because I did not want to think of myself as cowardly or letting our People down. And in the end ... I chose not to bring or wear my Star of David, my Chai, or my Kippah. In the end, I also chose not to think of myself as cowardly or letting our People down. In the end, I chose to be smart and safe about it – just like Jeffrey was being, not cowardly. I came to the realization that **I** know who I am – a proud Jewess – and I don't need to "announce" it to the world. I can just "be" one – and that will speak for itself.

Now that I was comfortable, truly felt safe to meet these four Germans, all that remained was some mild anxiety about traveling to Germany (or anywhere in Europe) as a Jew. That was overridden by my sense of adventure, my greater anticipation of the spiritual nature of this once-in-a-lifetime journey, and by my desire to know as much as possible about the fates of our family members – in order to perhaps "come to closure"?, though I didn't particularly feel such a need for closure at that time.

Oh, and by the way, here's an unexpected irony I encountered in January 2019 while writing this book – ironic, because I (a lifelong Baltimorean, having lived in the city for the first 17 years of my life!) was worried about safety traveling to Germany. I googled the distance from Baltimore, Maryland to Meinerzhagen, Germany, to see how far we'd actually traveled, in order to include it in this book. I found that Google answer as well as these other common questions:

"People also ask: ...

Is **Baltimore,** Maryland safe?

Is it safe to walk around Baltimore?

Is Baltimore safe at night?

Is Maryland a safe state?
What areas of Baltimore are safe?"

Ha – and **I** was worried about safety in GERMANY?! Not to mention all the mass shootings America has experienced.

And so it was, that on August 21, 2014, Jeffrey, Gail and I flew to Munich, Germany together, where we began our journey by ourselves – by design, just the three of us – taking day tours in and around the city – before meeting up with Ira and Oliver on August 25, to begin our personal and Family Heritage journeys alongside our Significant 4.

Chapter 6

MUNICH, NUREMBERG, AND DACHAU

I journaled almost every day when we were in Germany, at the
end of every evening – even if I couldn't keep my eyes open,
because I wanted to document what we experienced and how it
impacted me, so I would "remember." Because I was physically
and emotionally drained most evenings, yet equally eager to start
every new day to experience more, I recall that sometimes my
entries were very brief. However, despite recurrent searching, I
was unable to find that travel journal while writing this book for
the past seven years or so, figuring I'd probably find it once this
was already published! Hallelujah – I did find it finally, in a file
drawer in January 2021 as I was purging my home office during
the global COVID-19 pandemic! The entries that I wrote between
August 21, 2014 – August 31, 2014 are now included with each
day's journey!

Germany Itinerary
8/21 – 8/22/14

Thursday, August 21
Newark, NJ to Munich – 5:25 pm – 7:40 am; United UA
Friday, August 22
Private Pick-up Munich Airport-VIATOR; Flemings, 3 nights

From my Travel Journal, written 8/21/14 – 8/22/14:
Fly to Germany and 1ˢᵗ Day

8/21/14, 5-6 pm USA EST: So many emotions, so many
thoughts have led to this day aboard United Airlines, flying
to Germany with Jeffrey and Gail. It's 5 pm USA EST, aboard,
pending departure to Munich first – just us three – after which
we'll spend our last six days with Ira, Oliver, Rolf and Christina

guiding us through Ralph's-Dad's family's life experiences (8/25-8/30). So much tragedy and horror comes to mind first, but I also hope to find their Spirits and their joys as well, when they were able to live and practice Judaism freely and safely in their Homeland, as Jews, as Germans, treated as the human beings that they were, just like everyone else – enjoying the same rights, responsibilities, and privileges as all Germans.

Listening to the airline announcements in German (They actually did it in English first, as we're still in America.) – which I'd anticipated, led to an experience different than I'd expected – a pleasant one. I'd thought that I might feel fearful hearing the German language because of what it might evoke for me about the time of WWII, the Shoah, fear, tragedy, torture, despair, hopelessness, and deaths. But it pleasantly and blessedly did not take me there. Instead, and I'm not "looking a Gift Horse in the mouth" (what an odd American slang expression!) – I find myself engaged and listening because of my interest in different cultures, hearing a language spoken by others across the ocean in Europe. Hopefully my curiosity will reduce my fear, and in the process – perhaps delight me a bit… and it does. Now there's lovely classical music playing. I could go negative and fearful here, recalling movies I've seen in which concentration camp prisoners in their meager prison clothes and shaved heads played instruments for their captors. Instead, I choose freely not to dwell on that, although it was a true fact of life long ago. I choose instead to be full of Gratitude for my freedom of choice, my financial status that affords me to travel and enjoy adventures, be here in this airplane Economy Plus seat, at this moment in time, free and safe to move about the world, to trace the roots of Dad and his family, and our People, during that time in history.

As well, I am full of Gratitude for my current state of peace of mind, especially considering the events of recent weeks, and my reactions to them. Truly a testament to my humanity, the frailty of the human condition, my Spirituality, my Spiritual Guides/Protectors, and my Faith and Hope. Hope lights my path, for me, and others… I want to resume/continue my trust in the basic goodness of others, without being naïve, while staying alert, checking things out, and taking natural safety precautions. I pray for Healing and Peace, which I believe can come about through

Love and Forgiveness:

Love + Forgiveness = Healing and Peace

I want to professionally speak, write, teach, mentor, and inspire other women and men to self-empowerment for personal peace, as a means towards World Peace. I pray for everyone, Veterans, women, men, children, colleagues, myself, family, friends, the USA, Israel, the World – to begin and continue to live in tolerance of each other [1] glorifying in both our differences as well as our similarities, live and let live in Peace as neighbors, all of us members of the Human race, with grace, dignity, and respect.

SHALOM – Hello to Peace and Healing through Love and Forgiveness, goodbye to intolerance, hatred, fear, persecution, fanaticism, xenophobia, evil, inhumane actions, genocide, crime, poverty, hunger, illness, etc.

Friday 8/22 day & eve: Incredible arrival day, staying awake together so we can sleep at the normal German bedtime! We went to the Jewish Museum in Munich, and saw both Stern and Strauss (my mother-in-law Shirley's maiden name) names together, on a restored but still broken Synagogue donation plaque memorializing WWI Jewish Veterans. Outside we saw a functioning 2006-built Synagogue, near the JCC (Jewish Community Center) in Munich. Sad stuff, but as Gail said then: "This was the one 'fun' day built into this vacation!" We had a great dinner at our hotel (Flemings): Jeff and I had Weiner Schnitzel for the first time, and Gail also tasted it for the first time. We all enjoyed the fried breaded veal, the wine, good conversation, and great service. All in all, an outstanding first day and eve. Off to Nuremberg/long day tomorrow ...

PS: Last evening, Jeff noticed a mezuzah outside our hotel on the right-side of the doorway entrance. I kissed it publicly and said the Shema Prayer silently to myself, as I do back home. Then I remembered where I was, in Germany! No problem, it's who I am.

Of particular interest to me was that I saw many women wearing scarves/headcoverings-hijabs, with their children in

---

1   Today I would instead write "acceptance", for it is not enough for us to be just "tolerant" of each other.

strollers. Beautiful, stunning. Interesting that there's a multi-cultural population here, seems to be way more here than in the USA. The USA needs to get with the program! Not really sure what I mean by that, because we do accept regularly-screened people into our country. Goodnight.

end of my 2014 Travel Journal entries for 8/21 and 8/22

Saturday 8/23/14: Nuremberg – 8:40 am: Today, I stood exactly where Adolf Hitler stood on multiple occasions, and so did Jeff and a number of other Jews. We took pictures there at Zeppelin Field where he'd (Hitler) hosted members of his Nationalist Workers Party, and spoke from a concrete stage, inciting his fellow party members to collaborate with him to do his evil bidding – while his evil Nazi soldiers/SS men marched in the wide paved aisle in the center of the field. [2]

We Jews stood exactly where Hitler stood, not in his shoes, not in support of his thoughts or actions, but in direct and triumphant contrast – because we are alive and well, survivors, growing and prospering and living lives well-lived, despite his evil killing and torturing of so many of our brothers and sisters, aunts and uncles, children, parents, grandparents, and great-grandparents and cousins and friends. Not just Jews, but anyone different from him – gypsies, homosexuals, those with mental illness, political partisans of other parties who disagreed with his blasphemy and evil. We have survived, and continue to procreate *L'Dor v'dor* (Hebrew), from generation to generation, and be successful and healthy and happy and live productive lives while he is long dead, and remembered as evil-personified, an egomaniac who seized control and spread evil for more than 12 years of hell.

Clearly, Jeffrey and Gail, and frankly all of us Jews are here... because Hitler lost. He committed suicide before he could be

---

2   Author's Note added 1/25/21: Wow! As I copy my own words now from my 8/23/14 journal entry into this manuscript, any American and our global neighbors may experience the same "deja vu" as I just did. Although I wrote those words on 8/23/2014, they sound eerily similar to what we all witnessed on 1/6/2021 at the steps of our Capitol in Washington, DC: the violent insurrection that attempted to overturn fair and secure election results and overthrow Democracy itself.

captured, though way too long after he'd already inflicted tragedy, pain, torture, and death amongst millions.

It was scary (Gail's word – "freaky") to hear the soccer fans in the nearby arena "rock" the arena with their loud chants for their favorite soccer team when we were entering Zeppelin Fields. It was surreal, making me think it was against us, and that they might break out at any moment to wreak evil havoc. I couldn't understand their words, only heard loud raucous male voices in loud unison chanting in German. It couldn't help but take me back to what it must've been like in the 30s and 40s.

Then I saw the history lesson in black and white, real life-101, of which I took pictures showing the swastika being toppled down and burned by US Army Soldiers in 1945 when the Allies' Victory was declared. I was very emotional.

Later in the day, back at the Train Station, while walking upstairs to the outside, I passed a young man with multiple tattoos, multiple earrings and facial piercings, an angry facial expression, a blond Mohawk cut, with a German Shepherd dog on a leash walking practically next to us. I wasn't scared or worried until I saw him turn around, change direction purposefully, and with venom in his facial expression and behaviors, he visibly and forcefully/purposefully spat at or onto another person or object. I saw neither the person nor the object he spat at, nor what triggered his spitting. He paused, and then continued walking upstairs just behind us. Jeff did not witness this. I was scared, did nothing except walk briskly away and make sure Jeff was right by me. Gail was at a separate location, not with us. Once upstairs and outside, he joined a bald-shaved-head young man, both of them in black leather with multiple zippers and chains, multiple tattoos and earring and facial piercings, and angry looks on their faces. I saw them chest-bump, smile, and hug, and talk for awhile. Jeff and I were at least one entrance away by then.

Besides feeling scared, I realized only afterwards that I took no action against his behavior, no action in support of the other possible individual or individuals (I couldn't see who or at what target his hatred and venom was aimed. That made me feel scared, too, because I realized I am human – and self-preservation for me and Jeff came first. Now I did not see him touch or harm anyone other than the spit, nor did I even see if it was a person/persons whom he spit at. I do know that if I saw him or anyone harm or threaten harm to another human being, I would've searched and run for the closest security/police officers and notified them so they could do their jobs. I would be smart and not confront them myself, but report them to someone who can safely and professionally address the situation right then! Of that, I feel good/proud. That is the right thing to do, the humane thing. But that experience showed me how it may have been for the many other human beings who bore witness to the pain and torture of the Holocaust, and did nothing out of fear for their own lives, out of self-preservation.

Finally, in Nuremberg, I "turned the Ring" at a historical gate with Gail and made a wish: for Health, Happiness and Safety for my Family and others, and Love + Forgiveness = Healing and Peace – for every individual on the Planet – right here, right now. This is a custom at a historic site in Nuremberg, that says your wish will come true if you "turn the Ring" on this gate.

I've cried a bit today, and given thanks and blessings and prayers, as I do every day, filled with Gratitude for my many blessings, and wishing Peace and safety and plenty for every human being. *Baruch Ha'shem ...Shema Yisrael Adonai eloheynu Adonai echad. Baruch shaim k'vod malchuto l'olam va'ed* – Thank G-d ... Hear O Israel, the Lord our G-d, the Lord is One. Blessed be the name of His glorious kingdom forever and all time.

Goodnite. ...to Dachau tomorrow

end of my 2014 Travel Journal entries for 8/23

More on 8/22-23/2014, Munich and Nuremberg (written from my memories in the years after our trip 9/2014 – 2020, before I found my Travel Journal): [3]

Munich is a beautiful old city. We joke here in the USA that our country's history is "old" – over 200 years old, but Europe's history is thousands of years old! The architecture is incredible, detailed, and unbelievably still standing after all these centuries (and multiple wars).

---

3   Particularly since our trip to Germany, whenever I write the date using numbers, in this format, as we do in America – Month, Day, Year – I'm reminded of how Europeans write the date differently, by placing the Day ahead of the Month: Day, Month, Year.

Beautiful German architecture.

We arrived in Munich on Friday 8/22/14. A few memories from these three days stand out for me above the others.

The hotel Gail had booked us in, for its location near the train station, was Flemings. When we entered the modern hotel, Jeffrey was the one who noticed there was a mezuzah on the right side of the doorway entry, indicating a Jewish "home" where people live Jewish lives.

Jews affix a mezuzah (which holds prayers written on a parchment inside) to the outside and inside doorposts of their homes to fulfill the mitzvah, a good deed done from religious duty / Biblical commandment, "to write the words of G-d on the gates and doorposts of your house." Whenever passing through the doorway, many people touch their fingers to the mezuzah, say a prayer silently, and then kiss their fingers as a way of showing respect to G-d. I've been doing this for years, having learned it from watching my mother do it since my childhood.

Of course, Jeffrey googled Fleming's, and found out that the owner is Jewish! That's one of Jeffrey's "hobbies" – he loves to look up owners, businesses, games, actors and actresses, etc, and is always excited and very proud whenever he finds out that they are Jewish.

Wow – how incredible! Decades post-Holocaust, a Jewish man and his family not only own a hotel in Germany, they've placed a mezuzah upon its doorpost – in GERMANY, on a public street! I'm not sure what I'd expected, Jews in hiding, Jews not showing up publicly as Jews? (likely a lingering remnant from chapter 5 when paranoia set in!), but I certainly didn't expect a modern intact (not destroyed or removed) mezuzah on a doorpost for all to see on a building on a busy street in Germany! Sheri, this is 2014 – I had to remind myself, pleasantly. We have come a long way! And yet, per the documented statistical evidence, often from the ADL organization, anti-Semitism is once again increasing markedly in 2021.

So now, here I am, in Germany, having just arrived, a little anxious about being "openly" Jewish here. Yet you'll recall that I was **angry** about **not** wearing my Chai and Star of David, angry because I was advised **not** to "announce" myself as a Jew in Germany, which I **so** wanted and viscerally **needed** to do. But was it safe to repeat that practice of "kissing the mezuzah" **here, in Germany**?

I'm **embarrassed** to tell you that I did hesitate, while debating in my head "to kiss, or not to kiss, that is the question". I'm **proud** to tell you that the hesitation lasted only seconds, after which I enthusiastically and quite publicly on a busy street in Munich, Germany in August 2014 (almost 70 years after the Shoah ended) – kissed that mezuzah and recited the prayer silently! And I felt so good, so proud, so free, so unafraid for having done it! One for me! Then all at once, my next reaction was mixed: joy and pride for having done it, but sadness and grief for all those who were not allowed to do it decades prior, and during the Roman era, and during the Spanish Inquisition, and, and, and – and all that had happened to them, just because they were Jewish. Was this a very minor experience of what is meant by "Survivor Guilt"? As I review this passage in my manuscript on 11/30/2020, and again 5/12/21, I become tearful – again.

Over the next three days, we visited many historical and architectural sites in Munich, including Zeppelin Field and the town of Nuremberg. Although I often had the Shoah in my mind as we toured, there were some tours that appropriately mentioned it and other tours that were just about the "rest" of Germany's history and architecture (Imagine that!). I tasted (and enjoyed) my first chicken Wienerschnitzel at a lovely restaurant, ate dinner in an authentic German Beerhaus (where we met a Chinese tourist traveling for her first time in Germany, and joined her for dinner and conversation) – where we watched tables of college soccer players drinking from a German beer keg and singing very loudly to celebrate their victory. Seeing these young German men singing loudly with smiles on their faces, demonstrating inebriated joy at an apparent soccer game victory, I smiled and celebrated with them.

Nuremberg's history is notable for these two particular significant events:

Hitler's Nuremberg Race Laws, implemented September 1935, which was discussed in Chapter 3, and **the famous Nuremberg Trials** which occurred after WWII, between 1945 and 1949, for the purpose of bringing Nazi war criminals to justice. The defendants were indicted on crimes against peace and crimes against humanity." [4]

Our first of two troubling experiences occurred when we were at the Nuremberg Train Station, described in my Travel Journal above (the young man spitting). I was scared for Gail, I was scared for Jeffrey and me, and I was scared for what that man may have stood for and what he might do. Had I just seen my first "skin-head" in Germany?

When I see the two guys chest-bumping and laughing, I still feel scared, because I have no idea if they're "planning" anything to hurt anyone. I feel scared as a Jew, but also simply as a human being, because sadly – "terrorist" incidents of mass murder and casualties are now occurring all too frequently within the USA and abroad. What should we do? Have they planted a dirty bomb in this very public place? Should we run, should we alert other innocent bystanders, should we find the police, would/could the police do anything? I believe this time that my thinking is not paranoid, but possibly real – based on the reality of our World

---

4   Nuremberg Trials. June 7, 2019. history.com.

in 2014 (in which domestic and international terrorist acts have only increased exponentially since then: the Pittsburgh Synagogue murders, the Mosque murders in Sri Lanka, the Church murders in North Carolina and elsewhere, and too many others).

Nothing bad happened. If they'd planted a bomb, or planned to attack people, not only would it have likely already occurred, but they certainly wouldn't be hanging around at the site leisurely. I realize that although one spit vehemently before, and I have no idea what that was about, perhaps ... they're just two young men who are friends, hanging out at the train station, maybe not even German?! They could be anti-Semites from any country, as anti-Semitism is certainly not limited to Germany. Or, they may not be anti-Semitic at all. This is what our World has brought me to: paranoia based on possible incidents, true fear based on real incidents, and yes – "profiling" others based on little to no factual information. But I do have a choice in how I think and act. I can choose to collect as many facts as possible about an experience, and then instead - choose to think and act upon the belief that while some people who dress, look, and act as these two young men did may have indeed believed White Supremacist doctrine and acted upon it, too often with tragic outcomes, that doesn't mean that all people who dress, look, and act as these two young men did are White Supremacists. Finally, Gail arrives, and we walk together to meet our group at the train track to return to Munich ... and to safety?

Also in Nuremberg, we three experienced our second frightening experience in Germany – while at Zeppelin Field: the site of Hitler's Nazi rallies. This is where Hitler stood on his grandstand overlooking the large field with masses of Nazi soldiers, verbalizing his evil blasphemous propaganda full of hate. Whenever I've seen old newsreels of this field, the "grandstand" upon which Hitler stood appeared so large and threatening. In fact, once I saw it up close and personal, and stood upon it, it's actually quite small; not more than a dozen people could stand on it packed together. And I realized that I needed to stand on it, right then, as one of those people – in August 2014, on that warm sunny day, by myself, in the presence of my family (who were only able to be born and present because

Julius and Auguste Stern were able, by the Grace of G-d, to get their first-born child, their only son – my then 15 1/2-year-old father-in-law Rolf/Ralph – onto a HIAS Kindertransport leaving from France in September 1938, just two months before Hitler gave the orders for Germany's Kristallnacht (The Night of Broken Glass). I needed to stand on that platform in the presence of unknown tourists, in the presence of G-d – decades after Hitler had stood on it, decades after the Shoah in which Hitler ordered that my father-in-law Rolf/Ralph's family (and so many others) be tortured, experimented on, starved, forced into hard labor, and murdered ...simply because they were Jewish or "other". I cannot tell you I felt a sense of Peace in that moment, because I did not. I felt extreme grief, and cried, perhaps the first of many times on this journey. But soon, I felt an overwhelming sense of triumph – because we three were here, to bear witness – Rolf-Ralph's son, daughter, and daughter-in-law. We were actually HERE, ALIVE, JEWISH, IN GERMANY – STANDING WHERE HITLER STOOD MANY TIMES, more than seven decades ago. This was just as overwhelming as the grief, and I cried, again – but happy tears of triumph this time.

As our tour guide continued to share information with us, including assuring that we all saw the poster pictures of when the American Allies arrived in 1945 and blew up the swastika on the building in Zeppelin Field, suddenly we became aware of a loud rhythmic chanting coming from another building across the field. It sounded like a large group of young men yelling something over and over again. Of course, it was German, so we couldn't understand what they were saying. I looked around at my family, and the other tourists – of which we'd learned through chatting that one other family was also Jewish – and no one else seemed to be concerned.

I was! This experience of "young men singing/chanting in German" was completely different for me than the beer hall experience, a completely different context. In the beer hall, I could see the young men, smiling, clearly celebrating their soccer victory; there was no need for me to feel fear. But here at Zeppelin Field, with the other building (within walking distance) as the source of the loud chanting, I could not see anyone, so I had no context for what they might be chanting or why. For me, it instantly became a surreal moment, as if I was transported back in time 70-plus years ago, yet consciously aware that it was actually 2014 and I was in Germany. My knee-jerk thought was "Oh my G-d! These are German men, possibly Nazis or neo-Nazis, shouting epithets against Jews. We need to run and hide!" I immediately and unexpectedly again experienced a surge of the "fight-flight or freeze" response – physiologically and emotionally – and was preparing in my body and mind to flee and hide with my family and others who needed to hide. My knee-jerk emotions were true fears, not paranoia, for me, my family, and the others with us. My second thought, shortly thereafter, was "Really, Sheri? Come on – this is 2014 – this doesn't happen anymore... Right? But what if it does, and it's happening right here, right now?" I instinctively began to scan the perimeter for exits to safety and hiding – "in case". Visions of German Shepherds on leashes being held by Nazi soldiers in uniform "appeared" in my mind. Is this what happens to someone who has PTSD whenever they're triggered (Post-Traumatic Stress Disorder)? I was very aware of the PTSD diagnostic criterion, because I continued to partner with many brave veterans with that diagnosis during my career at our local Department of Veterans Affairs – which was ongoing when we took this trip.

I looked to Gail and Jeffrey with the unspoken question clearly on my face: "What is that, and should we run?" Before I could speak it aloud, Gail surprised me by asking our Australian (go figure!) tour guide, "Uh, what are they saying?" Our guide quickly replied that they were cheering for their soccer team within the stadium building where town sports events are held.

Gail responded aloud, "OK, that's freaky", which immediately made me feel a little "better", because I realized I wasn't the only one who was feeling worried. Just as we do in America for our sports' teams, these German people were cheering for their favorite sports team! Then for a very brief moment, I did have thoughts of concern, thinking paranoidly that perhaps the Australian tour guide was in cahoots with the Germans chanting, and wasn't telling us the truth. And besides, he's AUSTRALIAN – how do I know he is fluent in German?! Then finally, as in the past, but this time more quickly and not-quite-alone with my paranoid thoughts, I began to calm down and think rationally: no one was running out of that building towards us, no sirens were going off (Really, Sheri? Do you think if they were Nazis they'd "announce" their presence before rounding you up?), nothing appeared, smelled, or sounded out-of-sorts, and there was nothing else to see except our small group of tourists with our Australian tour guide – safely walking together in the footsteps of Germany's history.

Even today, I don't really know where that "autonomic and visceral" fear was coming from – and actually still comes from occasionally, if "triggered." For example, as I'm writing this particular entry on my deck at home, surrounded by green trees and peaceful silence – except for chirping birds – in May 2019, I also suddenly hear dogs barking loudly in my neighborhood, and yet again – I find my heart racing a bit, and unexpected, unbidden thoughts of Nazis and their German Shepherd dogs on leashes, but at least I don't feel that I need to run and hide.

My only "rational" rationale is that this recurrent autonomic and visceral fear must be from a combination of the factors below, which created that "hard-wiring" in my brain. I know that all of our brains are hard-wired to respond this way to any perception of threat. But in this case with my recurrent responses to "triggers" reminding me of the Holocaust, I wonder if that was occurring because of "inherent trauma" and/or sensory overload developed from my recurrent indoctrination about the Holocaust from childhood through the present?

Potential rationale:
- hearing so many testimonies of actual Holocaust Survivors at the Washington DC Holocaust Museum years ago, and on numerous other occasions since,
- reading a number of history books as well as novels about the Holocaust,
- remembering what I'd learned in Sunday School and Jewish adult-education classes about the Shoah,
- watching "Schindler's List" and "Sophie's Choice" and other Holocaust related movies or documentaries (Both are heart-wrenching depictions of peoples' lives during the Shoah, "Schindler's List" being based on a true story.),

- the fact that I'm highly "suggestible" with a creative imagination, and
- the fact that this whole "vacation" in Germany so far (and at this point, it's only the "beginning") is filled literally with the ashes of the Shoah right alongside beautiful architectural wonders that have been preserved for millennia, great food, and beer. It was already feeling like a bit of a paradox. Could the tragic history of WWII and the Shoah really stand alongside the beauty found in the same country? Indeed, yes.

Germany Itinerary
8/24/2014

Dachau – 9:15 am; Munich Walking Tour – 3 pm

Sunday 8/24/14: Dachau, my Travel Log Entry:
Where do I begin? Sad, devastating, grief-filled, regrets, surreal, tragic, history that must never be repeated – yet is with other peoples even as we speak – horrific, man's inhumanity to man. Yet ... triumph. Dad and so many others like him who were able to get out in time, all those who survived and were liberated – are living proof of men, women, and children's abilities to cope successfully and experience and demonstrate post-traumatic growth, survival, and thriving. Dad did all of that when he returned home from the war. He fell in love, married, worked, provided for the loving family he'd created, supported charitable organizations, and worshipped G-d and practiced Judaism for the rest of his productive Mensch life.

I said Kaddish at least five times today alone, for those who may have no one to speak for them or remember them. We should work towards the messages of these quotes on Holocaust Memorials we saw at the Dachau concentration camp in Germany: "Forgive, but never forget"; "Remember that we lived. Remember how we died ...and never forget." Man's inhumanities to man.

What can I do today, now? **I** am responsible for my brothers and sisters across the globe. I **am** responsible to be a Voice for those who have none, who have been silenced. I **must** do something!

I do not know what exactly, how I can help, how I can make a difference. I only know that I am compelled to do so, called to do so. If I save but one Life, it is as if I have saved the World. I know I am but one person, but I must stand up and speak out, I must represent, I must do something.

I will ...

Tomorrow, onward to our Family Heritage Trip with Ira, Oliver, Rolf and Christina, more Bearing Witness, more life experiences.

I am glad I came. I couldn't NOT come. I must Bear Witness. I must take Action. I must not be complacent or silent. That's why G-d/Hashem created me – to do something. Good night . . .

(Author's Note added 2/7/21: *Talmud*: "When you save one life, it is as if you saved the entire world."

Jewish Proverb: "If you save the life of one person, it is as if you saved the world entire."

Arrahman Arraheem, Al-Quran: 5-Surat Al-Ma-idah-Ayat 32: "And whoever saves the life of one person, it is as if he has saved the entire humanity.")

end of my 2014 Travel Log entry for 8/24

Dachau memorial at the site of the former concentration camp.

More on Dachau (written during the years after our trip from my memories, 9/2014-2020, before I found my Travel Journal):

On Sunday 8/24/14, we traveled to Dachau Concentration Camp – which we'd planned ahead before we left the USA, because I wanted, needed to go to one concentration camp, to see, to bear witness to some of the horrors of the Shoah. Gail had already been to other concentration camps prior to this trip; Jeffrey – like me – had been to none. I chose Dachau because it was in Germany and fit into our itinerary geographically (not far from Munich), but primarily because Dad (Ralph) was one of the US Army Soldiers who had helped liberate Dachau with his unit of fellow Soldiers – the 42nd Rainbow Infantry Division. Imagine the irony of that!

At Dachau, other concentration camps, in the isolated Jewish ghettos where Jews were forced to "live", everywhere – they were required to wear a "Jewish badge" identifying them publicly as Jews.

Nazi officials implemented the Jewish badge ... between 1939 and 1945. They did so in a systematic manner, as a prelude to deporting Jews to ghettos and killing centers in Germany-occupied eastern Europe. Over the course of more than ten centuries, Muslim caliphs, medieval bishops, and, eventually, Nazi leaders used an identifying badge to mark Jews.

Decrees ordering identifying badges were ... often part of a series of anti-Jewish measures designed to segregate Jews from the rest of the population and reinforce their inferior status. ...

During the Nazi era, German authorities reintroduced the Jewish badge as a key element in their plan to persecute and eventually to destroy the Jewish population of Europe. They used the badge not only to stigmatize and humiliate Jews but also to segregate them and to watch and control their movements. The badge also facilitated deportation. [5]

---

5   https://encyclopedia.ushmm.org/content/en/article/jewish-badge-during-the-nazi-era. United States Holocaust Memorial Museum logo, Holocaust encyclopedia.

Dehumanizing Dachau concentration camp prisoners' badges.

Dachau "Arbeit Macht Frei – Work sets you free" entry gate.

As we entered what remains of Dachau, I saw the infamous iron entry gates which read: *"Arbeit Macht Frei –* Work sets you free." I also saw the one bright spot – for me – at Dachau: a bronze plaque on the entry wall just past these gates, recognizing the 42nd Rainbow Infantry Division, Dad's US Army Unit, as Liberators of the Dachau Camp. This was one of few things Dad had shared with us about his time at war in Germany. While it didn't name the soldiers individually, we know that Dad helped liberate Holocaust victims at Dachau along with his fellow combat soldiers!

We also found out much later in Dad's life that he had earned a Bronze Star from the Military to honor his heroic service in a combat zone. When we found his Bronze Star, we had to pry the story out of Dad (who was always humble) to find out why it was awarded to him. During WWII, stationed in Germany, Dad was initially assigned to be a Medic, and his partner was assigned to be the ambulance driver. Their job was to pick up their wounded battle buddies and transport them in their ambulance to safety and medical care. They had to drive with their lights off once dark, or else they could be discovered by the enemy. Dad told us that he didn't much like being a Medic, and his partner didn't

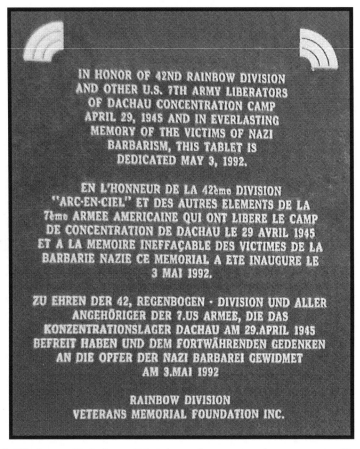

42nd US Army Rainbow Division plaque at the entry to Dachau (Dad's unit, 1 Band of Brothers' Liberators of Dachau prisoners on 4/29/1945).

much like being the Driver. So they checked with their COs (Commanding Officers), about exchanging their assignments – which was granted. Dad quickly realized, as the Driver, that his Army battle buddies were suffering and sometimes dying unnecessarily because he was only able to drive up to a limited area to pick the wounded up due to the risk of going closer to the front lines. However, the wounds were obviously occurring on the front lines. Dad was convinced that if they could drive closer to the front lines and pick their wounded soldiers up sooner, the wounded soldiers would be able to receive pain medications and emergency treatments sooner – thus possibly saving their lives because of initiating treatment more quickly. Despite the dangers inherent in that, going closer to the front lines and risking their own lives, their CO agreed to a trial of Dad's idea. It worked, and Dad helped to save the lives of many Americans and Allies. For that, he was awarded the Bronze Star. This concept of "reaching the wounded sooner" may sound familiar to some. Decades later – we know it as the rationale behind the Shock Trauma Center in Maryland, with Dr. R. Adams Cowley's belief that there was a "Golden Hour" after traumatic injury that made the difference between life and death.

When I saw that plaque, preserved for us and the world to see for all posterity, I remember it was bittersweet: I was and am proud of Dad and all of our American and Ally soldiers for all the good they've done for us, our nation, and our world. I am devastated and angry at what they discovered, what they had to bear witness to, how many had already been tortured and murdered before the Allies arrived at the gates, and how many more lives could've been saved if they'd arrived earlier, and if America, the British who then-controlled Palestine, and more countries had allowed the Jewish and other immigrants entry earlier – once they'd been made aware of the truth: that genocide was occurring in the name of Hitler's Nazi party regime.

When I saw that plaque honoring Dad and his unit, I remember thinking... Dad knew nothing about the welfare or whereabouts of his parents, sister, or other family at that time, April 1945. His last letter to them years prior had been returned to him unopened, clearly his family was Jewish, and many of these prisoners were Jewish – emaciated, barely alive. What could he have been thinking when he saw those prisoners and their conditions? Did he imagine that this may have happened to his parents and sister too? Did he wonder whether they were still alive and if so – what condition they must be in, did he wonder if the three of them were in this camp and that he could find them?

I can't imagine the pain and torture Dad went through bearing witness to all this, in those moments of Liberation, in his memories (and nightmares?) once he returned home after the war ended, and possibly for the rest of his life, in memories when he returned to Germany after the war – courtesy of the US Army with one fellow US soldier on "Compassionate Leave" for

Dehumanizing Dachau toilets.

six months – in order to try to find out what had happened to his family, and when he served in the US Army post-war as an Intelligence Officer – selected because he spoke German fluently which helped him to complete his assigned mission to find out which German soldiers were Nazis by choice (freely joining the Nazi Party early on) or by conscription – mandatory enlistment, like the draft – which occurred per Hitler's orders later in 1935.

Despite Red Cross searches for his family once he returned home, which came up empty, and Gail and Jeffrey's recurrent searches over the years – Dad died 11/27/2009 in his own home, at the age of 86, with Gail by his side, without ever knowing the final details of his parents' and sister's deaths (which were presumed, since he couldn't find them and had not received any communication from them for almost seven decades).

This, I believe, was likely a blessing in many ways – for Dad. Gail thinks it could have actually helped Dad to know exactly what happened to his family, instead of his "imagining" multiple scenarios – every one of them tragic – for all those decades. Jeffrey isn't sure of which he thinks would've been better for Dad: to know, or not to know. Either way, it's done, and Dad never knew. I was actually ambivalent about "finding out" myself. At the time, I believed I absolutely wanted to know if the information

Crematoriums in Dachau.

was available, although I knew it wouldn't be a good outcome. I believed I'd want the information because it could help Jeffrey, Gail, and me come to "closure".

Also while at Dachau, I saw the very gas chambers and crematoriums where victims were gassed and burned, actual wooden bunks where multiple prisoners "slept" cramped together, suffering, starving, malnourished, the towers from which prisoners were watched day and night and shot dead if they tried to escape, the deep trenches purposefully carved inside the front of all surrounding camp walls and the barbed wire used to keep prisoners from escaping, and rows and rows of buildings where prisoners were kept. As disturbing as all of these sites were, there was an aura of organization and sterilization, which clearly belied all of the horrors that had occurred there.

Gail mentioned that now that she saw Dachau – compared to some of the other camps post-liberation – Dachau had been "cleaned up for tourists". Nonetheless, it remains engraved in my mind as one of too many examples of man's inhumanities to man.

That said, after our three days of being American tourists in and around Munich, Nuremberg, and the Dachau Concentration Camp – seeing and experiencing all that we did, we flew to

Frankfurt on Monday morning 8/25/14, uneventfully – to meet Ira and Oliver and begin the next chapter of our life-altering journey to Germany: our personal Family Heritage Journey. So far, except for the food, hotels, and the architecture, this was not a "vacation." To be fair, I hadn't expected it to be Disneyland. Little did I know what was yet in store for us, which to be completely fair – we had asked for – to learn and bear witness to for ourselves.

Gas Chamber in Dachau. (Brausebad – German for shower.)

Chapter 7

OUR FAMILY HERITAGE JOURNEY
(8/25/14-8/30/14)

Itinerary for Monday, August 25: Fly to Frankfurt, meet Ira/ Oliver, Rexingen: Lufthansa, 10-11:05 am, Munich to Frankfurt; Ira/Oliver Pick-up; Drive to Rexingen; Worms, evening: 1 night/4 rooms at Parkhotel Prinz Carl

Monday 8/25/14: Travel Log Entry: Fly to Frankfurt, meet Ira and Oliver at airport, drive to Rexingen together:

Ira and Oliver met us at Frankfurt Airport, as planned. They look exactly like their pictures. Any worries I had pre-trip reduced once we met, yet when we split up cars (Gail with Ira, Jeff and I with Oliver), I must be honest that I was concerned – though it made sense – and of course, once I saw Ira and Gail were behind us the whole time, and we stopped together on the road for lunch, my anxiety melted away.

Rexingen was incredible, but more incredible are Barbara and Heinz – who've passionately devoted their later years to buying and building a Jewish Museum to show what occurred and pay respects to our people. They are warm and caring, honest and compassionate, appalled at what Hitler and the Nazis did to Jews, Romas, etc. even before 1933-1945. There's a synagogue (now a church) and a Jewish cemetery, with many of our relatives! Then, on to Worms for the night: great late dinner, then sleep. LONG driving times.

end of my Travel Log entry for 8/25/14

More on 8/25/14, from my memories after the trip (9/2014-2020), before I found my Travel Journal:

We three left Munich Monday morning 8/25 to fly to Frankfurt, where Ira and Oliver were to pick us up at the airport, driving the three of us and our luggage to our first stop on this personal

Journey – Rexingen, where Auguste (Dad's mother) and her Weil Family lived before the war and the Shoah. We'd suggested to them that two people pick us up in two separate cars, since there were three of us and several pieces of luggage – and so they did. They didn't need to hold signs saying "Stern", because we had pictures of them which we'd requested (Okay – only I requested their pictures!). They already had a picture of all three of us, from Gail's Law School graduation, that Oliver had found on the internet when he was searching for information about our cousin Erwin and possible descendants.

Here is where my paranoia resurfaced for a few hours. Old habitual thinking dies hard, old habitual thinking which I hadn't even realized was in my head until this journey began. I recall vividly a Jewish event Jeffrey and I had attended through our Jewish youth group when we were 16 years old (Yes, we were high school sweethearts.). As we entered the auditorium, holding hands, distracted by the adolescent chatter of our peers, we were abruptly separated by other peers dressed as soldiers with rifles (not real) standing guard – speaking in a language we didn't understand. They quickly forced our hands apart, pushing Jeffrey to the left, and me to the right – to sit on different sides of the room. They were doing this to everyone as they walked in, gesturing them angrily with their rifles and loud language that no one could understand. If we continued to talk (as we all did, trying to figure out what was going on), they nudged us with their rifles to keep quiet. Once all were separated and seated, the program began. It was a program about the Shoah, and that initial "exercise" upon our entry was a simulation of what the Nazis did when Jews and other prisoners entered the camps – sent them into different lines, separating men from women, children from parents, those capable of working and those not. As part of the program, we were asked to share how that exercise impacted us. I remember being frightened, wanting to stay with Jeffrey and our other friends, wondering what was happening, and why. For me, the organizers hit the nail on the head with that exercise.

I'd told Jeffrey even before we left home that although Ira and Oliver would each be driving their own cars to pick us up, I believed that we should split up as follows: all of the luggage in one of the cars, then Gail, Jeffrey, and me in the other car, together. Of course, he'd asked me why. I told him clearly, "NO ONE is going to separate the three of us! You know, like the Nazis did during the Shoah. We're all staying together in one car." I was deadly serious. Jeffrey had the good nature (and the wisdom of a wise man married to me for 39 years at that time) to simply say "okay".

However, once we arrived and found Ira and Oliver – as planned – at baggage claim, and spontaneously hugged each other, Gail said, "OK, so I'll go with Ira, and you two (Jeffrey and me) go with Oliver." I realized that I couldn't very well say anything, because if we all went in one car, then one of them (Ira or Oliver) would end up driving the several hours to our next stop – alone, with only our luggage as companions! That wasn't exactly fair. Not to mention, I would've sounded paranoid and unkind for not trusting them after everything they'd already done for us in the past eight months – as well as what they were doing for us now during this week together. So now, I had to worry about Gail being separated from us, and what to talk about in a car with a "partial" stranger (We all "knew" Oliver and the others partially, because of our budding eight-month email relationship.)! Interestingly, I was never afraid to actually be alone with Oliver or with Ira (or Rolf or Christina, for that matter) at any time. It was just some visceral delusional fear about being separated from Gail, my family – due to the history of that having occurred in the earlier part of the prior century, by GERMAN NAZIS, WAR CRIMINALS, Sheri – not "ordinary" people. Except ... it was indeed "ordinary" people who became Nazis. However, from what I "knew" so far of our Significant 4, I had nothing to fear. What I was still learning ... was that none of our Significant 4 were "ordinary."

That said, Gail got into Ira's car, and Jeffrey and I got into Oliver's car, and off we went. I think I might've even hugged Gail "goodbye" and said "I love you" as we each walked to our respective chauffeur's car. However, I must also confess: every 15-20 minutes, I turned around to assure that Ira's car was behind us (with Gail in it!). And it wasn't until almost three hours later, when we stopped for gas, parked, and all got out to get lunch – together – that I exhaled! Because Gail and Ira, of course, were right there with us. We'd not been "separated" by Ira, Oliver, or any imaginary "Nazis", only "separated" by the logistics of the car ride. Our family was still intact and together. And after that, I never had another thought about being separated or something bad happening to us while we were with these people in Germany. In fact, I now walked into lunch with the sense that if something bad were ever to occur, these people would protect us.

I never told Gail or any of our Significant 4 about my visceral irrational car ride experience with them – until my return trip in 2018. I think I may've felt like I needed to "confess" to them, be honest and forthright with them, perhaps as a way to show how I indeed do trust them, how I'd "grown" since I'd met them, and/or perhaps to "get it off my chest", heal, and move forward!

As each of them placed gas into their cars, Gail and I pulled out our credit card to pay for it – but neither of them would permit it. Gail and I acquiesced, and returned our credit cards to our wallets. This would become a pattern at every opportunity where money was necessary, whether at gas stations, museums, or restaurants when it was time to pay the bill: We'd offer to pay, they'd politely say "No thanks, we've got it." After a number of times, it became a sort of contest whereby Gail or I would rush to the gas pump and insert our card first, or notify the waiter to give one of us the bill after our meal. As we had done initially, our Significant 4 graciously acquiesced each of those few times we were "allowed" to pay. However, one time – towards the end of our days together – Gail again hurried to the gas pump with her credit card, ahead of Ira. This time, Ira really insisted on paying, and in response – so did Gail. I'd "6th-sensed" over our days together – without any one of them saying the actual words – that it was very important to them to "take care" of our expenses, to "take care" of us. Not because they could make "amends" by bringing our loved ones back, not because it would recreate or erase history, but perhaps because of what I whispered in Gail's ear: "I think they have a great need to do this, to show us these kindnesses – both because of our 'shared' history and because we are their 'guests'. I think we should let them." Gail acquiesced, and Ira paid. I believe this was one of the human kindnesses we showed them in return.

Inside the cafeteria, Oliver and Ira explained to us what the different food choices were, and the prices, as naturally everything was written in German with German currency prices. We broke bread together, chatted about our adventures in Munich, and the plans for the next day or so – becoming further acquainted with each other. There was no language barrier, for both speak English fluently. There were no communication barriers; we each spoke freely and fluently, as if we'd known each other a long time – though we'd only just met in-person at the Frankfurt Airport hours ago. But truly, we had "met" and begun to "know" each other through our zillions of back-and-forth-emails over the prior eight months.

After our lunch and refueling stop, Oliver and Ira drove us to Rexingen, our first stop, where Dad's mother Auguste was born and raised. Upon arrival there, we met Barbara and Heinz (who I serendipitously "met" again on a Zoom Memorial for Rexingen residents, 11/2020, and had the honor to thank them again for

Rexingen, Germany: empty space remaining where a mezuzah was once placed on the doorpost, (circled) according to Jewish commandment; example of previous Jewish life in Rexingen pre-Holocaust.

*Rexingen, Germany: At Barbara and Heinz's Holocaust Museum.
L-R: Heinz, Jeffrey, Sheri, Gail, and Barbara.*

who they are and the good they continue to do by telling the facts and stories of our People in their special museum), two extraordinary individuals who've created and continue to manage a small museum in their town dedicated to the lives of those who were impacted by the Shoah, because they believe it's "the right thing to do". They taught us about the brave contingent of young Jewish people who left everything and everyone that was dear to them in Rexingen by choosing to emigrate to what was then called Palestine, hoping life would be safer for them there. (Israel did not become a state until 1948.) There they created the Shavei Tzion community in the desert in 1938 – which continues to thrive today in Eretz Yisrael (Hebrew: the Land of Israel).

Every day I was in Germany, I learned more and more about how the Shoah and WWII has continued to impact Germans – both individually and as a nation. As well, I learned from my German Skype-pal Beate in 2016 how the Shoah had affected her parents who'd immigrated to Germany at the end of WWII ("To escape the Russians," she told me.), as well as how it had affected her growing up/her sibling/husband/and children. The generations of Germans we met during our Germany 2014 Journey (from school-age at the several Stolpersteine Ceremonies we attended, to Septuagenarians (those in their 70s), Octogenarians (those in their 80s), and Nonagenarians (those in their 90s)), either personally lived during that time in history, or are being educated at their schools about this time in their Nation's history. Just like our Significant 4, Barbara and Heinz did not stray from the truth, but rather spoke of and showed us actual pictures and documents in their museum of that tragic time in their nation's history – in all its horror.

The ADL [1] release that follows describes America's recent legislation to enhance resources for teachers across our country to teach about the Holocaust in their classrooms.

ADL Welcomes Senate Passage of Never Again Education Act

New York, NY, May 13, 2020 ... ADL (the Anti-Defamation League) today welcomed Senate passage of the Never Again Education Act, H.R. 943, which would provide federal funding to help give teachers across the country the necessary resources to teach about the Holocaust in their classrooms. The bill passed the House on January 27 and now goes to the President for his signature. (Author's Note: Then-President Donald Trump signed the bill into law on Friday May 29, 2020.)

'I am grateful for the leadership of Senators Jacky Rosen and Kevin Cramer, and Representatives Carolyn Maloney and Elise Stefanik, and to all Senators for passing this bill today, during

---

1   From the ADL website (www.adl.org) : ADL is a leading anti-hate organization. Founded in 1913 in response to an escalating climate of antisemitism and bigotry, its timeless mission is to protect the Jewish people and to secure justice and fair treatment for all. Today, ADL continues to fight all forms of hate with the same vigor and passion. ADL is the first call when acts of antisemitism occur. A global leader in exposing extremism, delivering anti-bias education and fighting hate online, ADL's ultimate goal is a world in which no group or individual suffers from bias, discrimination or hate.

Jewish American Heritage Month, to ensure that the lessons of the Holocaust will be passed from one generation to the next,' said ADL CEO Jonathan A. Greenblatt. 'Through the study of the Holocaust, students can grow as responsible citizens in a democratic society and develop critical thinking, empathy, and social justice skills for the future.' ...

H.R. 943, which passed today, was introduced by Representatives Carolyn Maloney (D-NY) and Elise Stefanik (R-NY). The Senate companion, S. 2085, was introduced by Senators Jacky Rosen (D-NV), Kevin Cramer (R-ND), Marco Rubio (R-FL) and Richard Blumenthal (D-CT).

The Never Again Education Act would address the gap in knowledge by expanding the U.S. Holocaust Memorial Museum's education programming to teachers across the country, requiring the Museum to develop and disseminate accurate, relevant, and accessible resources to improve awareness and understanding of the Holocaust and educate individuals on the lessons of the Holocaust as a means to promote the importance of preventing genocide, hate, and bigotry against any group of people.

The bill also authorizes $10 million over five years to go to these activities. ADL supported a letter led by Senators Ben Cardin (D-MD) and Jacky Rosen to the Senate Appropriations Subcommittee on Interior, Environment, and Related Agencies, asking for the funding to ensure implementation of Holocaust education programming. [2]

An article in the Business Insider by Michal Kranz on 11/22/17 entitled: "5 genocides that are still going on today", describes those genocides ongoing in 2017: the Rohingya (Muslims) in Myanmar, the Dinka-Nuer and other ethnic groups in South Sudan since 2013, the Assyrian Christians/Shiites/and Yazidis peoples in Iraq and Syria, the Christians and Muslims in the Central African Republic since 2013, and the Darfuris in Sudan since 2003. [3]

---

2   https://www.adl.org/news/press-releases/adl-welcomes-senate-passage-of-never-again-education-act; May 13, 2020.

3   https://www. businessinsider.com/genocides-still-going-on-today-bosnia-2017-11#darfuris-in-sudan-5

I attended a protest march years ago in Washington, DC for the latter, feeling that I must stand up and speak out against the same evil that killed Jews and others during the Shoah, when many people did not speak up. This time it was happening to the "others'" ethnic groups (and we are ALL "others").

"In December 2020, the Simon-Skjodt Center for the Prevention of Genocide of the Holocaust Memorial Museum in Washington DC, published a new report 'Countries at Risk for Mass Killing 2020–21: Early Warning Project Statistical Risk Assessment Results', prepared in cooperation with Dartmouth College's Dickey Center for International Understanding. (It) shines a spotlight on countries where mass killings have not begun, but where the risk of such violence is high. Some countries remain absent from the assessment, including Myanmar and Syria. The report focuses on new instances of mass killings ... not countries where an existing mass killing continues. In Myanmar and Syria mass killings continue." [4]

I discovered an article (April 16, 2021) that describes two ongoing genocides: the Rohingya people in Myanmar (see above, still ongoing) and the Uyghur people in China. It also notes that every April is Genocide Awareness Month. [5]

Of relevance, "the internationally recognized date for Holocaust Remembrance Day corresponds to the 27th day of Nisan on the Hebrew calendar, (which) marks the anniversary of the Warsaw Ghetto Uprising. This usually coincides with an annual April date on the secular calendar." [6]

An organization called Genocide Watch classifies three levels of Genocide Alerts:

- A Genocide Watch is declared when there are signs of the early stages of the genocidal process. ...
- A Genocide Warning is called when the genocidal process

---

4   https://www.forbes.com/sites/ewelinaochab/2021/01/18/what-are-the-countries-at-risk-of-mass-killings-in-2021/?sh=4ed1cde93c35
5   https://www. facinghistory.org/educator-resources/current-events/genocide-still-happens
6   https://www.ushmm.org/remember/days-of-remembrance/resources/calendar; retrieved 6/19/21

has reached the stages of preparation by perpetrators and persecution of a targeted group.

- A Genocide Emergency is declared when the genocidal process has reached the stage of genocidal massacres and other acts of genocide.

As of 6/19/21, there are 21 countries included on their list. [7]

Remember Martin Niemöller's poem cited at the beginning of this book ... "when they came for me, there was no one left to speak for me."

Maya Angelou said, "Hate, it has caused a lot of problems in the world, but has not solved one yet."

Hillel, a leading Biblical Jewish scholar and sage, said: "If I am not for myself, who will be for me? And being only for myself, what am I? And if not now, when?" [8]

I continue to be pleasantly surprised by those German individuals who I listen to when discussing the Shoah, surprised by their consistently spoken truths, and so grateful for their choosing to educate themselves and others, as well as take positive actions to:

1) "Never forget" and "Never again", by working to minimize the risks and prevent another Shoah from occurring, though unfortunately there remain many examples of ongoing genocide today (noted above).

2) Combat the Holocaust denials that remain prevalent in this 21st century, by preserving and sharing the research and facts about the Shoah, and

3) In some way memorialize and pay their respects to those who were murdered as well as those who survived, and include their family descendants in this process. Clearly, the damage cannot be undone, because they can never bring back those who were murdered, never "repair" the effects of the absences of parents, grandparents, siblings, and other relatives who were

---

7   https://www. genocidewatch.com/copy-of-current-genocide-watch-aler, retrieved 6/19/21
8   Ethics of the Fathers: 1:14

not a part of their descendants' lives, nor erase the memories and nightmares that may continue to torture Holocaust Survivors ever since. However, their actions validated what we already knew: each of our loved ones' lives were significant and mattered. I respect them immensely, especially during these troubling times when anti-semitism is re-exploding.

Though Barbara and Heinz, as well as Ira and Oliver, gave us the facts and true stories, clearly we know from history books, the news, and our Significant 4 that there are other people – including Germans – who choose not to talk of the Shoah – and if they do, it is brief, diluted, and/or sugar-coated (as if it was "not so bad", "the numbers were exaggerated") rather than blatantly truthful. We also know that some Germans, as well as people of different nationalities, did help Jews and others by hiding them, bringing them food, helping them escape. I would think that some Germans would want to put this painful period of their history out of their thoughts, and continue to live their lives, i.e. that they'd not want to speak about their "dirty laundry" nor continue to "re-live" it.

However, I imagine it is similar in some ways to any country's shameful parts of history. For example, the United States certainly has its own number of shameful historical periods and events – past, present, and ongoing. Starting with slavery, systemic racism and bigotry (with past lynchings of brown and black people of color, "whites" and "coloreds" signs at water fountains and entrances, and "no negroes admitted"), more recent examples include the Charlottesville Rally and George Floyd's murder. Many watched in horror as the Unite the Right rally on August 11-12, 2017, in Charlottesville, Virginia occurred. A group of white males carrying fiery tiki torches marched through the streets shouting racist, xenophobic, anti-semitic, and homophobic epithets such as "Jews will not replace us" and "F*ck you faggots". One counter protester, standing up for rights for all, was killed, and others were injured. We also watched in horror as George Floyd was murdered May 25, 2020 in Minneapolis, Minnesota by a police officer who kept his knee on Mr. Floyd's neck for more than 9 minutes while Mr. Floyd repeatedly cried, "I can't breathe", until he took his last desperate breath and died.

On 6/1/20, law enforcement officers were ordered amid the George Floyd protests in Washington, DC to use tear gas and other riot control tactics to forcefully clear peaceful protesters to create a path for the former President and senior administration officials to walk from the White House to St. John's Episcopal Church for a photo op.

Prejudice, gender issues, and multiple episodes of injustice and inequality are not new in America. America has experienced brother against brother in the Civil War, sex trafficking, sexual harassment and assault, the deplorable treatment of our Vietnam Veterans upon their return home from war to the USA in the 60s-70s, and quite a number of unjust laws/language/ and behaviors executed by the previous Administration, i.e. the "Muslim Ban", restricting immigration numbers and immigrants' abilities to seek asylum legally from the violence and poverty of their countries, calling Mexican immigrants "bad hombres", ordering immigrant children to be kept in cages and detention camps, separating immigrant children and parents by deporting the parents back to their own country (some of whom have still not been reunited with their families at the time of this writing in February 2021), and terminating DACA (**D**eferred **A**ction for **C**hildhood **A**rrivals) – just to name a few. By speaking about these shameful behaviors, we choose to remember rather than forget – just as our German Mishpacha do. In doing so, we each have multiple opportunities to learn and act differently, positively, so that history does not repeat itself. By choosing to forget and not talk about these shameful behaviors, we "sweep it under the carpet", and that begets the real risks and probabilities of repeating those very same shameful behaviors – as we regretfully continue to see today.

Fortunately, when the new American Administration began on 1/20/21 at noon with President Joe Biden and Vice-President Kamala Harris, President Biden immediately wrote Executive Orders that effectively cancelled the "Muslim Ban", reinstated DACA so that the "Dreamers" could stay in the United States and follow a legal path forward to attain US Citizenship, and many others that "cancelled" policies and laws of intolerance and injustice towards "others" which had been promulgated by the prior Administration.

Back to Rexingen: It looked like a small town frozen in time, with classic German style architecture and design. In the small cemetery, there were many of our relatives and other Jewish people, none of whom we "knew". I said Kaddish for all of them, the first of many cemeteries we visited almost daily with our Significant 4, several of many Kaddish Prayers I recited throughout our week with our Significant 4.

This is where Auguste had grown up. However, she could not be laid to rest in this cemetery with her other relatives, nor in a Hohenlimburg cemetery, nor in any cemetery – because she was murdered and buried in a mass grave, a death pit, along with her husband, their teenage daughter, and so many other Jewish people, in a town far away from her homeland, at the prime of her life.

That first evening together with Oliver and Ira (Monday, 8/25/14) began our nightly ritual of learning about and bearing witness to our family's, our People's, and German history during the day, then celebrating life and developing our ongoing relationships with our Significant 4 with good German food and wine every evening – something that helped to lighten the burdens from where we'd "been" during each day – for all of us. Following dinner, we were driven to the town of Worms where we stayed overnight to learn and explore more the following day.

Itinerary 8/26/14:
Tuesday, August 26 Worms
Bad Godesberg (1 night/3 rooms)
Hotel Dreesen, Rheinstr. 45-49

Tuesday 8/26/14: Travel Log entry, Worms: A Synagogue and cemeteries:

I said Kaddish multiple more times, although there is no one we personally know in these cemeteries either. The mikweh from the 11th century (in German; in English, it's transliterated as mikvah) was "filled" partially with some rainwater from yesterday. I had Gail take a picture of me stooping in the mikweh on the steps, with just both my hands immersed in the little bit of rainwater while I said the Shema Prayer. The first time I've been "in", symbolically, a mikvah. It's something I'd like to do when I return to the states. [9]

Everything and everyone is so moving. I've cried briefly every day. Feeling very "heavy" emotionally, remembrances of all the torture, despair, devastation, and deaths, all the losses, all the pain, all the indignities to human beings. I've had little appetite, and 1-2 glasses of wine each night which relax me. The first few nights, I fell asleep fine, but awakened often during the night and slept intermittently falling back to sleep.

Too tired tonight and next couple days to journal, but saved space in Journal to do so.

Every evening with Ira and Oliver is fun, informative, relaxing. Europeans dine for several hours, no rushing like in America. Also, much walking, great exercise, many hills, many steps. Can't remember if we met Rolf and Christina today or if we'll meet them tomorrow. Nite . . .

end of my 2014 Travel Log entry for 8/26

More memories for 8/26/14, written after our trip (before finding my Travel Journal):

Throughout the day in Worms, we continued to listen and talk

---

9 The mikvah is a ritual pool with a body of natural water in which Jewish women immerse to be purified from a state of ritual impurity. https://www.chabad.org/library/article_cdo/aid/961505/jewish/Positive-Commandment-109.htm). Before we left for Germany, I looked into going to a mikvah in or near Worms. I contacted a Chabad Synagogue about it, but because of the rigorous preparation-purification process necessary prior to immersing in a mikvah and my unfamiliarity with it – especially in Germany – I decided to wait until I returned to the USA to pursue this option. Several years later, I took a course at my local Chabad, and was offered the opportunity to participate in the mikvah process; it was indeed the spiritual experience I'd expected, and I also gained new respect for Orthodox Jewish women who perform this mitzvah on a monthly basis.

with Ira and Oliver, learning more about each other and German and Jewish history. As I recall, this day was mostly a Jewish "sightseeing" tour of interest, without any specific focus on our family. These cemetery visits, too, like the evenings we spent together dining, drinking, "letting go" of what we'd experienced during the day, and celebrating life with our Significant 4, were now becoming another "ritual" of our Germany journey. At each Jewish cemetery we visited, whether our relatives were buried there or not, I felt the need to recite the Kaddish Prayer [10] softly to myself, but audible to anyone nearby.

This day, I explained the prayer to Ira and Oliver, who stood by silently and respectfully as I recited it, describing my need to say it even if I didn't know the deceased – because it's likely that they may no longer have anyone living who continues to remember and honor them by reciting Kaddish for them, and I wanted to do this as a Jewish woman for "our People". Although these were not Jewish individuals killed in the Holocaust (for those individuals were incinerated or shot and buried in mass graves, with no tombstones to identify them), this was still an emotional experience for me.

After our day in Worms, we drove to Bad Godesberg that evening. We'd mentioned to Ira and Oliver prior to our trip that we wanted to come here, and stay overnight at the Hotel Dreesen. There were three reasons we wanted to visit there in August 2014:

1) Bad Godesberg is the town where Dad and cousin Erwin had enjoyed their summers living with their uncle who raised cattle. It was a time when they were happy and carefree.

2) We'd all been to Bad Godesberg for 1 day on January 1, 2009 when we'd traveled with our adult kids and Dad to Amsterdam and London. Gail had planned a day to surprise Dad by going there. I remember him staring in disbelief at the site where his uncle's home had been more than 70 years ago, when he'd last seen it; although he cognitively realized that many decades had passed, not to mention the occurrence of WWII and the

---

10   The Jewish prayer regularly recited in the daily synagogue service, and on other occasions for the dead, it also includes giving thanks and praise, concluding with a prayer for universal peace.

Holocaust, and new residences were built there now, it must've felt surreal to him – somewhat of a cognitive dissonance – that the home he remembered was gone.

3) As well, we have a picture of Dad in his US Army uniform during WWII standing in front of a wooden gate overlooking the Rhine River behind the Hotel Dreesen! Even more fascinating is that we took another picture with all of us standing with Dad on that cold day on January 1, 2009 in front of the Hotel Dreesen sign overlooking the Rhine River! That second picture was taken more than 60 years later, after he'd been there fighting alongside the US Allies in the early 1940s! Also, although Dad didn't speak much about that time in his life, I clearly remember him telling this story many times about Hotel Dreesen's place in history during WWII: "It was here that Hitler met with Prime Minister Chamberlain and promised that he would not invade Czechoslovakia, but then broke his promise and did so."

Although this was now decades later, I had conflicting emotions about this day: glad to be where Dad had once walked – actually he walked there twice, both during WWII with his military buddies – long before we were born, and again on January 1, 2009 with us. However, we were also staying overnight in the same hotel that Hitler had stayed in many times.

After the daytime events, per our newly established routine, we had a lovely dinner at a restaurant. Typically, Europeans dine later than we do here in the USA, and so that is what we did – every night. We reviewed what we'd learned that day, asked more questions, and shared our lives with each other, breaking bread together and continuing to get to know each other. We slept overnight at the Hotel Dreesen, had breakfast there together the following morning, and drove on to Bonn and Meckenheim.

Bad Godesberg, Germany, 1940s during WW II and the Holocaust: Dad in US Army uniform, leaning on wooden railing with the Rhine River behind him, with Hotel Dreesen in the background.

Bad Godesberg, Germany, August 2014, L-R: Gail, Sheri, Jeff, leaning on that same railing (which is now iron) with the Rhine River behind us, across from Hotel Dreesen (Hotel not visible in this photo.).

Bad Godesberg, Germany, 1/1/2009: Dad with us during our family trip to Europe, standing together outside of Hotel Dreesen. L-R: Jeff, Dad, Gail, Sheri.

Bad Godesberg, Germany, August 2014, L-R: Gail, Jeff, Sheri, standing at same spot as the photo with Dad on 1/1/2009 outside of Hotel Dreesen.

Itinerary for 8/27 – 8/29/14:
Wednesday, August 27-29: Gummersbach (3 nights/2rooms)
Wyndham Garden, Huckeswagener
Wednesday 8/27/14 – Bonn Meckenheim Strasse 4

Wednesday 8/27: My Travel Log entry: Bonn: Convent and Memorial Center (rain)

Group dinner August 27. L-R, back: Oliver, Jeffrey, Sheri, Christina and Rolf. L-R, front: Ira, Gail, Shaked.

Meckenheim, Jewish cemetery, former synagogue site, Selma's house, and a representative from Meckenheim. This was the site of one of the temporary residences of Julius, Auguste, Margot, and Dad. We saw four stones/Stolpersteine today: three Sterns plus Selma, as well as two new stones to be placed once construction's completed on the torn-up street: for Rolf (Dad) and Aunt Jenny Weil – for Bahnhofstr 15. Though the house is no longer there, an upholstery store is now present. We met the owner and chatted.

Rolf and Christina were definitely with us today all day. I became emotionally overwhelmed at the Bonn Memorial Center, especially when I went into the restroom and Christina came looking for me. She immediately saw I'd been crying, hugged me, and empathized that this was so hard for us seeing and hearing about the atrocities of the Shoah, all of our losses, and the losses of millions of others. I just melted in her arms, felt so comforted, loved, and "apologized-to" for what her homeland's people did to our families, Jews, and so many others. I felt so understood and respected.

In the evening, we drove on to Meinerzhagen. Great fun international dinner at a French restaurant in Meinerzhagen, "Oliver's" restaurant. I believe we met Shaked tonight. Three cities in one day (Meckenheim, Bonn, and Meinerzhagen)!

end of my 2014 Travel Log entry for 8/27

Memories of 8/27/14, written after our Journey, before finding my Travel Log:

The Museum Hug

Several days into our Family Heritage Journey, we visited a local Holocaust museum – Bonn Memorial Center – featuring pictures, exhibits, and information about local people who were murdered or otherwise died during the Holocaust. Mind you, this occurred after we'd already visited multiple Jewish cemeteries that day and daily for the past few days, and I'd been reciting Kaddish multiple times daily – constantly being reminded of death. We'd been inundated with Holocaust education all day, every day – at our request, to be fair – since arriving in Germany. Just the very name of that country – GERMANY – initiated the Pavlovian response in which my mind automatically "traveled" to the word "HOLOCAUST." These two words had been indelibly linked together, practically as synonyms in my mind since childhood. I really knew absolutely nothing else about Germany except the Holocaust – the Shoah.

As our museum tour guide – a young man who looked to be in his 30s – took us from exhibit to exhibit, I remember feeling rather numb and dead inside from our experiences of the last few days. At the same time, I felt overwhelmed from the continuous bombardment of Holocaust information – which we had requested of our Significant 4, and boy did they deliver!

Looking back, I remember they were each quite sensitive to our emotions, yet I never felt that they were "watching" or observing our reactions in a sterile way. We were just a group of people touring a museum together.

As we entered one of the rooms, the young tour guide explained that this was the room that highlighted those who were from the town of Hohenlimburg. My ears perked up, my mind became more alert as it fought its way up through the fog of numbness. As he spoke, my eyes looked at the exhibit of pictures on the wall in a blurred kind of way. Since 8/23, we'd chosen to be inundated by Holocaust history, and as a result my mind was silently saying: "Yeah, yeah, yeah, more pictures of Holocaust victims, more lives lost, more dead people, this is just more of the same horror, is this going to be something I haven't already seen ten times?" And just then, to my horror, I did see something I hadn't already seen: my eyes focused on Julius, Auguste, and Margot's pictures framed on the wall alongside other pictures of their neighbors who were also Holocaust victims.

I froze. I couldn't stop staring. I "knew" these three people, these exact three individual pictures: They'd apparently been cut out separately for this display, but the way I recognized them was because they were each 1/3 of one picture I have hanging on my dining room wall of the three of them together – Julius, Auguste, and Margot. This was likely the last picture Dad had of the three of them together, which he'd brought with him to America. Since he was not in that picture, it's even likely that he'd taken that picture while still living in Germany. There they were – the paternal grandparents and aunt that Jeffrey and Gail (and I) had never met, had never had in their lives. These were the loving parents who'd done whatever it took to secure passage for their oldest child Rolf (Ralph, my father-in-law) – their only son, on a Kindertransport, hopefully to safety with a relative in America. There was the younger sister who was to eventually follow her older brother to safety in America along with her parents, but instead suffered and died brutally with her parents at the hands of Hitler's Nazis before she became sweet-16.

Those three, and so many more relatives, friends, and neighbors, were never allowed to make that trip to safety. Two months after Rolf/Ralph-Dad left for the USA on a Kindertransport,

Julius, Auguste and Margot Stern's photos (sent by Gail) displayed in Bonn Memorial Center, as Hohenlimburg Shoah victims.

Kristallnacht ("The Night of the Broken Glass") occurred: Hitler ordered the pogroms that occurred in Jewish German towns – Nazis burned down synagogues, broke glass storefronts and windows of homes, vandalized, and arrested and imprisoned Jewish men.

And then, I felt the tears abruptly and uncontrollably coming. I excused myself before the tears began to flow, telling Jeff and Gail that I was going to the bathroom. Once there, I let it all out – sobbing silently, tears and mascara running down my face, arms crossed and folded across my stomach, as if to hold myself together instead of breaking apart – because that's what I felt was happening to me. ENOUGH... ENOUGH... HOW could this have happened, AND CONTINUED for 13 years (1933-1945)?! HOW could "human" beings DO THIS to other human beings?!

I don't know how long I stood like that in the bathroom vestibule. Then suddenly, Christina (Rolf's wife) entered the bathroom. She threw her arms around me, hugged me tightly and silently for a long time, and then whispered in my ear: "It was wrong. I'm sorry." Even at this writing, 8/20/2019, 5 years after Christina's embrace, and 77 years after the deaths of Julius, Auguste, and Margot – I am crying again. And again when reviewing this on 4/13/2021, I am tearful remembering all the cruelty, tragedy, pain, hate, and loss. How very different our lives – and millions of others' lives – and the World would be today, if those who were imprisoned, killed, incinerated, and died at the hands of the Nazis from infection, starvation, neglect, torture, heinous medical experiments, hard labor, and death marches had been allowed to continue living their productive lives in peace, with justice, equality, and freedom for all, loving their families and contributing to society. And I'm crying also, from accepting the compassionate acts of kindness, Christina's hug and apology for something she certainly did not do, for something that her "people" did to my "people" less than a century ago. Christina continued to hold me in her loving embrace until I stopped crying, dried my face, and thanked her as graciously as I could. Then we rejoined our group in the Memorial Center. While my "thank you" felt so inadequate for what our Significant 4 had already given us (and there was more to come), I can only imagine that Christina may have felt a similar inadequacy about her embrace and apology. Any possible perceived inadequacies made no difference, because her actions spoke volumes. Maya Angelou said: "I've learned that people will forget what you said, people will forget what you did, but people will never forget how you made them feel."

Once rejoining our group, I remember asking our 30-something German museum guide: "Why do you choose to keep doing this, day after day, working here year after year, when it's so depressing?" Without a moment's hesitation, his compelling response was: "Because the young kids in school today need to hear this, and remember that it did happen – so that it never happens again." Chilling, even still today (2/22/21) as I'm reviewing the manuscript. Frankly, I don't want there ever to come a time in my life when that statement isn't chilling.

The Convent
One of the few stories Jeffrey remembers his father telling them about war-time Germany was about how his family (and so

many others) was forced by Hitler's orders to move to different areas of Germany. Can you imagine having your belongings, home, neighbors, friends, job, business, source of income, everything that's precious to you, everything that's "home" to you, everything that's part of your identity – taken from you, and being forced to move to places unknown, determined by Hitler and the Nazis, to await an unknown future? One particular place Dad had described, that Jeffrey could never understand, was "a building where entire families lived crowded together in one room." We found out from Ira and the others, through their scrupulous research about our family, that Dad must've been talking about "the convent," so they took us there on our Family Heritage Journey.

Once we entered this convent (In other emails, some of our Significant 4 have also used the word "monastery" for this same building.), our guide that our Significant 4 had arranged explained that Hitler and the Nazis had taken it over, kicked the Nuns out, and used it as a way-station to hold and imprison thousands of Jews temporarily until they could be deported elsewhere. Some of the Jewish prisoners, often the men, had temporary authorization during work hours to leave the convent only to go to "work" – which was the Nazis' term for forced labor without any compensation, and return to the convent daily by a predetermined time. In one email, Oliver explained that he believed "our" Julius Stern, Dad's father, was one of those men who had this "privilege" to come and go for his forced labor "job," while Auguste and the other women had to remain all day, every day, in the convent.

Jeffrey has always believed that his father lived in the convent together with his family, based on the fact that Dad was able to "describe" the crowded one-room-surroundings to him and Gail. However, per Ira and Oliver's research of well-kept German documentation and the historical facts of that time, it's clear now that Dad could not have lived in the convent with his family, because Julius, Auguste, and Margot were not ordered to live there until 1942, several years after Dad had already "rescued" to the US via Kindertransport in September 1938. "Rescued" is another word often used in Germany, along with "escaped" or "fled". On the other hand, I believed that the reason Dad was able to describe the living conditions so well is that his parents must have shared that information in a letter they sent him. But that can't be true either, because Dad's 12/7/1941 last letter to his parents came back to him unopened, months later. Even though Hitler's law forbidding Jewish emigration didn't occur until 1941, it was still very difficult for people to leave Germany during the years between Dad's emigration in September 1938 and that law in 1941. Though we were finding so many of the "puzzle pieces" that were "missing" about Dad's and his family's life through our Significant 4's research efforts, we still had many questions, to which we will likely never learn the answers.

The convent was "empty" now, transformed into a museum, to show and remember what had occurred. Each room looked like a prison cell, small, spare, perhaps room for one bed for an entire family. This was where families ate, slept, and passed the day contemplating their dismal circumstances. While there were no gates, locks, or fences, the prisoners "knew" that if they attempted to walk out (in other words, escape), they would be captured and tortured, and/or shot immediately.

From Ira's research, we know that Julius, Auguste, and Margot, like so many others, awaited their final fates here. Months prior to leaving for our trip to Germany, we'd learned from Ira's research that it was from here – the Bonn-Endenich convent – that Dad's parents and sister were deported with 1161 others (German documentation noted there were 1164 passengers deported on their train transport.) on 7/20/1942 to their final destination – Minsk, which was part of the "Soviet Union" at that time.

Itinerary 8/28/14: 8/28 – Meinerzhagen

Thursday 8/28/14: Travel Log entry: Meinerzhagen walking tour

We went to another Jewish cemetery where Shaked's family is buried, and the site of a prior synagogue, as well as Ira's office where the Archives are kept. There are many records of our families.

Shaked (A Sabra, a native-born Israeli, in his early 20s, who's actually related to us because someone in his family married a Stern in the past!) joined us for the day, having recently arrived to visit and stay with Rolf and Christina as he's done in the past as well. Upon seeing me recite Kaddish at multiple cemeteries, step back and bend to the left, right, and center when reciting the last sentence of the prayer, as is custom, he said to me, "I never saw a woman pray like that in Israel." He was in awe, and respectful, walking only on the cemetery path rather than the grass: "I don't want to walk on their graves."

Tonight is the night before the Stolpersteine Ceremonies, so there will be a dinner in town with members of the Meinerzhagen Stolpersteine Initiative. I wonder if I will feel "on exhibit" there. How many will be there? Will some of them have mixed emotions, supportive of the Project or not? I'm not naïve enough to believe all citizens are okay with these commemorations, but I believe and hope that those attending tonight and tomorrow will be.

Travel Log Entry after the Stolpersteine Dinner 8/28/14

They were incredible – truly and verbally sorry for what happened to our family and the 12 million others during WWII and the Shoah. They took pictures of us, were interested in hearing what we had to say, asked us questions, hugged us, cried with us, told the truth without sugar-coating it, kept referring to the Holocaust as "our (their) problem to deal with." One woman gave us pictures from her Dad (deceased) of Hohenlimburg to keep. Another joyfully shared her religious beliefs about Jews bringing redemption in the next era, and blessed us. Another greeted me and said, "I hope tonight and your trip here is not too hard for you." Several others apologized by saying, "It was awful, it was wrong," and they cried. Still others spoke of how they'd taught their children tolerance and about the horrors of the German Nazi regime. I actually comforted a small German lady about 70-some years old, a retired teacher; we cried together, and I said, "Now, it is okay." – because I felt her pain and wanted to comfort her. I wanted people to understand that I/we are working toward the present and the future, remembering the past, but working towards creating an environment of tolerance and Peace such that we will "Never forget" – but rather that we will live and love our neighbors.'

Memories of 8/28, written after the trip, and before finding my Travel Log:

Shining the Stolpersteine

The first time I saw any Stolpersteine in the pavement, rather than just in pictures, was during the first few days of our Family Heritage Journey. Rolf was guiding us through a small outdoor mall in Meinerzhagen, and pointed to a group of Stolpersteine in the pavement outside a store. As we got closer, we saw that they were actually for some of our extended family.

Cousin Bella's store had been right where these Stolpersteine were placed. Rolf explained that she and her family lived above her storefront, which was common during that time, so this site represented both her home and her workplace. Bella was cousin Alma's mother, and she and her family were able to get out of Germany much earlier, when leaving was still an option. Bella and her family were the ones who "sponsored" my 15-year-old father-in-law Ralph when he arrived in the USA years later via Kindertransport, in September 1938. Dad lived with them in Ohio for some time. Later, he joined the US Army after the USA joined our Allies in WWII. Yes, a German native who became a naturalized US Citizen by virtue of pledging his allegiance to the United States of America when he joined the US Army during WWII!

As if seeing some of our family's actual Stolpersteine was not emotionally intense enough, I watched as Rolf got down on his knees, silently lifted his hand up to his wife Christina, took the clean white cloth and jar of brass polish from her, and began cleaning our family's Stolpersteine (which blacken over time from the elements and from people walking on them through the mall, which makes it difficult to read the inscriptions).

I was speechless. My tears flowed. Rolf's "simple" act of human kindness – polishing the first of our family's Stolpersteine that we were to see – was instantaneously neshama/soul-touching, and spoke volumes. It was an act of simple generosity, dignity, and respect, for which we had no words, though we descendants tried to thank him. But once again, "thank you" felt so terribly inadequate. And once again, I can only imagine that for Rolf,

Rolf, shining our family's Stolpersteine, which were laid prior to 2014, of which we had no idea these existed. (Uncle Wilhelm Weil and Aunt Jenny Weil's Stolpersteine, two of Auguste's siblings.)

his shining our family's Stolpersteine felt equally if not more inadequate for the atrocities and loss of their lives caused by his countrymen. Again, I cried – both for the pain of it, as well as the kindness of it.

Maya Angelou said: "Life is not measured by the number of breaths you take but by the moments that take your breath away." This was one of many breath-taking moments for me during our journey.

Multiple Jewish Cemeteries Every Day

One Jewish cemetery, of so many we visited, was particularly well-manicured and lush with a carpet of green grass. We had a town official with us, and he began to read a brochure passage aloud to us with information about the cemetery. At one point he abruptly stopped, and we observed a look of shock on his face. We asked him to please continue, and to interpret it for us. Ira and Oliver translated as well. The passage stated that in this cemetery, Nazis dug up Jewish tombstones, desecrated them, and then stole them. This official couldn't believe that people would do such a thing, clearly hadn't known about it previously, and was apparently appalled and horrified, likely ashamed and embarrassed too. Though we felt "violated" because of this Nazi behavior against our People (certainly not for the first time in this country), I also felt some sense of human compassion and support both for and from this town official, for he was clearly human, and like us – was appalled by this particular fact of history he'd just unexpectedly uncovered and shared with us three American Jews and our Significant 4.

Other Jewish cemeteries we visited were in decent shape, from before the War, and held some of our relatives in their final resting places – including Dad's grandparents, Jeffrey and Gail's great-grandparents, who'd died before or during the early parts of WWII – not as a result of the Holocaust. Each cemetery we visited, Ira would pull out her map and direct us to Row ___ and gravesite ___, telling us which of our relatives were laid to rest there. Such time it must've taken her to research all of this, and create maps to make our experiences so meaningful and personal. Other graves held the dust of prominent Jewish citizens. I cried as I recited Kaddish for each of them, at each gravesite, for I did not know if there was anyone left who knew them and recited Kaddish for them. These were all my People, every one of them, related biologically or not, for our People all came from Abraham and Sarah.

And yet, despite the horrors of history that we confronted multiple times on a daily basis in Germany, each evening, when our daily field trips were done, we dined and drank together, and laughed – yes, laughed, together! Whether it was a conscious effort on each of our parts or not, it was as if we were trying to blur, but not erase, what we'd seen and heard and felt that day. Surely, we can not erase the facts of history and our family's fate. For then, we would only be fueling the fire of the Holocaust deniers, those who deny that the Shoah ever happened, or that it wasn't as bad as we "make it out to be." For then, we could not learn from our past and commit to "Never again." For then, we would be putting our heads in the sand, wearing blindfolds, and therefore unable to see danger and inhumanity as it is brewing – and take action to stop it.

Yes, every evening, we would drink and dine together. I was aware that the people we were dining with were not the ones who took away the rights and lives of Julius, Auguste, Margot, and so many others – tortured, starved, and murdered them. What I do recall thinking was how kind and sensitive – and yes, "apologetic" our Significant 4 were for their countrymen's beliefs and actions. Their words and actions, throughout the eight months of emails (paraphrased here: I am sorry to tell you this... I am sorry this is hard for you again ...I do not have words for this ...I hope I can interpret this letter with the emotions with which it was written ...how could this happen? – it was a time when the World went mad.) and ongoing once we were in their homeland, made it clear that – like us, they too were appalled, horrified, shamed, and sickened by the historical facts and true stories of the Shoah.

Empathetically, wouldn't I feel "shame" if our ancestors and countrymen had done such things to fellow human beings? Of course! But just like our Significant 4 are not responsible for the Shoah, I am not responsible for America's history of slavery, Jim Crow laws, housing "redlining", the way our Vietnam Veterans were treated when they returned from war, or the murders of so many black and brown men at the end of a policeman's gun. And just like our Significant 4 and other Germans, I too feel shame for our past and ongoing wrongs perpetrated in America. But during our time together, I did not think about that – perhaps because it may have been too painful, but more likely because I was drawn to focus on the genuine respect, dignity, compassion, and kindness with which our Significant 4 treated us. So I focused on the present, while "remembering" the past.

The Stolpersteine Dinner, 8/28/14
On the night before our family's Stolpersteine Ceremony, the Meinerzhagen Chapter of the Stolpersteine Initiative hosted a dinner and program for us in a local church. We had no idea what

to expect, what we would say or do, what they would say or do, how many would be there. I wasn't nervous at all, just curious.

As we entered the room filled with Germans and the program began, two singers welcomed us by playing the guitar and singing the Hebrew song "Shalom Aleichem", followed by the rest of the chapter members joining in the singing, and then the three of us (Yes, I was crying! You already knew that by this part of the book, of course!). I could never have imagined in my lifetime that we three American Jews would be singing Shalom Aleichem with multiple Germans who were not Jewish, a number of whom were likely descendants of Nazi parents and/or grandparents – standing side by side together, wishing each other Peace!

Shalom Aleichem is a spoken greeting in Hebrew, meaning "peace be upon you." The appropriate response is Aleichem

Stolpersteine dinner August 28 at local Meinerzhagen church, the evening before the ceremonies. L-R, back: Rolf, Oliver, Shaked, Jeffrey, Herbert. L-R, front: Christina (Rolf's wife), Gail, Ira, Sheri, Christina (Dietmar's wife).

Shalom ("unto you peace"). Shalom Aleichem is also a traditional song sung by Jews every Friday night upon returning home from synagogue prayer, signaling the arrival of the Jewish Sabbath.

The program explained the creation and purpose of the Stolpersteine Initiative, the vision of the Artist Gunter Demnig who created it, the ceremonies that would take place tomorrow in different sections of the town, and introduced the individual members. I clearly recall that the Master and Mistress of the Ceremony, Dietmar and his wife Christina, spoke in English first, as a sign of respect for the three of us, followed by each of the same passages in German – for the participants. Then Christina introduced each of us, and we stood one at a time as she called our names – mentioning that Gail is Jeffrey's "shvester" (sister; this is also the Yiddish word for sister!), Jeffrey is Gail's "bruder" (brother, also the Yiddish word for brother), they both are the "kinder" (children) of Rolf (Ralph) Stern, and I am the "veyb" (wife) of Jeffrey. I did feel a bit awkward at first, as if we were "on display" as "the three American Jews whose family members were murdered during the Holocaust," who journeyed to Germany for the purpose of participating and bearing witness to the laying of the Stolpersteine for our immediate and extended family – and I wondered if perhaps they were looking at us with pity, contempt, or as "specimens" of some sort. I could not have been further from the truth.

•••

Welcome to all at the Stolpersteine Program August 28, 2014
(The eve before the laying of our families' Stolpersteine, August 29, with a welcome by Dietmar's wife, Christina)

My name is Christina and I'd like to give a warm welcome to you – Ms. Gail Stern, to your brother, Mr. Jeffrey Stern and his wife, Mrs. Sheri Stern. A special welcome to Shaked, who already attended – together with 16 family members – last year's laying for their ancestors, family ___.

The Stolpersteine Initiative feels very honored by the presence of descendants of the Jewish citizens of Meinerzhagen and Hohenlimburg. All of you undertook such a long journey to come to a place where your ancestors were defamed, tortured, driven to suicide, or murdered in concentration camps. Even those who survived – being expelled to countries all over the world – often never (got) over depressing homesickness and the trauma of having lost all their family members during the Holocaust. No matter which fate they suffered, they all were victims of the Nazi regime.

There are many ways to keep the remembrance alive to prevent such injustice and cruelty from ever happening again in Germany. One way is sharing the past with witnesses of that time. But of course they are getting fewer. Last year five (elderly) people from Meinerzhagen could attend the ceremonies and meeting; this year only two of them are still capable to join us. I'd like to give a warm welcome to ___ and ___ ... They all will be glad to talk to you later.

To keep remembrance as a warning, many memorials have been built, books were written filled with historical facts and enormous figures that take your breath – if read. But many mass memorials keep victims faceless and facts and figures bear the danger of being pushed aside by never-ending news of catastrophes, civil wars and cruelties happening all over the world.

The artist Gunter Demnig had some 15 years ago the outstanding idea to give each victim – no matter which way they suffered – their own remembrance by laying individual stumbling blocks at their last chosen home. This idea has meanwhile spread all over Germany and even Europe and is a somehow brilliant means to give each victim not only their dignity and a decent and proper remembrance, but moreover – as Shaked's father said last year: 'You don't know what the laying of these stones means to us! It's like coming home. I think now my father will be able to rest in peace!' So maybe these blocks can help to heal descendants' wounds and the biographical information attached may answer some of the questions about their (family members') fate(s) and family roots. Like in this June when the (name) family from (town) was here... (She) told us that she had been wanting to come here since 10 years ago, when she first realized that the family tree she should draw for school ended in the second generation – no grand-uncles, no cousins.

But we are quite aware that coming to Germany can be very

hard, especially for younger descendants like (name's) brother or for Shaked, who could hardly stand the confrontation with all the cruel details, seeing their grandparents' houses, hearing about the large numbers of lost relatives, for the first time. Experiencing their families' histories so vividly that it felt almost unbearable.

So we are deeply touched by your visits and thankful that you came here. We feel obliged to do our very best to pass memory to future generations, raising our children to become democratic and tolerant individuals. Looking not only for their own best but for society's best. Not only by teaching them self-confidence that doesn't follow authorities' orders blindly. Teach students how it all started. Being role models for them. The Stolpersteine Initiative in some way had to and still is fighting for the laying because there are still fears and prejudices among the population. When times get rough, people and some politicians start looking for someone to put the blame on. These scapegoats have been Jewish people far too often in history, but in general people of different religious beliefs or skin color. Teach them to stand up and speak up, even via internet, when minorities suffer from prejudice and intolerance. Get engaged for people less privileged, looked down upon or somehow excluded from society.

•••

Before we came to Germany, we learned that Stolpersteine brass plaques already existed in many countries where Hitler exterminated people, not just Germany. As well, unbeknownst to us, we learned that Julius, Auguste, Margot, and Aunt Jenny already had their own Stolpersteine placed in other locations in Germany where they'd been forced to live per Hitler's orders, between the time they were forced from their own home and when they were eventually deported. We'd learned from Ira and the others before arriving in Germany that Dad, though considered a Holocaust Survivor according to the criteria determined by Yad Vashem in Israel as well as the Stolpersteine Initiative criteria (because he was forced to flee his home and country due to religious persecution and genocide), did not have a Stolperstein anywhere, and that there were no Stolpersteine laid at the site of their last freely-chosen home in Hohenlimburg (now Hagen)

– the last place where Dad, his sister, and their parents had lived happily and freely together, before Hitler and his Nazi party came to power. Before coming to Germany, we'd requested the Meinerzhagen committee to please place a Stolperstein for Dad, alongside Stolpersteine for Margot, Auguste, and Julius, so that they could be "together at last" – at their Hohenlimburg home. We'd been told that it was unlikely to be authorized by the town's officials who made those decisions, since the other three family members already had Stolpersteine laid at other sites where they'd lived. However, we'd also learned that the actual criteria for placing a Stolperstein is to have it laid at the last known place where the residents had lived and freely chosen that property –not at the last known place where they were forced to live per Hitler's orders. Rolf had told us that he would take it up with the appropriate authorities in Meinerzhagen, and before arriving in Germany – since we'd not heard back from Rolf about it, we assumed it would not occur.

That's exactly how I remembered it before flying to Germany, and up to the time we actually drove to Hohenlimburg on Friday 8/29/2014 for the Stolpersteine Ceremony. Therefore, I was "surprised", elated, and very touched when I believed I was first hearing about it moments before the 8/29 Hohenlimburg Stolpersteine Ceremony. It's interesting that I had no memory of the fact that Oliver and Rolf had actually let us know months before our arrival that Dad would have his own Stolperstein, and that it would be laid together with his parents and sister at their last freely-chosen home in Hohenlimburg (in their May 5th and 6th emails respectively, shared in Chapter 4), as well as another Stolperstein for Dad with his family in Meckenheim! Additionally, apparently after we'd returned from Germany, when writing this book – I still wrote it as above, that "since we'd not heard back from Rolf about it, we assumed it would not occur." Whatever the reason for not remembering that I knew ahead of time, it was a bittersweet experience for me all over again when I finally realized that Dad, his sister Margot, and his parents Julius and Auguste – would finally be together again after 76 years, resting in peace, back home.

Back to the ceremony at the dinner event 8/28, the night before the laying of our family's Stolpersteine. After the first part of the ceremony, a pot-luck dinner followed, for which each of the participants had not only cooked a dish – but they'd displayed each dish with an identifying tag – in English – noting whether there were any pork or shellfish ingredients or not, so that for keeping kosher – we would not accidentally eat something that contained those items. Once again, my eyes filled with tears – for their painstaking attention to details to accommodate us and respect our Judaism, and their collaborative communication with our Significant 4 – as we had told only Ira (when she had asked, by email, sometime before we left the USA for Germany) about Jeffrey's keeping kosher/not eating shellfish or pork; that way, they could prepare for which restaurants they could take us to throughout our Family Heritage Trip and which pot-luck dishes he could eat.

During and after the community meal, some of the members came and sat by us to eat and talk. They didn't talk much about our reason for being there, although some of them did apologize for what happened to our family at Hitler's hands. Most of the members were likely between their 50s-70s. I recall one member sharing that she is an ardent lover of Jewish people and Judaism because Jesus had been a Jew, and in fact her adult daughter was wearing a Star of David ring! I asked her daughter if she felt uncomfortable or afraid wearing the ring publicly, and she looked at me as if I had three heads! "No, no – no worries at all, why should I?" I shared with her that a number of Jewish people in our town had advised us not to wear anything in Germany that identified us clearly as Jewish, per concerns about recurrent or ongoing anti-semitism in many places in Europe – not just in Germany. She did not appear to know anything about that, or maybe she didn't want to talk about it.

Another member particularly touched my neshama, Gudrun, a petite woman in her 70s who is even shorter than me. Gudrun wanted me to know that she was a retired school teacher, and that she always taught her students throughout her decades of teaching about acceptance and love for one another. I don't recall which one of us put our arms out first to embrace each other, nor which one of us began crying first. But what does it matter which "stranger" spontaneously re-ignited an ongoing process of healing? And for whom? What mattered at that moment, on that evening, in August 2014 – and still now – is that this Jewish American woman and that Christian German woman embraced each other warmly and willingly, each grieving for ourselves and for each other, together, for all who were lost, for all that was lost – at the hands of her countrymen in the previous century. And as we cried and dried each other's tears, I like to believe that our tears were cleansing, a big healthy "exhale" following an old but "present" trauma. And that perhaps some of our tears could be tears of joy that we were now together, supporting each other, and that she and the other members of the Stolpersteine Initiative were doing their best to make whatever "amends" or atonement they could through their present actions ...for all that we had both lost. Surely, they could not bring back our loved ones who were murdered, nor the naïve beliefs that no human being could possibly treat another human being like that, nor could we erase the pain and nightmares from those who witnessed and survived. But they could and did recognize the significance of our loved ones' lives by memorializing that they lived and mattered, with the placement of the Stolpersteine, by stating and demonstrating repeatedly through their actions that the Holocaust did occur, by not forgetting those who were lost, and by joining forces within their community to take actions together so that the horrors of the Holocaust will never happen again ...anytime, anywhere, against any group of human beings – any of our Brothers and Sisters.

Itinerary 8/29/14 – Meinerzhagen / Hohenlimburg

Friday 8/29/14: My Travel Log entry: 3 separate Stolpersteine Ceremonies (our last full day)

#1: In Meinerzhagen, Cousins Erna and Erwin (brother and sister, both who made it to the USA), Cilly and Julius (Erna and Erwin's parents; Cilly and Auguste were sisters), Aunt Jenny (another sister of Auguste), and Siegfried (husband of cousin Erna).

#2: Also in Meinerzhagen, other Sterns, whose families did not come, and whom we did not know, but we're likely related.

#3: In Hohenlimburg, Dad with family.

Everything was "perfect". I didn't cry when reciting the Kaddish at the first two ceremonies. It wasn't until we arrived at the final (third) Stolpersteine Ceremony that Rolf told us that Dad WAS indeed going to receive his own Stolperstein. (Author's note: reminder that I did know this in May 2014, but had forgotten.). I cried and forgot the words of the Kaddish. Jeff got me back on track and I was able to complete it. Each time I recited the Kaddish, I wished everyone in attendance healing and peace – for both them and us. I was quoted in their local newspaper with pictures of me, Jeff, and Gail.

We had a really fun dinner with a local official of Meinerzhagen and his wife along with our Significant 4. I said my "special goodbye" privately to Ira, Rolf, Christina, and Oliver – placing my hand over their hearts and my own: "With Love and Forgiveness, comes Healing and Peace."

During the daytime Hohenlimburg Stolpersteine ceremony, at Dad's family's home, Rolf came and stood beside me, put his arm around me, and I just melted and cried, sobbing quietly such that my body heaved and shook. It was as if Dad – "our" Rolf/Ralph was there with me, comforting me, loving me, keeping me safe, protecting me. I am sad to be leaving them. I will miss them.

Note from Author, 2/6/21: I am so glad that I finally found my original Germany Travel Log Journal. As I am typing this journal entry into my manuscript on 2/6/21, I cry all over again at this touching memory of Rolf putting his arm around me – which I had actually forgotten. So finding this Journal and this particular entry helped me relive this beautiful memory. "Beshert" (Yiddish) – it was meant to be.

Memories of 8/29, written after our Journey, and before I found my Travel Journal:

The 3 Stolpersteine Ceremonies
Then suddenly, it was 8/29, our last day of our Journey, and our last day to be spent with our Significant 4 – at three separate Stolpersteine Ceremonies.

We were driven to the Meinerzhagen Town Center that

morning, where people were already setting up for the initial Ceremony. About 100 townspeople plus members of the Meinerzhagen Stolpersteine Initiative attended. Rolf and the others were setting up at each of three locations for the laying of Stolpersteine, for multiple Jews who'd been murdered in the Holocaust as well as some who'd survived, escaped, and made it to America.

As folks were setting up at the Town Square, and Jeffrey, Gail, and I were idly standing by, I suddenly got this urge, this need, to recite the Kaddish Prayer aloud. First and foremost, I wanted the deceased individuals who were receiving Stolpersteine today – both the relatives I'd known and loved, the relatives I didn't get to meet because they were victims of the Holocaust, and the strangers I'd never met – to still be remembered by someone who would recite Kaddish for them, which is one of many mitzvot (plural of mitzvah – good deed) Jewish people are commanded by G-d to perform. I wanted to mark their lives as having been significant on this Earth, because they mattered. Secondly, I realized I had this visceral need or calling to speak Hebrew aloud in a public place in front of many German people – in Germany. Perhaps some had heard Hebrew spoken before, but more likely – some never had. I wanted them to hear Hebrew Prayers being recited aloud, reverently, proudly, and fearlessly, in their town – by a Jewess.

I didn't realize until after I'd recited the Kaddish in that Town Square, that I myself would feel empowered, would claim a victory over my prior and any residual fears – once and for all – in this place, in 2014, almost 70 years after WWII and the Shoah ended in 1945. In this place ... where Jews and other human beings were once rounded up like animals and deported to concentration camps throughout Europe, where they would be tortured, starved, experimented upon, murdered, burned in crematoriums, and buried in mass graves. In this place ...where Jews were not allowed to openly practice their religious beliefs, or celebrate their holidays, or speak their Hebrew or Yiddish languages aloud, without dire consequences. In this place ...I chose to speak our Hebrew language, say our Kaddish Prayer for our dead and continue to sanctify G-d – despite, and/or perhaps because of, our many losses. I needed to respectfully

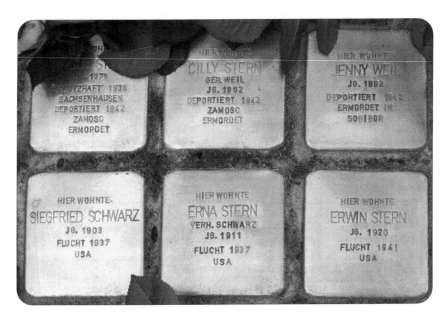

6 Meinerzhagen Stolpersteine, 1ˢᵗ ceremony August 29: The family and stones they'd originally sought us out for in 1/2014:

Julius (not "our" Julius) and Cilly Stern: cousin Judi's maternal grandparents.

*   * Julius's Stolpersteine says: Here lived Julius Stern, born 1886; protective custody 1938, Sachsenhausen; deported 1942 to Zamosc; murdered.*

*   * Cilly's Stolpersteine says: Here lived Cilly Stern, nee Weil, born 1882; deported 1942 to Zamosc; murdered.*

Aunt Jenny Weil's Stolpersteine says: Here lived Jenny Weil, born 1892; deported 1942, murdered in Sobibor.

Siegfried Schwarz's (Judi's father) Stolpersteine says: Here lived Siegfried Schwarz, born 1903; flight/escaped 1937, USA.

Erna Stern's (Judi's mother) Stolpersteine says: Here lived Erna Stern, married name Schwarz, born 1911; flight/escaped 1937, USA.

Erwin Stern's (Erna's brother, Judi's maternal uncle) Stolpersteine says: Here lived Erwin Stern, born 1920; flight/escaped 1941, USA.

honor the memories of every person who was significant, of every person who died at the hands of Hitler and his Nazis. I needed to stand up and speak out in proud and fearless defiance of every Holocaust denier and anyone today who still clings to neo-Nazi nationalist beliefs that not only exclude "the others", but too often aim to wipe "the others" off the face of the Earth. In this place ...perhaps reciting the Kaddish Prayer was my steady anchor ...that paradoxically allowed me to feel free.

And so, strengthened with these thoughts, I walked over to Rolf and asked if I could recite the Kaddish Prayer aloud at the end of each of the three Ceremonies that day. He replied, "Of course. We will make it so." And off he went to the other officials, to make it happen.

As each Stolpersteine Ceremony began in German, true to form – Oliver gravitated to our English-speaking sides and softly whispered the interpretations for us. Dietmar and his wife Christina softly played music in the background, as school children held up pictures of those being memorialized while sharing stories about them – who they were, the lives they led before the Shoah, and what happened to them. All the while, Gunter Demnig and his assistant dug out small portions of the pavement and laid the Stolpersteine in place, careful to clean every speck of dust and dirt from the site ...silently and reverently. Then, the young school children placed yellow roses around the Stolpersteine. It was incredibly moving.

Then Rolf walked over to me and handed me the microphone – silently, nodding in assent and reassurance. I looked out at everyone gathered, doing my best to make eye contact with as many of them as possible, as I recited the Hebrew Kaddish Prayer. It only took a minute, but it was one of the proudest victorious minutes of my life. I may not have worn my Jewish Star of David necklace to Germany out of fear, but here I was – in this place – in Germany, almost 70 years after the Shoah ended, reciting a Hebrew Prayer aloud, fearlessly, proudly and publicly. In the respectful silence afterwards, Rolf briefly explained in German to those gathered that I'd just recited the Hebrew Kaddish Prayer in memory of our dead and in sanctification of G-d. I was proud of cousins Bella, Erna, Siegfried, and Erwin, who had made it safely to America, each by a different path. And while saddened by not having had the privilege to know our other relatives, I felt a distinct sense of closure and saying "goodbye" to them ...with honor, love, and in peace.

It was much the same at the second ceremony, for which we walked a few blocks. At this one, we did not know any of these individuals for whom Stolpersteine were laid, but their stories were tragically the same: healthy productive law-abiding German citizens, many of them men who had served their country honorably and even received The Iron Cross for their valor during WWI, were persecuted and arrested by the Nazis because they were Jews, deported to concentration camps along with the Jewish women and children in that town, and many died in the camps or on their way there. This second ceremony also memorialized a family of Sterns, likely related to us in some way – though unknown to us. We were told by our Significant 4 that the one male Stern of this family who'd survived the Shoah had told each of his descendants: "No one in this family shall ever set foot in Germany again." And so they did not. No one from his family was there. For that reason, because they were Sterns, and for so many other reasons, I recited the Kaddish here for them as well.

Finally, it was time for the third and final Stolpersteine Ceremony that day, just before sundown and Shabbat. This would also be our last full day in Germany with our Significant 4. Though the Stolpersteine for our family in Meckenheim were already engraved, they were not going to be installed there until after construction on the streets was complete. We were able to actually see and touch the Meckenheim Stolpersteine in a visit to the Mayor's office where the plaques were laid out on his carpeted office floor for us to view. Those plaques were later installed around October 2014, in front of the current upholstery store which had been the previous site of the apartment where Dad had lived with his nuclear and extended family (because his father no longer had any income, per Nazi laws forbidding Germans to patronize Jewish-owned businesses). We were sent pictures of these Stolpersteine after their installation in October 2014, once we were already back home.

As we all got out of our cars in Hohenlimburg for this final Stolpersteine Ceremony, onto a steep narrow street, Jeffrey,

Gail, and I immediately recognized the now-overgrown "garden" of which we had a number of pictures with Dad and Margot as young children, and some family friends, in this "garden" before the War and the Shoah! But the house was no longer there, demolished long ago. However, right next door – as Dad had talked about – as in days of old, there stood the synagogue that their family and neighbors had attended, now a Museum of Jewish artifacts arranged according to Holiday celebrations (i.e., wine cups, seder plates, and a Haggadah Prayer Book for Pesach, apples and honey for Rosh Hashana, groggers and costumes for Purim). Jeffrey said jokingly: "No wonder Dad always said he could never skip Hebrew School even in bad weather ...because the synagogue was literally right next door to his home!"

Prior to the ceremony, we all entered the Hohenlimburg Synagogue where a German gentleman shared the synagogue's history of destruction during WWII, and how it was restored post-war by the community's non-Jewish residents and converted to a Jewish museum. I realized that this was the synagogue where my father-in-law became a Bar Mitzvah (a Jewish religious ritual and family celebration commemorating the religious adulthood of a boy on his 13th birthday), which would've been 1936 – already a dangerous time for Jews to live in Germany, more than 78 years ago from the time we were there in 2014. I was so excited, and I asked Jeffrey if he wanted to go stand at the Beama (the pulpit) at the front, exactly where his father had stood those many years ago. Whether it was too painful for him, and/or for other reasons – he said "no." I absolutely wanted to stand where Dad had once stood, becoming a "Man" according to Jewish tradition handed down *L'dor v'Dor* (from generation to generation), and reflect and "absorb" the moment. I did so, and felt called to recite the Shema Prayer as I stood where Dad and his father would've stood on that proud day so long ago – "*Shema Yisrael Adonai Eloheinu Adonai Ehad* – Hear O Israel, the Lord our G-d, the Lord is One."

As we walked outside, I looked back at the doorway entrance and noticed that the synagogue did not have a mezuzah on the outside doorpost. So Gail and I told our Significant 4 that we would like to purchase a mezuzah as a gift to be placed there, in memory of our family. While they expressed their appreciation for our proposed gift, they said no thank you, because there was

Dad's Bar Mitzvah, 1936. (He was 13 years old.) Family and Friends' celebrating at their Hohenlimburg family home. Family members identified in the photograph. In 1936, it was already difficult for Jews living in Germany.

no mezuzah there for a specific reason: the townspeople were afraid that a visible mezuzah could provoke vandalism and terror, still, in 2014 – almost 70 years after WWII and the Shoah formally ended.

And then it was time to walk to the pavement site for the Stolpersteine Ceremony, the last one of the day, and the culmination of our Journey to Germany – our reason for coming here. We were leaving the next day for Frankfurt, to stay overnight to fly home the following day. Though Dad's actual family home was gone, the Stolpersteine were going to be placed in the pavement directly in front of the "garden" of their home – pure and true to the Stolpersteine Initiative's criteria – because this was the family's last known residence that they had chosen freely.

•••

Herbert's Speech in Hagen-Hohenlimburg at Stolpersteine Ceremony for Julius and Auguste Stern, Rolf/Ralph (Dad) and Margot Stern, and Aunt Jenny Weil

August 29, 2014

Honored ladies and gentlemen, dear students:

I sincerely welcome you – also in the name of Gunter Demnig – to this laying of Stumbling Blocks here in Hagen-Hohenlimburg.

A special welcome goes to (Author's note: several town officials). And we are particularly happy that descendants of the victims we honor today have made the long journey from (the) USA, to be our guests and participate in this laying of Stumbling Blocks: Ms Gail Stern, and her brother Mr. Jeffrey Stern with his wife Sheri. Your visit is a highlight, and a special honor for us.

I also welcome the members of the media.

The presence of all of you demonstrates that this "Stolperstein-Verlegung" is an important event for Hagen-Hohenlimburg.

Let me say a few words about "Stumbling Blocks." By means of the "Stolpersteine" Project, the "culture of remembrance" we need takes a unique shape. Other than the usual memorial monuments or tablets (which, too, are significant), we may encounter Stumbling Blocks in our everyday lives – walking by or hitting upon them, "stumbling on" them on our daily way to work or from shopping. These blocks lie where we usually walk, where people live, and where the victims whose fate we remember have lived. With these blocks, in a way, they are back amongst us.

Every Stumbling Block is produced individually, and identifies the person whose name is engraved as a part of his or her family. Thus, families separated and individuals reduced to mere numbers during the Nazi regime, are symbolically reunited, and given back their names and identities at the place of their last real "home." To the descendants, they indicate that we won't forget what happened to their ancestors. We hope that the Stumbling Blocks that will be laid here today tell our guests from (the USA) exactly this.

Gail and Jeffrey Stern are the children of Rolf Stern. Born here in Hohenlimburg in 1923, at the age of 15 he could escape with a child transport to the USA in 1938. His family, trading in iron and steel, had lived here for generations. When the Nazis cut off their economic basis, they moved to Meckenheim to find shelter with relatives. From there, all of them were deported, the whole family annihilated. These Stumbling Blocks symbolically bring their family back together.

For this, we have Gunter Demnig to thank. About 15 years ago, he started his project in Cologne and it has spread far and wide since. "Stolpersteine" have been laid in more than 800 cities all over Germany as well as in neighboring countries. For this extraordinary project, he has received almost every award our country has to offer. Laying the "Stolpersteine" himself, up to six days a week, gives proof to his dedication. We are glad to have him here.

"Stumbling Blocks" make you stumble – not literally, that is. A student, asked about the risk of stumbling because of the "Stolpersteine", once said: 'Oh, no, you don't stumble and fall down, you stumble in your heart and mind!'

(A member of) the Central Council of Jews in Germany speaks from his own experience when he says: 'Traveling through all of Germany for the laying of Stumbling Blocks, I have realized that this project helps to face the Nazi tyranny, and to bring this part of history before the eyes and to the mind of the people. The fate of the murdered Jewish citizens arouses interest and sympathies. The laying of Stumbling Blocks often lets relatives of the victims and dedicated citizens meet, so that together they build bridges to commemorate the Jewish families, a commemoration that more and more has to be done without eyewitnesses. I therefore strongly endorse the project of Mr. Demnig as an important contribution against neglect and oblivion.'

There is still another dimension of memorial – the significance for the future. Memorial shall keep us alert: never again must this be allowed to happen! History classes in our schools have an important lesson to teach here. And the Stumbling Blocks are suitable helpers with this, because history only gets 'real' when connected to individuals, biographies, and places. Mrs. Ira ___, archivist of the City of Meinerzhagen, and Dr. Oliver ___, historian from Meinerzhagen – a special welcome to both of them – have compiled a documentation of the Julius Stern family of Hohenlimburg. They presented it to the descendants of Julius Stern, and they make it available for schools, for the media, and for the city archives of Hagen as well. Basing on this documentation, the Stumbling Blocks to be laid today have been made.

We thank all who have helped preparing this laying of Stumbling Blocks. Thank you for your attention.

Herbert

(Translated by Initiative Stolpersteine Meinerzhagen)

•••

Just as in the previous two ceremonies, school children were standing at the site, this time holding pictures of Julius, Auguste, Margot, and Dad (that Gail had sent to our Significant 4 for this purpose, along with a requested description of the man Dad was) while reading aloud about their lives pre-Shoah, Julius/Auguste/and Margot's ultimate fates of murder at the hands of the Nazis, and Dad's escape via a Kindertransport to the USA at the age of 15 – just two months before Kristallnacht. As before, the children spoke in German, and as always – Oliver interpreted for us without being asked. Next, a local Hagen official spoke. He needed to stop several times due to his tears. So already, I was crying softly – between looking at the pictures of our family members that the children were holding up, hearing Oliver's interpretation of what was being said in German, seeing the German official crying, and my acute realization that this was the culmination for us of an eight-month journey that had begun in January with Oliver's initial email to Gail, that this was our last day with our Significant 4 whom we could never repay for their many kindnesses, and that this ceremony was now for Dad's nuclear family whom he'd seen for the last time in September 1938 – and for Dad, his own first Stolperstein. And finally, I cried because I realized that our spiritual hope was coming true.

With the laying of these Stolpersteine, Dad's neshama was once again and for all eternity "back together" with his parents' and younger sister's neshamas, reunited at last, right where they belonged: at the last home where they'd lived happily together before their world – and the entire world – was forever and irrevocably changed.

Below are the English translations of the Meinerzhagen and Hohenlimburg articles that appeared in their local newspapers with pictures of us and the German citizens who participated. As they'd appeared in their local newspapers following the ceremonies, our Significant 4 sent these to us sometime after we'd returned home. Reading them then, and re-reading them now as I enter them into this book (March 2021)... still packs an emotional punch.

•••

"Stand up against discrimination"
(Author's Note: the first two of three Stolpersteine ceremonies 8/29/14):
"Solemn laying of Stumbling Blocks with much local participation and valuable interactions with relatives.
(Translated by the 'Initiative Stolpersteine Meinerzhagen')

Meinerzhagen. 'Healing and peace to all of you – Heilung und Frieden fur Sie alle!' That was the wish that Sheri Stern expressed after reciting the Kaddish – the most familiar of Jewish prayers – at both Stumbling-Block installation locations. Her words captured, at the same time, the very principle that motivates the members of the 'Initiative Stolpersteine Meinerzhagen' to work for this kind of memorial.

About one year ago, 17 Stumbling Blocks were first laid in Meinerzhagen. Yesterday, 13 more were added in front of the residence at Zur Alten Post 8 (formerly Haupstrasse 6) and the business at Kirschstrasse 5. As before, these new blocks were laid by Cologne-based artist Gunter Demnig, supported again by a large number of locals. Also as before, relatives and descendants of the honored victims participated in the events.

(The) Mayor welcomed Gail Stern and her brother, Jeffrey Stern, along with his wife, Sheri. All three had come from Baltimore in the USA, following the trail of their ancestors. (The) Mayor also welcomed Shaked, the great-grandson of ___. (Shaked) had been present, with his entire family, at the first installation. 'These interactions are extremely valuable, as they strengthen the predominately positive relationships that our city and citizenry has had for many years with the descendants of our former fellow-citizens,' said (the Mayor). He expressed gratitude for the efforts of the 'Initiative Stolpersteine Meinerzhagen' in keeping alive the remembrance of the city's victims of National Socialism. 'Those who cannot remember the past are condemned to repeat it,' (he) made clear, using the words of George Santayana.

Herbert ___ of the 'Initiative Stolpersteine Meinerzhagen' called strongly in his address for further specific action, 'because never again can such atrocities as our fellow citizens suffered be allowed to occur.' (Herbert) described it as a task of childrearing and of the schools to strengthen in the coming generations their sense of self-worth, and to make clear the mechanisms that lead to discriminatory and inhumane behavior. 'It takes courage to stand up against discrimination. We must practice and develop this courage every day.' During the installation of the Stumbling-Blocks, students from various Meinerzhagen schools read short biographies of the individual members of the Stern Family. They were accompanied musically by members of the group, 'Among Friends,' as well as the young guitarist.

Photos:
Artist Gunter Demnig added yesterday 13 more Stumbling-Blocks in Meinerzhagen to the 48,000 that have been installed in Germany and Europe through the project that he initiated.

Grandniece and Grandnephew (with wife) (Author's note: cousins) of Erna observe the laying of the Stumbling Blocks.

The second installation of Stumbling Blocks occurred, as the first, with active participation of locals."

•••

"The Memorial in situ is Especially Effective

Official commemoration and interactions accompany installment of Stumbling Blocks

(Translated by the 'Initiative Stolpersteine Meinerzhagen')

Meinerzhagen. 'Memorial is most effective when it occurs in situ and is connected concretely with the destinies of those that it memorializes,' said Herbert ___ of the Citizen-Initiative yesterday at the second installment of Stumbling Blocks in the city. And this particular kind of memorialization in public space is obviously well-received by many Meinerzhagners, judging by the great number of locals that gathered first at Zur Alten Post (formerly Haupstrasse) and then at Kirchstrasse to hear the life histories of the members of the Stern family.

Members of the Bundestag, ... of the Social Democratic Party and ... of the Christian Democratic Union, were in attendance as were relatives of the victims of the Nazi regime. Gail Stern and her brother, Jeffrey Stern, along with his wife, Sheri were welcomed on Thursday at the evangelical congregation-house. There they were treated to a buffet and had the opportunity to converse with three eyewitnesses of that time. Unfortunately, ___, who lives in Hamburg and was a classmate of Erwin and (___), could not be in attendance on account of a foot injury. 'In 1983 Erwin visited Meinerzhagen and hugged warmly everyone that he knew. He was an amicable and joyful classmate of mine,' wrote ___ along with his regrets. Erwin and Erna (... the grandaunt (Author's note: cousins) of the guests from the USA) had fled Germany for Baltimore. Gail and Jeffrey Stern are the children of Ralph (Rolf) Stern, who lived in Hohenlimburg and was the sole survivor of the family, the result of his successful escape to the USA. Stumbling-Blocks were laid as well in that part of Hagen in honor of the Stern Family.

Pictures:
Sheri (left) and Gail Stern (right) were visibly moved as they took a moment next to their family's memorial stones. Their grandaunt (Author's note: cousin) Erna ... was also a member of the family.

The guests from the USA were received by members of the 'Initiative Stolpersteine Meinerzhagen' in the evangelical congregation-house on Thursday. The mayor made a brief appearance.

The ceremony was accompanied musically by members of the group, 'Among Friends,' as well as the guitarist, ...

Herbert ___ (right) sees need for action in the present day."

•••

"Stumble with Head and Heart

(Authors note: Hohenlimburg Ceremony, 8/29/14)

Memorial stones are laid in remembrance of the Stern Family, victims of the Holocaust. Descendants from the USA present as guests.

(Translated by the 'Initiative Stolpersteine Meinerzhagen')

Hohenlimburg. He had just turned 15 years old – still a child – when Rolf Stern fled Germany for the USA in 1938. He would never see his family, which for generations had lived in Hohenlimburg, again. His parents, Auguste and Julius, his younger sister, Margot, as well as his aunt Jenny ..., were taken by the Nazis and murdered. Yesterday, in commemoration of the victims, as well as the displaced Rolf Stern, the artist Gunter Demnig laid five Stumbling Blocks in front of Wesselbachstrasse 4, where the Stern Family's home once stood.

It was a moving ceremony, all the more so as Rolf Stern's children, Gail and Jeffrey, as well as his daughter-in-law, Sheri, had traveled from Baltimore in the USA in order to take part in this action against forgetting. The commemoration took on a distinguished form: some one hundred students had come, as well as numerous citizens and representatives of the city, including (the) Mayor and Borough President....

Herbert ___ of the 'Initiative Stolpersteine' explained that the name of these 'Stumbling Blocks,' which feature the names and dates of the victims engraved upon a brass plate, was not to be taken literally. (Herbert) quoted Demnig, who had previously explained the term, by saying, 'one doesn't 'stumble' and fall over; instead, one 'stumbles' with head and with heart.'

A visibly moved mayor. (The) Mayor was visibly moved when he recalled in his speech that millions of people were robbed of their names, their dignity, and their lives during the terror of National Socialism. 'They were reduced to mere numbers', said (the Mayor), 'so that they would appear, in the end, merely as a statistic on a piece of paper. However, the belief of the 'Death-Bureaucrats' that they could hide the names of their victims behind these numbers did not come to fulfillment. And it is and remains our mission and our never-ending duty to ensure that this can never be the case.'

After students had presented the life-stories of each member of the Stern Family, Sheri Stern spoke, with tears in her eyes, the Kaddish – one of the most important prayers in Judaism. Equally emotional was the communal singing of the Jewish song, "Shalom Chaverim," and the laying of flowers upon the Stumbling Blocks by young students. This part of the event marked the importance of educating the younger generations about the darkest chapter in Germany's history, in order to fight against forgetting. When Gail and Sheri Stern laid small stones on the recently installed blocks, it appeared as if the Stern Family had, for just a moment, been reunited. Following the solemn occasion, the visitors from Baltimore wrote their names in the guestbook of the city of Hagen. Upon their arrival at City Hall in Hohenlimburg, the Sterns received a fitting welcome: the American National Anthem was played on the bell tower, followed by "Hewenu shalom alejchem," a song that calls all people to peace. Perhaps, after yesterday's ceremony, we might more reasonably hope that this call will someday be heard.

Insert: Over 800 Stumbling Blocks in Germany and abroad (translator's note: I think the heading should read "over 45,000 Stumbling Blocks in more than 800 cities")

The artist Gunter Demnig began the 'Stumbling Blocks' project 15 years ago in Cologne.

Since then, more than 45,000 Stumbling Blocks have been laid in more than 800 cities, mostly in Germany but also in neighboring countries.

Gunter Demnig lays the Stumbling Blocks himself, often working six days a week.

Pictures:

Gail and Sheri Stern lay, according to Jewish tradition, small stones on the bronze plates (Author's note: brass plates) that are engraved with the names of their ancestors. It was a moment that visibly moved many of those in attendance. Numerous children from Hohenlimburg decorated the Stumbling Blocks with flowers in remembrance of the Stern Family."

end of the local newspaper articles about our 8/29/14
Stolpersteine Ceremonies

•••

After the children placed yellow and red roses around their Stolpersteine, Gail and I knelt down to the Stolpersteine, laid stones on them, and touched the plaques – as if that could help us "feel" Dad's presence, and that of his family that we'd never met, except in pictures. At that moment, the local newspaper took a photo as the tears were running down my cheeks. I didn't feel awkward, or like people were gawking at us or intruding on our private – yet oh so public – grief. Rather, I felt it was an important moment for the Germans who were present and all of us – as we were coming together to memorialize, recognize the significance of our loved ones' lives, recognize who and what was lost, and grieve together ...now, with a picture for their newspaper and for us to mark this day, this ceremony, all those who were present ...and all those who were lost.

Now, as Rolf handed me the microphone to recite the Kaddish Prayer (for the third time that day, and likely hundreds of times in my lifetime), surrounded by Jeffrey and Gail, our Significant 4, and local Germans, I began to say the words in a trembling voice with tears running down my face: "Yisgadal v'yiskaddash shemay rabbah." And then, NOTHING! Suddenly, I couldn't remember the rest of the words! I started again, "Yisgadal v'yiskaddash shemay rabbah". Again, nothing. In my head, I thought, "Oh my G-d, I HAVE to complete this Prayer for our family, for Dad." Gail put her arms around me from behind, and softly whispered in my ear, "It's okay, you remember it, try again." Then Jeffrey whispered the next three words to me: "B'almah divrah cheerusay...", and then I remembered the rest of the Prayer, stopped crying, and recited it with all the dignity, respect, and love in my heart for our family.

After the ceremony, our Significant 4 took us to meet the next-door neighbor, not the one who'd lived next door to Dad's family in the 30s, but one who'd moved there more recently – so we could meet him and see the inside of his home, which would've been similar to what Dad's family home looked like inside. The neighbor was very gracious and allowed us to look around. We spoke some pleasantries in English, and he mentioned he was glad to meet us – though not for the reason we were meeting, more than seven decades later. And then our Significant 4 drove us back to our hotel to finish packing, and to prepare for our last dinner together before leaving Germany.

We had a lovely dinner together at a local restaurant, where as always – Oliver either interpreted the menu for us, and/or our friends described several of the dishes to us and what was very delicious so that we could decide what to select, or there was a menu in English in some of the restaurants (which I

Gunter Demnig (behind us) with Gail, Jeffrey, and Sheri as we sign the Hohenlimburg Guest Book following Dad's family's Stolpersteine Verlegung 8/29/2014.

thought was very accommodating). We spoke of our past week together, getting to know each other beyond the eight prior months of email relationships, learning more facts and stories about WWII and the Holocaust than we'd ever known before, visiting more cemeteries and reciting Kaddish than ever before within one week, and especially learning so much more about Dad and his family during that time. "Thank you" simply seemed so inadequate to express the depth of our gratitude for all they had done for us, all they had given us, how our lives had been forever altered – but along with special gifts we'd purchased for each of them while in Germany, those were the words we said nonetheless, as we promised to stay in touch once back in the States.

As we walked outside into the dark starry night, I felt "unfinished", as if something was incomplete. While we'd spoken about how their kindnesses and generosity had impacted us, I don't recall them speaking much about how they'd felt being with us this week, seeing our reactions, sharing sad information – other than to say they were glad to meet us and to be able to personally provide our Family Heritage Trip that we'd requested. And that's okay, because not everybody is transparent or comfortable sharing their emotions. And this had been an incredibly intense week together, so perhaps they still needed to process all that they and we had experienced, just as we still needed to do once back home. In the physical world, they knew and we knew that none of them had personally captured, tortured, or killed our People, and yet ... it's likely they knew of others who had, their own German countrymen. And so in the spiritual world, I "sensed" that there was a need to speak to them about the shame, about forgiveness and healing – face-to-face, to perhaps relieve some of their burden, right now, before we left to return home. Looking back, perhaps it was my own need to speak to them about forgiveness and healing.

I gathered our Significant 4 outside the restaurant and told them I wanted to speak to them privately. I started by sharing that I had been very scared about coming to Germany, both initially as well as pretty close to when we boarded our plane in the States, and yet I'd known even then that I couldn't say "no" to what I'd anticipated would be a once-in-a-lifetime experience that could

Rolf, Gail, and Sheri – on the eve of our last dinner together with everyone at a local Meinerzhagen Biergarten Restaurant (Beer Garden).

never be repeated. Before I went on, Ira said, "Of course you were scared. You were traveling to a country whose people killed your family." She hit that right out of the ballpark! I nodded in assent, and continued. I told them I didn't "know" them in January, but that as we'd developed our "email-relationships" over the past eight months – I came to know their "neshamas, their souls." I "knew" them from the compassionate way they each wrote, from all the time they'd spent researching specific information for us about our family as well as placing that in the context of German history, from their choosing to be our tour guides for our personal Family Heritage Journey, from their integrity, their passion, their choosing to spend their own time out of work, away from their families, at their own cost, and their telling the stark truths of the Shoah – no matter how difficult that is to do. I told them I had been scared to fly thousands of miles across the ocean to meet "strangers" and get in their cars in a country where I did not know the language or how to get around. But I couldn't have stayed home. It was not only worth the journey for me to take it, but the journey exceeded my imagined expectations, and they each exceeded my expectations, I was so glad that I'd met them, and "thank you" just seemed so pathetically insufficient a response for their contributions to our life-altering experience.

I told them that I personally felt no need to forgive any of them. Not only had they not personally perpetrated what the Nazis did decades ago, but they had individually and collectively chosen to make some form of amends – through the Stolpersteine Initiative, seeking us out, inviting us to the Stolpersteine Ceremonies for our family, and especially by offering to be our Family Heritage tour guides, which involved their extra time researching our Family members, taking off of work this week, and being available to us 24/7 without accepting compensation. However, I said that throughout the week I'd sensed that they felt pain, darkness, and shame for what their countrymen had done, as any human being would. I asked if I could place my hand on their heart as I spoke, and each said yes. I placed my other hand on my own heart. Starting with Oliver, with tears on my cheeks, I said: "Although you personally have done nothing to harm me or my family, now or in the past, I believe that Love + Forgiveness can bring Healing and Peace. That is my wish for you."

Next, I spoke these words and placed one hand on my heart and the other hand on each of theirs in turn: Ira, then Christina, and finally Rolf. Some of them had tears glistening in their eyes too.

After Rolf, we spontaneously formed a group hug and held each other silently for a moment. They thanked me, I told them how much they'd given me/us, and that I would miss them. I promised them I would tell others back in the States about them – because the World needed to hear this, now more than ever.

"Until we have seen someone's darkness we don't really know who they are. Until we have forgiven someone's darkness, we don't really know what love is."

– Marianne Williamson

Itinerary 8/30:
Saturday, August 30 Frankfurt
(Day open – TBD) Frankfurt Niederrad, Lyoner Strasse 5

Saturday 8/30/14:
Travel Log entry, Leaving Meinerzhagen:

Today we will be leaving Meinerzhagen to go back to Frankfurt to fly home. We go with Oliver, Rolf and Christina (Ira must work today, so last night was our last night with her.) to a nearby lake, talking and walking around it, sometimes silently walking and taking it all in. (I truly had difficulty physically keeping up with Rolf, who at 72 is very sprite and walks briskly even up and down hills!) After our workout, we have lunch together with Shaked at Christina and Rolf's home. Here I share my favorite Jewish prayer with everyone, as the spirit guides me, the *Shehecheyanu: "Baruch atah Adonai, Eloheinu melech ha-olam, shehecheyanu v'key'manu v'higiyanu lazman hazeh. Amen* – Blessed are You, Adonai our G-d, Sovereign of all, who has granted us life, sustained us, and brought us to this season / this moment."

Although we usually reserve this prayer for "firsts", i.e. the first night of a holiday, I feel great comfort and joy when reciting it for any momentous occasion – including at this time, the "end" – or the "new beginning" after our life-altering Germany Journey.

After lunch, Herbert (the Meinerzhagen leader who founded the Meinerzhagen chapter of the Stolpersteine Initiative) will be driving us to Frankfurt, at his request, and Shaked will accompany us, as he said: "Of course, I will spend up to the last minute with you!"

Author's note 2/6/21: Of course on 8/30/14, I had no idea of our future relationships, but I suspected that we would remain in touch. Spoiler Alert: our relationships are certainly ongoing, both in emails up to and including the global COVID pandemic, Gail's multiple return trips to Germany and her trip to Minsk with Ira, and my return trip to Germany with Gail in the spring of 2018.

More memories of 8/30, written in the years after our Journey, before I found my Travel Log:

While at Rolf and Christina's home, we enjoyed lunch and each others' company one last time. After all, who knows if any of us will ever return here – not because of the painful memories, but simply because coming back to Germany is not like driving or even flying somewhere nearby in the USA. It requires more time off from work, and is more expensive. My heart would love to return and spend more time with our Significant 4 again, but I just don't know if that's possible or practical.

Shaked has been yet another unexpected surprise during our Journey, especially since we found out that one of his male relatives married one of our female Stern relatives long ago – so we're related. When I recite the Shehecheyanu prayer and what it means in English (because just like Oliver always interpreted for us automatically, I'm aware that no one else except Jeffrey and Shaked would understand what I've just recited in Hebrew), Shaked is once again surprised. Maybe in his lifetime in Israel, he's never heard a woman recite prayers – though of course he's heard women speak Hebrew every day of his life. Maybe he is Orthodox, so when he goes to the synagogue the women pray in a separate area that is divided by a mechitzah, so he's unable to actually see them praying. [11]

It's hard to leave Germany. It's hard to "leave" Dad, Margot, Auguste, Julius, and the rest of our family. I feel like we "just" got to know Margot, Auguste, and Julius, during our time there and during the past eight months of ricocheting emails. It's never enough time with loved ones, even though we've never met these. And Jeffrey and Gail were robbed of growing up with their paternal aunt and grandparents, being spoiled by them, celebrating birthdays and anniversaries and graduations together over a lifetime. They were robbed of their great aunts and great uncles. Robbed... by Hitler and the Nazis, who murdered them all – because they were Jewish. How very different so many people's lives would be today, if only those neighbors, friends, siblings,

11   A mechitzah is a physical partition separating men and women in an Orthodox synagogue service, according to Orthodox law.

parents, and grandparents had been allowed to live their lives to the fullest - in the same way that those people who were not persecuted and massacred were allowed to do. For each person matters, and impacts and shapes the lives of those around them. And in their absences in our lives, they continue to impact and shape us as well.

I miss our Significant 4, I miss our other Stolpersteine Friends. I don't know if I will ever see them again. Although it was time to return to our lives in America, it feels like barely any time at all that we were in Germany, barely enough time to continue searching for words adequate enough to thank them for what they have done for us, what they have given us – from their hearts to ours. That... is what matters. That... is what touches my neshama.

"History, despite its wrenching pain, cannot be unlived, but if faced with courage, need not be lived again."

Maya Angelou

Itinerary: Sunday, August 31
Frankfurt to Newark – 11:20am – 1:55pm; United UA

Sunday 8/31/14:
Travel Log entry, Frankfurt (written aboard the plane):

We arrived here last evening, so that we could stay overnight near the airport. We left Germany today, following our "breakfast-included" (Jeffrey rarely travels without booking hotels that have "breakfast-included"! Family joke!).

So many thoughts, so many emotions, such incredible experiences. So many new friends, so many kind people.

Just finished watching the "Heaven is for Real" movie aboard the plane. It all boils down to Love. I do believe that Love + Forgiveness = Healing and Peace (Shalom – Hebrew, Frieden – German). I imagined and created that "equation" at the very beginning of this Journey, and said it aloud for the first time when I was sharing my private goodbye with Ira, Oliver, Rolf and Christina on 8/29/14.

I believe that equation can empower each of us to find our Authentic Voice, to speak our truth, and to be an Instrument of our Higher Power to create our own "Heaven on Earth". That will be the basis of my next Life Passage, I know it, I am certain of it. I just don't know the details yet, other than possibly public speaking and retreats. And it will involve at some point my writing a book "and you having the mirror." I don't know where that phrase just came from. It came to me as I'm dozing off and writing on the plane. I don't know at the moment what it means!

end of my 2014 Travel Log Journal entries, 8/31

That was my last Germany travel log Journal entry, on 8/31/14, as I was flying home from Germany to the US.

Today, 2/6/21, almost six and a half years later as I enter this into my manuscript, I still have no recollection of that "mirror" phrase nor what it means... if anything. However, I am indeed writing this book, the one I am called to write following my life-altering experiences in Germany during August 2014.

"There is no greater agony than bearing an untold story inside you."

Maya Angelou

The above quote by Maya Angelou is particularly meaningful to me, and explains why writing this book continues to be so important to me. This book is my instrument for sharing my universal message: Love + Forgiveness = Healing and Peace. I hope it remains as meaningful to our Significant 4 – and now to you and yours – as it is to me. After all, we are all sisters and brothers in the family of Humanity. Let's remember to treat each other that way.

Chapter 8

WALKING IN FOOTSTEPS – THE FINAL JOURNEY

by Gail Stern

Learning about my Dad's family has been a wonderful, but also painful, journey. As you know by now, it started with an email from Oliver on January 3, 2014, to which I responded immediately. In less than a year, we were off to Germany to meet our new friends, and in a certain way, our ancestors.

On the first trip, we started in Rexingen, where Auguste was born, and moved on to Meinerzhagen, Hohenlimburg and Meckenheim, where Dad lived for a short while before escaping to the United States. We went to Bad Godesberg, where the amazing archivist in Bonn walked with us, showing us the various houses where Dad's aunts and uncles had lived, and taking us to the nunnery, where Auguste, Julius and Margot lived in one room for a very short time before being taken to the train station in Cologne to start their final journey to the forest in Minsk, Belarus, where they were murdered.

Sometimes I think of my time in Germany as the tour of German cemeteries, starting with Rexingen, where Auguste's grandparents and many other relatives are buried. We also visited, and had re-engraved, and landscaped with the help of our friends, the graves of Berthold and Sophie Levi (nee Weil), Auguste's parents, in Bad Godesberg. And, of course, we visited the old and new Jewish cemeteries in Meinerzhagen, where many of my ancestors currently reside. Of course, no cemetery exists for Auguste, Julius and Margot, who were shoveled into a pit in Minsk.

On each trip to Germany, the feeling of walking in the footsteps of my Dad and his family became more and more prominent and emotional. I had avoided asking my Dad many questions, not because of how painful it might be for him, but because of how painful it was for me. This became my chance to learn and understand, although I wish I could have taken the journey with my Dad.

In Meckenheim, we walked from the house where my Dad lived to the small train station, the exact walk he went on with his parents when they took him, at 15, to begin his journey, alone, to the United States. Each step was painful. It is overwhelmingly sad to think of parents walking their son to the train to escape, knowing in their hearts that they will never see him again. We know from letters that they did not share this with him, but left him with hope that they would reunite soon in the United States. The sense of following in footsteps became more poignant after one trip to Germany where Rolf, Christina and Ira took me to a castle sitting high above Hohenlimburg. I did not realize it at the time, but a picture that Ira took of me in the castle turret mirrored a picture that had been taken of my Dad at the same location.

On one of my trips, Rolf, Christina and Ira took me to the NS Documentation Centre of the City of Cologne, a regional site dedicated to research and teaching about Cologne's history during the time of the Nazis. Ironically, this wonderful Centre is housed in the former Gestapo headquarter buildings. One can almost hear the cries of the hundreds of people murdered in the building's courtyard while the Gestapo held meetings, organized more killings and ate lunch in the rooms overlooking the courtyard.

It was here where I was shown a copy of the actual typed manifest of the names of the people taken by train from Cologne to Minsk, including Auguste, Julius and Margot. To sit in a room and view the detailed documentation on the people to be murdered is an overwhelming feeling that stays with you forever.

I remember leaving the Centre, in somewhat of a daze, to walk around Cologne on a beautiful sunny day, with the aura of death following like a black cloud. We walked to the Cologne train station where there are two plaques memorializing the deportations from Cologne to Minsk. It was at that moment that I knew I had to complete the walk in my family's footsteps and go to the forest in Minsk.

Auguste, Julius and Margot were deported from Cologne on July 20, 1942, arriving four days later and immediately marched down a dirt road where they were murdered on July 24, 1942.

The forest is known as Blagowtschina, near Maly Trostenets, not far from Minsk. Maly Trostenets became a Nazi extermination site in 1942. It had no fixed killing facilities, so all killed there, including Jews deported from Europe, inhabitants of the Minsk Ghetto, and Soviet prisoners were murdered primarily by being shot while lined up around pits. Mobile gas vans were also used. Estimates of the number of people killed range from 100,000 to in excess of 300,000. The Nazis, in an attempt to cover up their crimes, opened many of the pits in late 1943 and burned the bodies, adding to the difficulty of determining the number of people killed there. More than 30 grave pits have been discovered.

The dirt road to Blagowtschina.

Small memorials and oblique signage were erected at Maly Trostenets beginning in 1963, but it was not until 2015, that a larger memorial was erected at Maly Trostenets. None of the memorials acknowledged that the majority killed in the forest were Jewish, instead just noting the Soviet POWs, Minsk residents and "civilians" deported from Europe. This, however, did not stop families of those killed from tying yellow paper memorials to the trees, erecting a potentially temporary but powerful remembrance of some who were killed in the forest.

I went to Minsk in 2017, with Ira. I hired a local guide in Minsk to take us around the area. Although he has been guiding in Belarus for many years, he was unaware of the Blagowtschina forest "yellow sign" memorial. This was most likely due to the Soviet view of the "Great Patriotic War," a limited story told of the Soviet Union as victim of the German aggressors. This is not an entirely false view; millions of Belarusian people were slaughtered in their towns and villages, not while working as soldiers. What is left out, to this day, is that possibly a third of those murdered were Jewish.

Our guide was wonderful, and is still guiding in Belarus today. I looked at his current site, and he has more offerings on Jewish history in Belarus than he had even a few years ago. Perhaps things are slowly changing.

Ira and I spent our first full day with our guide trying to find the forest. We found the small, early and scattered Maly Trostenets memorials, including the obelisk, the Pit and the two railroad cars seemingly located randomly near Maly Trostenets. We then drove for hours in ever increasingly larger circles trying to find the Blagowtschina forest and the road leading to it.

At times I was almost ready to give up finding it, but not Ira. She had researched it in detail (as she always does) and insisted we could find it. Our guide was game, and we drove randomly down roads, knowing only that we were in the right general area. We finally drove down to a dirt road, where two hikers were coming up. Our guide spoke to them, and then excitedly motioned to us to follow him down the path. We did, and came upon a small memorial, surrounded by candles and wreaths, standing in front of the yellow paper forest. The area is covered

Blagowtschina Yellow Paper Memorial.

by weeds and trees, one of which has a small plaque describing the deportations from Europe. We walked through the area reading the yellow paper memorials, some of which also had pictures of Stolpersteine memorializing some killed in Maly Trostenets. We found a tree with paper for four family members that were on the same train from Cologne as my family, and with the help of always ready Ira, attached papers with the names and history of Auguste, Julius and Margot to the tree. Our guide, who knew nothing of the history of the forest, was visibly moved.

Another Blagowtschina Memorial,
in front of the Yellow Paper Memorial.

While standing there, I suddenly realized that it was 75 years to the month that my relatives were murdered in the forest in cold blood, by seemingly normal people. I was standing in the forest of the dead, on soil mixed with their blood, three-quarters of a century later.

How did I feel? Along with horror and great sadness, I also felt relief, and a strange kind of happiness. It had taken 75 years from the date that they had been slaughtered, but through the efforts of many new friends, and some strangers, I was able to complete my journey, walking in my family's footsteps, and silently sending them a message that they will never be forgotten. I hope that they will take some comfort from this, and can rest in peace.

Gail's personally created Blagowtschina Memorial to Julius, Auguste, and Margot.

Ira and I spent the next day at the Minsk Historic Workshop "Leonid Lewin," located in the Minsk Jewish Ghetto. The Workshop is committed to, among other things, preserving and memorializing the Jewish citizens of Minsk and their culture, research and preserving information on the atrocities that were committed by the Nazis in Minsk, and assisting the families of those murdered by the Nazis at Maly Trostenets and elsewhere in Minsk. A statement from the Workshop says it all: the Workshop is where "Belarusians and Germans work together to create a good future by remembering the past."

Across the street from the Workshop is a poignant memorial

to those who died in the Minsk Ghetto, titled the "Broken Hearth." It is a broken table and chair, symbolizing the destruction of the Jewish families and homes in the Minsk Ghetto. It sits on the site of the former Jewish Minsk cemetery, along with a nearby Holocaust memorial.

What do I remember about that day? Not much. The researcher at the Workshop spoke Belarusian and German, Ira speaks German and English, and I only speak English, so all information transmitted had to be translated. I remember little, except the wonderful commitment that both had to remembrance, preserving and educating, and passing on so much to me. It does give one hope, which can be challenging to hold on to as the Workshop is across from the Jewish cemetery started in Minsk in 1867, closed permanently in 1951, and destroyed permanently in the late 1900s. There is nothing left there but a few gravestones that survived and are gathered in a small area. There were plans to erect a dance pavilion on the site of the cemetery, but those plans were stopped only after the intervention of a number of world Jewish organizations.

The train to Minsk was Auguste, Julius and Margot's last journey, but not mine. I have returned to Germany a number of times and will return again later this year. I will return again to Minsk because it was too difficult to absorb everything, information and emotions, the first time. I will continue to honor and respect my Dad and his family, and will repeat the promise often to never forget.

I will continue every day to remember that if you do not speak and act when you see wrong, in the words of Martin Niemöller, there may be "no one left" to speak for you.

Chapter 9

BEYOND OUR AUGUST 2014 JOURNEY TO GERMANY

Von: Sheri
Gesendet: Montag (Monday), 1. September 2014
An: Oliver, Ira, Rolf (Christina), Herbert, Shaked, Gail, Jeffrey
Betreff: arrived Home!

Wanted to let you know we are home, following our Incredible Journey to Germany.

And what a life-altering Journey it has been, which will continue to impact us and our children and their children – for we will speak of you and Christina and Gretel and the people of the Stolpersteine Initiative with family and friends, emphasizing your hospitality, lovingkindness, compassion, and sense of Integrity and Justice. Please know what a difference you have made in our lives, by recognizing and honoring the significance of the lives of our loved ones and all Jews and other victims of the Shoah – acknowledging that they each lived, and they each mattered. Please know that you have each enriched our lives in countless ways. And we are honored to count you among our Friends, among our Blessings.

With Love & Affection, and Gratitude for your ongoing Passion and efforts...

Shalom, Frieden (Author's note: Peace, in German), Peace, Sheri, Jeffrey, and Gail Stern

From: Ira
To: all
Subject: AW: arrived Home!
Date: Tue, Sep 2, 2014

Dear Sheri,
I am very happy that you arrived home well. Thank you

very much for your warm and cordial words. We thank you for your visit and the time we could spend with you. It was a very impressing week together with you. ...

Shalom, Frieden,

Peace to all of you and around the world, Ira

From: Rolf
To: Sheri, Jeffrey, Gail
Subject: Thanks for your visit
Date: Tue, Sep 2, 2014

Dear Sheri, Jeffrey and dear Gail,

We are so glad to know that you reached your home safely.

It was so exciting to meet you here in Germany. We learned so much. Your interest, your sympathy and warmth, your numerous questions gave us the feeling to do something good for you. So we are so much honored.

We (will) never forget these days in our whole life accompanying you.

Many warm greetings to you, Rolf and Christina

From: Oliver
To: all
Subject: Thanks!
Date: Tue, Sep 2, 2014

Dear All,

Many thanks for your wonderful email! I am very happy that you returned well to the US. We returned to Paris on Sunday and arrived here rather late. Yesterday, I was very busy, that's why I am sending you this email today.

Yes, it was an incredible week indeed and I am happy and proud I was a part of this wonderful experience. When I had breakfast on Sunday morning I immediately knew something and someone were missing, and I therefore hope there will be many other occasions to see each other. And I would like to thank you again for your generous present, although I had told you in the first place not to do that...

I will go on with research on your family, on Hohenlimburg and on issues related with World War II, the Weimar Republic, the Nazi period and the immediate post-war years ("denazification" and restitution of seized property), and I will also contact Judi because new questions have come up concerning Julius and Cilly in Meinerzhagen and the ___ family in Rexingen as well. Maybe, there will even be an article in English one day when I have gathered enough material.

To start with, I attach a photograph showing the bakery in Meinerzhagen (Kirchstrasse), where we had dinner on Thursday (unfortunately, it is no longer like this). Then I checked again what is available on Meckenheim 1933-1945 and found interesting stuff published by the historical association in town. It sounds different from what the Meckenheim archivist said (information on seized property, "Kristallnacht", the Nazi mayor etc.). Moreover, Rolf gave me a book on the Jewish cemetery in Hohenlimburg and another one from 1988 on Jews in Hohenlimburg in the 1930s and 1940s. The latter contains accounts by witnesses, interesting details on the Jewish families in Hohenlimburg, their shops, the synagogue etc. One account deals with "Kristallnacht" in Hohenlimburg in detail.

Another account states that the religious service took place in the Hohenlimburg synagogue on Saturday morning. There was no rabbi, but the teacher of the Jewish school, ___ (d. 1928), was in charge. Apparently, it was sometimes difficult to have the minyan because most shops owned by Jews were also open on Saturday. There used to be a small organ in the synagogue which, however, was not in use. The Jewish community comprised Liberal and Orthodox members alike. There is also a document on the forced sale of the synagogue in December 1938. The property was bought by an entrepreneur for 16, 300 Reichsmark (the ___ family also got Eggestr. 14 where your grandfather's warehouse was). The address of the synagogue was Eggestrasse. 6 at that time (today, the name is Jahnstrasse). There used to be a kosher butcher in Hohenlimburg.

I will come up with new information soon, I hope. All the best from Europe and take care, Oliver

On September 4, I emailed a meme that made me think of them to Ira, Oliver, Rolf, Christina and Shaked: "Unexpected Kindness is the most powerful, least costly, and most underrated way to change a Life."

On September 11, Ira replied: Dear Sheri, dear Jeff, dear Gail,
Thank you very much for your thoughts. Yes, for us it was the experience of unexpected kindness and it changes our life. Thank you very much, that you had the confidence to come here and spend your time with people you did not know. It was a very special, but a wonderful week with you – between laugh and cry, based on such a bad heritage. In sharing the remembrance on that may grow something new. May peace and friendship grow on this. Todah Rabah (Author's note: Thank you very much, in Hebrew), Ira

From: Gail
To: all
Subject: Thoughts
Date: Mon, Sep 15, 2014

Dear Ira, Oliver, Rolf, Christina, Herbert and Shaked,
I have been quiet for a few weeks (which as you all now know is not my natural state)..... just absorbing one of the most amazing and special weeks of my entire life. I really do not know how to thank each of you for your contributions to this journey (and it was a journey, not a trip).
There is a song that Jews sing at Passover called (phonetically) Di-A-Nu (Shaked can tell you how to write it in Hebrew). It is a song thanking G-d for getting us out of ... Egypt and for everything that came before and after. Di-A-Nu means "it would have been enough." If G-d had just gotten us out of Egypt, Di-A-Nu, if G-d had just parted the Red Sea, Di-A-Nu, if G-d had just fed us in the desert, Di-A-Nu, etc., etc., etc.
This is what keeps coming to my mind when I think of you and our week together ...
If Oliver had just found us,
If Ira had just given us information,

If Rolf had just arranged for stones in Hohenlimburg....or Meckenheim,

If you just took us to one cemetery,

If you just introduced us to ___ and took us to the convent,

If you just took us to my Dad's synagogue,

If you just laughed with us (yah, yah, yah),

If you just spent a week chauffeuring us,

If you just shared your beautiful lake with us...

And even more...

If you just introduced us to Shaked,

If you just showed us that people still remember... and care,

If you just polished our family's stones,

If you just sang Shalom Aleichem for us,

If you just "united" our family in Hohenlimburg,

If you just gave us back the family that we had lost ...

Any one of those things would have been enough ... more than enough ... but you did them all, and so much more ... and you did them with grace, and heart, and kindness, and, and, and.

I like words, and I can usually use them well, but this time they seem so very inadequate.

I think the only thing I can say is thank you for truly changing our lives.

I love you all, and I will be back (promise, not threat). Give ___ my best.

Love, Gail (your Mishpacha) (Author's note: So Gail named us as Mishpacha.)

From: Ira
To: Gail, Jeffrey, Sheri
Subject: AW: Thoughts
Date: Wed, Sep 17, 2014

Dear Gail, dear Jeff, dear Sheri,

First: thank you very much for your words. I am still impressed and I had to think about your thoughts before answering, but every answer seems to be so inadequate (specially in English, I have always doubts using really the right words – at least no dictionary can help). It is hard to express, what I mean or intend.

I am thinking on our dialogues in the car or somewhere else. The reason of our journey is – or was – so severe, that no "small talk" was possible. We talked as being friends for years in a very personal way and becoming friends.

I heard the song Di-A-Nu on the internet and I am thinking about your words. We thank you, because you had the willingness to get involved (not everyone wants to be faced with the malice of man or think about – because it is hard to see reality and destroys a part of our 'basic trust'). You had the willingness to come to the country, which murdered your family. And you shared your family history with us and allowed to make it public (in some way we are searching in your privacy – first of all it is your history). You have the greatness to look on your family history without hate, or bitterness, with sadness and with a look on the future, that such things should not happen any more. You had the confidence to plan a journey with people you did not know and you had the trust to sit in someone's car and hoping that the driver knows what he/she is doing. You just approached us very open-minded and you invited us (to the hotel, to some culinary delicacies...). You visited 6 cemeteries – in some towns the only what we could show you, because in some places it is the only which remained of a rich Jewish culture in Germany. You had the willingness to be part of a public event, with press and so many unknown people telling your very personal story. You just entertained us with your jokes and you made us thoughtfully with questions, observations and comments. And so much more... for what we want to say thank you.

You promised to come back – we take it seriously and we are glad to see you again.

Love, Ira

From: Oliver
To: all
Subject: Ellis Island
Date: Wed, Sep 17, 2014

Thank you very much for your touching last message! In fact, the wonderful reference to the 'Di-A-Nu' song proves that you use words and expressions extremely well. Anyway, they were more than adequate again.

I found additional information on your father's journey to the US on the website of Ellis Island [http://www.libertyellisfoundation.org/], which completes and corrects the information on Flickr. I do not know whether you have already visited this website and this information was not available in January when I checked it for the first time, but maybe the website is updated regularly and the passenger data are digitized bit by bit.

I typed "Rolf Stern" and found the following:

There are two passenger documents on the website, and copies can be ordered there. Your father travelled on the 'Ile de France' (information on the ship can be found here, in the section on the 1920s: http://www.thegreatoceanliners.com/index2.html) of the French "Compagnie Generale Transatlantique" (C.G.T.) from Le Havre to New York City. He left France on September 15, 1938, and arrived in New York on September 21, 1938. He had a ticket to his final destination in Delphos, Ohio (to his aunt Mrs Louis Sanders) (Author's note: Bella), but traveled apparently without any cash or had less than 50 $ with him because that is the amount the authorities ask about in the form. The name "Hohenlimburg" is not spelt correctly, and his parents, who paid the journey, are referred to as Mr and Mrs Aug. Stern, Meckenheim, Germany. His visa had been issued in Stuttgart on July 11, 1938. This is tricky because, according to the National Archives in Washington, D.C., there was no US consulate in Stuttgart in 1938, but I will have to check that again.

In the attachment, you will find photographs of the ship and of the port of Le Havre (i.e. the pier of the C.G.T.) destroyed by air raids in World War 2.

All the best from Europe, Oliver

From: Ira
To: Gail, Jeffrey, Sheri, Oliver
Subject: AW: Thanks ... and questions (of course)
Date: Wed, Sep 24, 2014

Dear Gail,

To your first question. I have the information that the Kindertransport was for children under 12 from you: www.flickr.com/photos/smoovej/6032862381/in/photostream/:

'On about September 7, 1938, just weeks before Kristallnacht, Ralph took a train from Meckenheim to Hamburg, where he met with a group of children from all over Germany who were migrating to America with the help of HIAS (Hebrew Immigrant Aid Society); this group usually only assisted the migration of children to the age of 12, however somehow Ralph's parents had arranged for him to join them even though he was too old'.

I wrote: 'Probably the money from selling the house was the key to make this possible.' That's wrong – cancel this sentence. Sorry, it was just a presumption without any evidence. I was thinking aloud. Your sentence: 'however somehow Ralph's parents had arranged for him to join them even though he was too old' is correct – nothing else. Where is the origin of your information?

I don't know if there are any documents about HIAS and where it could be.

I don't understand your sentence. I miss the context. The archivist from (that town) said there was no violence at Kristallnacht in (that town)? They destroyed shops and houses in (that town) like in most of the German towns and villages. I don't know if people were attacked or beaten. I think there must be more information about what happened in (that town) and I can try to find it out.

It was different from town to town. In Meinerzhagen they smashed the windows of __ Stern's shop (there were not other shops any more and the cattle traders had no shops) and members of the SS – (... it is just narrative, there was no trial after 1945) forced their way into __ Stern's house, took away the ritual objects of the Jewish community and burnt them in front of the house. I have reports of Jewish and not-Jewish eyewitnesses. The synagogue was closed in 1938 before Kristallnacht (there was no minyan any more and they could not pay the rent for the room any more), so the SS had no synagogue what they could burn down. Before – at nine o'clock in the morning – all Jewish men were arrested from policemen (against the order – the order was: no policemen, only gestapo should arrest). So the men were not at home, when the SS was on the street. Maybe that was good. I don't know if it was (on) purpose. Chief of the local police was ___. The SS men were not inside the houses or shops and there was nothing destroyed inside the houses or shops. So I know – no one was attacked or beaten in Meinerzhagen. I know, it is really bad enough, but it is remarkable – since I know what happened in other towns (murder, torture, rape and all kind of violence – with or without involvement of parts of the population). All Jewish men from Meinerzhagen were brought to Sachsenhausen. There it was really horrible.

Eyewitnesses To Kristallnacht

By Fred Gottlieb, from "My Childhood In Siegburg", Mazo Publishers, 2008

"When the terrible news came that a 17-year-old boy, Herschel Grynszpan, had assassinated a German official in Paris, we sensed Mother's foreboding. … My mother's premonition proved to be correct. In the early morning hours of November 10, 1938, our beautiful synagogue was torched, as were hundreds of synagogues all over Germany. The method of arson used was to toss canisters of flammable material into the sanctuary and strike it, from a safe distance, with a bullet.

From the attic of our house, the flames could be seen against the dark sky, but Mother shielded us from such a horrible sight. That morning, the windows of Jewish shops in Siegburg were smashed, and all Jewish males 16 to 60 in Siegburg were arrested and sent to Dachau. Almost all returned after several weeks, but many were broken in body and spirit. By that time, most of the Jews were trapped, trying desperately to get out of Germany, but finding no country that would accept them."

*By Brigitte Ringer Nenner, from "Brigitte's Angel Of Poetry",
Mazo Publishers, 2002*

Kristallnacht, *Or* Tale Of A Witness

I am a witness,
For I have seen.
I am a witness
Who lived in Berlin.

I saw those streets
Covered with glass.
I saw the Brown Shirts
Having viel Spasse. (Fun)

I saw Jewish men
Dragged out of bed.
Fifty years later
I cannot forget.

I saw those Jews
Hung by the neck.
Heard singing and shouting
Juda Verreck! (Jews Should Die!)

I saw the Temple
In flames, burning high.
I was a child
And asked myself, Why?

I saw the crowds
Watching the show.
I did not hear anyone
Saying "No!"

9th of November, 1988

From: Oliver
To: all (including us and Herbert, Ira, and Rolf)
Subject: Your questions
Date: Wed, Sep 24, 2014

Dear All, Thanks for your message! I will try to answer your questions:

1. Ira, in your materials, you indicated that the Kindertransport was for children under 12. Dad was 15? Did his parents bribe his way onto the ship? With the house money?

I found information saying that the term 'Kindertransport' refers to a programme of the British government in which German Jewish children were sent to foster families in the UK (and before the war to other European countries like the Netherlands, Belgium or France as well). In the US, there was the "One Thousand Children" programme. I think that your father's case was slightly different because his parents paid for the visa and the journey and sent him to a relative in the US. So, in his case, it was probably not a 'Kindertransport' in the proper sense of the word although he may have travelled with 'Kindertransport' children.

2. Oliver, if no consulate in Stuttgart in 1938, how did he get a visa? Was it likely a forgery?

I do not think it was a forgery. I do not know enough about the topic, but either the information on the website of the National Archives in Washington DC is not complete or there was another institution in Stuttgart issuing visa (e.g. a honorary consul or the like). I will have to look for more information and hopefully find something. Siegfried and Erna Schwarz as well as Erwin Stern also had visas issued in Stuttgart. ...

3. The info re (name's) deposit for Selma ... what was this a deposit for?

As I found this in the archives of the Joint Distribution Committee this must have been the deposit made for Isak and Selma's journey to the US. According to the JDC website, the bulk of these deposits were made between 1940 and 1942, but this one was obviously too late because Isak and Selma died in Theresienstadt as we know from the obituary in 'Der Aufbau'.

4. Any more info on the 'confused' archivist from (that town) who believes Kristallnacht skipped (that town)?

I do not know what this archivist wants to hide. There is a website of the local historical association (in German) which specifically mentions the 'Kristallnacht' in (that town). There is even an account by an eye-witness: (online reference). This document quotes sources from the ___ local archives and from the collection of the historical society (probably copies of these documents), and, as I told you, there must be something on (that town) in the State Archives in ___, too...

I will send another email shortly because I finally found data on Siegfried and Erna's as well as Erwin's flight to the US in 1937 and 1941.

I miss you, too.

Happy New Year (Rosh Hashanah is now, isn't it?), all the best and take care, Oliver

From: Oliver
Subject: Siegfried and Erna's as well as Erwin's escape to the US (Ellis Island Database)
Date: Sun, Sep 28, 2014

Dear Judi,

I hope you are fine.... I found some time to have another look at the database of the Ellis Island Foundation and I finally found information on your parents' and uncle's escape to the US (this information was probably not digitized yet when I tried in January). On the website (http://www.libertyellisfoundation. org/) you can look for individual passengers. Once you have found the name you can click on the 'I' on the right. A summary appears and you can log in. Once you have registered and logged in you can click on 'Ship Manifest' and have access to the scans of the documents (copies can also be ordered there). This is what I found (the errors are probably due to border police who did not catch the names etc.):

Siegfried and Erna Schwarz

Antwerp – New York City (Author's note: Judi states that her parents said they came directly to Baltimore, not through New York, and that the Baltimore Jewish Museum of Maryland has documentation validating that they came directly to Baltimore.)

S.S. Westernland (Red Star Line), leaving 15th May, 1937

Visas issued in Stuttgart on 23rd March, 1937

Siegfried had 40 $ with him.

They were going to stay at their cousin's place: New York City.

Siegfried's father (according to the document): ___ Schwarz, Rexingen

Arriving in New York City, 25th May, 1937

Erwin (Simon Israel) Stern

20 years old, tailor, Meinerzhagen

Visa issued in Stuttgart, 13th May or 15th March, 1941

Final destination: Baltimore, MD

Erwin had 30$ with him. Final destination: Erna and Siegfried Schwarz, Oakfield Ave., Baltimore

Arrival in New York City 23rd June, 1941

Sailing on the S.S. Serpa Pinto (Companhia Colonial de Navegacao, Portuguese line) from Lisbon on the 12th June, 1941

In the attachment, you will find photographs of the ships and the port of Antwerp (next to the Scheldt River) as well an article in English on US consulates in Germany. It proves – like several German authors – there was a consulate in Stuttgart in the 1930s which issued visas for German Jews who escaped to the US (however, I am not sure that all the files of this consulate are still in the National Archives in Washington D.C.).

I also would like to know whether you have letters of your parents concerning restitution claims of the (two) families in Rexingen after the war. Gail showed us very interesting letters her father had kept (correspondence with a law firm in Munich, letters containing file numbers etc.). If you should have similar letters and want them to have translated do not hesitate to send me the scans. As we did not stay very long in Rexingen in August, I did not have time to go to the state archives in nearby Sigmaringen (the archivists wrote me that they have documents on Rexingen in 1938, "Aryanization" and restitution claims). I would like to go there at a later date; if I had file numbers and other references it would be easier and quicker to order documents in the archives. Thank you very much and best regards from Paris, Oliver

From: Rolf
Subject: AW: saying hello
Date: Thu, Oct 2, 2014

Dear all,
Many many thanks for all the mails which touched our heart so much. We are well.

Like you we needed some days to recreate us from the intensive time we spent together. So we went with our caravan to the Netherlands without a laptop, without emails. After we have taken part in a wedding tomorrow we drive to Volkach on the river Main near Wurzburg to stay there for two weeks. If you want to, you can call us with the number ____). On October 19th we are back again . . . We often think of you.

We wish you all the best, Christina und Rolf

From: _____
Subject: Pictures from Meckenheim
Date: Tue, Oct 28, 2014

Dear Gail, Sheri and Jeffrey,
We finally made it! The "Hauptstrasse" (Author's note: the street and the mall) was reopened on last Saturday and the "Stolpersteine" are "in". I took some pictures for you as attachment to this e.mail. I hope, all of you are satisfied with the result!?

I also hope, that you have had a wonderful time in Germany after our meeting on august 27th and you had a good flight back to the U.S. All the best for you, with kind regards from Meckenheim! Yours, ____ Mit freundlichen Gruessen

Dad's and his family's 8 Stolpersteine, Meckenheim: Max, Selma, and Susanne, Julius and Auguste Stern, Aunt Jenny Weil, Rolf/Ralph – Dad, Margot Stern.

From: (an American cousin)
To: family
Sent: Sun, Nov 16, 2014 11:26 am
Subject: Rexingen

Ecumenical Service in memory of the night of the pogrom, (Kristallnacht) 1938 – Former Rexingen Synagogue
We had a reading from this memoir of (Viktor) at the recent

memorial I attended. Viktor was my father's best friend in this country and they got together often to play cards in the nearby park. He actually passed away playing cards with my father present. My father in fact notified his wife ... of the tragedy. (My sister) always said to me, of the occurrence, that my father was never the same afterwards and did pass away himself, late that year, 1976. I was an early arrival at the memorial and introduced myself to a gentleman who got there first... His last name was ___, shortened from ___. It was Viktor's son, who was about 4 years old at the time of 'Krystalnacht.' He came that day from another area to attend. Sat next to him at the brunch. He remembered my father and mentioned he had come several times during his father's Shiva (Author's note: 3 to 7 day mourning period in Judaism, when friends and family visit the bereaved to offer comfort).

It was Viktor who in fact received and then personally transported the Torah, at great risk, that came from the Schul in Rexingen and was saved from destruction by a Rexingen policeman, to Shavei Zion, Palestine.

From: Rolf
Sent   Monday, December 01, 2014

Hi All, 2014, November 29 we were in Hohenlimburg and November 30 we visited Meckenheim. We polished the Stolpersteine and made fotos. Many greetings ...to Baltimore! Yours, Christina und Rolf

From: Gail
Subject: RE: All good
Date: Tue, Dec 2, 2014

Thank you so much ... the stones are so beautiful ... even more so because they were polished with love. Every time I see them, my heart smiles and cries at the same time ... with sadness for what my family endured, with satisfaction that because of people like you they will never be forgotten.

We had a wonderful event on November 27, our Thanksgiving.

My niece (Jeffrey and Sheri's daughter) Michelle and her husband John had a beautiful, healthy baby girl. She was born on the date that my Dad passed away (5 years ago), and was named for him... The circle of life continues.

I hope you all have a happy and wonderful holiday season.

Gail

Von: Sheri
Gesendet: Dienstag, 2. Dezember 2014 04:53
An: all
Betreff: Fwd: We Joyously Welcome a New Generation!

We joyously welcomed baby girl Rowan Eden into our Family on Thanksgiving Day (Thursday 11/27 @ 1 a.m.)! She is healthy, strong, and beautiful, and our latest Blessing! She is named after Jeffrey and Gail's Dad (my father-in-law) Ralph, and John's Grandmother Barbara Ellen (It's a common practice of Judaism to name children after beloved relatives who've passed away.). Of note, Ralph died on 11/27/2009 – so Rowan Eden is Ralph's (and Barbara Ellen's) namesake, born exactly 5 years after Ralph passed away. Aunt Gail and Uncle Ryan (our son) are ecstatic!

As with your families, and families all over the World – no matter what language we speak, no matter what our culture or religious affiliation is – we all understand and speak the Language of Love.

Hope you all are well across the ocean and miles. No matter the distance or time apart, you are in our Hearts ...

Love, Bubbe Sheri and Pop-Pop Jeffrey (Bubbe is Yiddish for Grandmother.)

Each of them wrote their congratulations back, remembering when their children and/or grandchildren were born, what a joy it is, and similar cultural and/or religious baby-naming practices in their families and in Germany. If we simply stop and take time to think of it, how very similar we all are – all humans, with differences to be sure. Please, people – let us learn to embrace our similarities as well as our diversities – all of which can enrich us rather than separate us and sow hatred, intolerance, and even genocide.

On 12/4/2014, Oliver wrote condemning an anti-Semitic act in Paris that had recently taken place, noted here from a news source: "Brutal anti-Semitic rape and robbery 'an assault on all France holds dear', says President Francois Hollande. A young Jewish couple were tied up and robbed at gunpoint and the young woman was gang raped, authorities said (___) Thursday, 4 December 2014 ...

A brutal anti-Semitic rape and robbery in the Paris suburbs has been condemned by President Francois Hollande as 'intolerable' and an 'assault on all that France holds dear'. ... One of their alleged victims, identified only as ___, said it was clear the attackers had sought out a Jewish target. 'They said they knew we had cash in the flat because Jews have money and they never keep it in the bank', ___ told French radio. 'They said, over and over, 'We're robbing you and we are attacking Jews at the same time – the two things in one'". [1]

Yet again, I think: When will this stop, acts of violence like this towards anyone? How "old" this hatred is known to be. History has taught us when, why, how it began, and why it continues – not just against Jewish people, but against any group identified as "other" and a potential threat to those in the dominant caste. We must always be vigilant, stand up and speak out about hatred and intolerance towards anyone and everyone. We "humans" are harming and killing each other, wiping each other off the face of the Earth. STOP!

From: Rolf
To: Sheri and Jeff
Sent: Sun, Dec 21, 2014 5:30 am
Subject: Chanukah and 2015

Dear Sheri and Jeff, we hope you had a nice time celebrating Chanukah in your family.

We wish you a very happy new year 2015 with joy, health, effort and satisfaction and with peace for the whole world.

We are so glad that we were able to meet you this year. It was

---

1   http://www. independent.co.uk/news/world/europe/brutal-antisemitic-ra; December 2014.

so great for us and gave us so much. Thank you for this deep experience.

With kind regards, Christina und Rolf

From: Ira
To: all
Sent: Tue, Feb 10, 2015 3:18 pm
Subject: AW: pictures!

Dear Sheri, dear all, thank you very much for the nice pictures! I am still astonished that people whose roots are in the small town of Meinerzhagen meet in (___) and have fun. I am very glad that I was able to help to reunite you. I am thinking about you and miss you too.

All the best to you, Ira (Author's note: I'd sent them pictures of Judi and Bernie, and Yvonne and Rene at our home, sharing our experiences in Germany with them. Yvonne's ancestors lived at the last 2 homes in Meinerzhagen yet to have Stolpersteine laid. Ira "connected" us, and believe it or not – Yvonne and Rene live 10 minutes from us!)

From: Gail
Subject: Thoughts
Date: Sun, Apr 5, 2015

Thinking about all of you... I want you to know how much each of you have truly enriched my life. Words cannot really express how much everything you have done means to me, and how happy I am that you are in my life. I only wish that I had met you years earlier... I would have loved for you to have known my Dad, and for him to have known you.

Happy Easter, and love to all.

Can't wait to see you in September.

Gail

From: Oliver
Subject: Hohenlimburg in 1935
Date: Wed, Jun 24, 2015

Good morning everybody,

I received this photo this morning via facebook and would like to share it with you. It is from the collections of the Hagen (Author's note: region including Hohenlimburg) City Archives and shows the inauguration of the local historical museum ("Heimatmuseum") on May 12, 1935 in the centre of Hohenlimburg.

It clearly shows to what extent the local historical society ("Heimatverein") was actively involved in and supported by the Nazi regime. If I am not wrong, ___ was put on trial after the war and shortly imprisoned for his active participation in the 'Reichskristallnacht' in Hohenlimburg in November 1938. Best regards, Oliver

In November 2015, after Gail sent a number of Dad's papers to Ira for translation, Ira identified documents and forms between lawyers in Germany and Dad, who was seeking restitution/compensation for his family's many losses as a result of the Holocaust. Some of the highlights are noted here below:

27. June 1961:
Dear Mr. Stern, I'm sorry to say that the authority did not approve your right for compensation in the case of the death of your father ('Schaden an Leben' = (compensation for) losing the life). The copy of the decision is in the attachment.

Lawyer in Germany Aug 14 (year unknown): Mr. Rolf Stern, You have not yet replied to the inquiry from Munich, dated December last. They want to know from you which course of the High School you have left, why you left and witnesses who confirm your informations in a statement before a Notary Public. But before doing so, please report to me and then I shall prepare for you such statements.

Please report at an early date. Sincerely, ___

9. July 1962:

From Dad to law offices in Germany: Dear ___, To my regret, I did not answer your letter from 28. March 1962. I wrote to some former friends/acquaintances and asked them – for the purpose of answering your questions correctly. I got no answer. I answer your questions to the best of my knowledge on the attached paper. If you need documents or answers in the case of my mother's deprivation of liberty, please ask (bank connection). (Freiheitsschaden = the right for compensation for being arrested illegally). My father had his banking account by ___ bank in Hohenlimburg.

Respectfully yours, Ralph Stern

No date seen: The furnishing of my parents: 7 good furnished rooms and one furnished office. My parents possessed definitely Gold, Silver and jewelry. But I don't know in detail.

My mother always was working in the company of my father. The main occupation of my father was acquisition and sale of scrap iron. He also sold (non-ferrous) scrap metal and skins.[1] Some delivery men brought those articles (products) in our house. My mother almost only was responsible for the purchase of (these) goods. The house of my parents was rented to family ___ under the pressure of the racist persecution. I don't know, if the office premises (in the same house and yard) were rented too. Without any doubt the business was destroyed by the measures of the National-Socialists. The factories, my father bought the scrap iron, were not (allowed) to sell it to my father any more. Connecting the household goods, the furnishing und the furniture of the office: when I came back to Germany with the American occupation army in the year 1946, I heard that all (these) things were brought to a monastery in Meckenheim (per Ira – Bonn, not Meckenheim). There they were auctioned by the finance authority.

Footnote from Ira: 1. In the middle-ages Jews were not (allowed) to be a farmer (owner of land) or a craftsman (member of a guild), but they had the right to be a butcher (slaughtering kosher). So many Jews were butchers (selling meat for Jews and non-Jews – for example butchery ___, Meinerzhagen), cattle traders (some members Stern and ___, Meinerzhagen) or sold skins, guts (for making sausage, ___, Meinerzhagen) or bones, (for producing soap, ___, Meinerzhagen).

The iron was stored in the big yard. In the yard was a big, old railway freight car, where the scrap metal was stored. Inside of the house was a room, used as an office. I can not provide details about Gold and some other objects of value, which exist in the year 1938 and which had to be delivered.[2] My parents had a good, middle-class house. Without doubt my mother and my sister possessed jewelry, crystalware was in place.

Footnote from Ira: 2. Law February 1939: Jews had to deliver Gold, Silver, Jewelry.

My mother worked full-time in my father's business. Her main work was to buy skins and metal customers brought in the house. I can name witnesses (so they are alive): 2 workers, who worked in the business of my parents: ___ and ___, living in Hohenlimburg. In the rear house of the estate of my parents, Wesselbachstreet 4, a renter was living – I don't know his name any more. Over the way / on the other side of the street family ___ and family ___ was living. There was a policeman, his name was ___, sometimes he came to the estate.

Köln, 27.5.1964 (May 27.1964) ... Mr. Stern, your right for compensation in the case of your deceased mother ... You told us that your mother always worked in the business (of your father) in Hohenlimburg. Self-dependent she bought scrap metal and skins some customers brought to the store/firm ... we need a résumé (personnel data report of your mother's life) for the proceeding connecting your right for compensation because of disadvantage in making career in the case of your deceased mother. What school education and job training made she? Did she (have) a job before her marriage? You (were) very young at that time, but I am sure, that you know what profession your grandfather (on your mother's side = Berthold Weil) had. Did he have a business? Maybe your mother helped in your grandfather's business before she married. Please answer quickly...

Köln, den 7.2.1966 (February 7, 1966);
(Author's note: This happens to be Dad's birthday, February 7; he turned 43 years old on this date, married with 2 children, Jeffrey and Gail):
Dear Mr. Stern, ...your letter from December 1965. We got it. Thank you. We hope you got the money for the compensation that you had not as good chances for education as you would have had in Germany under other circumstances ("Ausbildungsschaden" = disadvantage in education / learning a profession; in Germany for Jews no chance to visit a high school or college, no chance for an apprenticeship (only in Jewish companies – which did not exist any more at the end of 1938)...)... your right for compensation connecting your mother. There is a copy of our letter (May 27. 1964). We think, that it did not reach you. So we send it again ... please answer the questions...we will prepare an affidavit...we hope that the proceeding connecting your right for compensation because of failing chances for progress in profession will be finalized (in the case of Auguste?) (Schaden am beruflichen Fortkommen = disadvantage in making career).
July 1966 Erwin Stern, (nephew of Auguste) born 13. July 192(0) in Meinerzhagen, often came to visit his aunt Auguste Stern in Hohenlimburg during his (school?) vacation. He saw that Auguste always was working in the business of her husband. ... on oath attested Baltimore MD. USA ... July 1966 (no signature / handwritten by Ralph Stern? / maybe a concept which Erwin Stern should sign?)

1. Aug. 1966 USA
Dear Mr. Lawyer! I think that you got my letter from July 18.
In the attachment you will find your questions answered in detail and an affidavit. The correctness can be confirmed by witnesses inside the country. ...greetings, Ralph Stern

Along with her translations of Dad's letters, Ira also explained the German word Wiedergutmachung – which after World War II refers specifically to the reparations that the German government agreed to pay to the direct survivors of the Holocaust, those who were made to work as forced labour, individuals who were persecuted for political, racial, religious or ideological reasons, interned in camps or ghettos, mandated to wear the Jude star badge, or who lived in hiding during the Nazi regime.

Sunday 11/29/2015, from Oliver:

...I had a first look at the pile of letters Gail gave me last Saturday (Author's note: Oliver had come to Philadelphia for a conference, and we met him there and took him to dinner with the three of us, and Judi and Bernie who met him for the first time.), and there is some very interesting stuff in it, indeed. Apart from the cynicism of West German authorities refusing to pay even small financial compensations after the war, there is some information on the tenant who lived in the house in Hohenlimburg. His name was ___, and he must have been a very good friend of your family because one letter mentions the fact that he went to visit them after they had already moved to Meckenheim. In another letter related to Meckenheim, the names ___ and ___ appear again. It becomes obvious that the ___ family were profiteers and took over property seized from your family....

Von: Sheri
Gesendet: Montag, 7. Dezember 2015

With all that's happening in our World, most recently Paris and San Bernardino, as well as our shared histories of the too-many-consequences of intolerance, and having just watched our President Obama address our Nation as to how "we" are continuing to fight terrorism at home and abroad with our French, German, and other Allies – I pause to find many beautiful Miracles (I believe these are not simply coincidences.), on this first night of Chanukah (The Jewish Festival of Lights and Miracles):

We 3 Jews (Well, we now know you were actually looking for the other Julius Stern's Family! Ach, we're ALL Mishpacha!) were sought out by you 4 Germans almost 2 years ago, January 2014 (Ira, Oliver, Rolf and Christina) for the purpose of memorializing and recognizing the significance of the lives of our loved ones who were killed by the Nazis during the Holocaust, sharing your many kindnesses, and sharing each others' feelings about what happened and where we go from here. And we continue this beautiful relationship and conversations today. And yet, it was not so very long ago that Jews were sought out by Nazis for a very different purpose.

Despite our shared prior histories, Germany and America are actually ALLIES today in the war against ISIS (and France, of course, has been a long-time American Ally).

And despite all that is happening in our World, as tragic as these occurrences are – although I sometimes struggle to do so, I still find Hope, because of people like you. If more people considered the many similarities between us all, and respected and valued the diversities of our cultures, and shared common basic values of respect for all humanity, equality, compassion, freedom, conflict resolution/negotiation, and worked TOWARD a common Goal of Peace – how very different all of our lives would be. It starts with 1 person, 1 Voice – joining with others. We're so glad to call you friends. And we appreciate the Stolpersteine Initiative, its Mission, and its dedicated Members. Thank you for looking for us across the miles! I will send this to Rolf and Christina as well.

With Love, Hope, and Healing, and wishes for PEACE and a very Merry Christmas Holiday season to our Mishpacha abroad, Sheri

From: Ira
Date: Tue, Dec 8, 2015

Dear Sheri, thank you so much for your very warm and kind words, which touched us deeply. We wish you 'Happy Hanukkah' and all the best for the holidays!

Love, Ira and family

From: Rolf
Subject: AW: Peace, Frieden, Shalom!
Date: Tue, Dec 15, 2015

Liebe Sheri, lieber Jeff und liebe Gail, (English: dear),

Thanks for the long email from December 7. 2015. I want to send it translated also to the members of the Initiative Stolpersteine. Your list with the problems of the world could be continued without getting to an end. In our country we are very busy in helping the big group of refugees from Syria and of emigrants from Iraq, Afghanistan and Africa. I am very afraid of the increase of nationalism, hostility to strangers and also of anti-semitism in European states. Do events in history recur? After Reichspogromnacht (Author's note: Kristallnacht), November 9. 1938, all countries closed their border and only Shanghai offered a place for shelter. This was the only place for five refugees from Meinerzhagen, among them the mother of ___, ___, ... with her husband___. Your father Rolf was lucky to escape a short time before to the USA in September 1938. Evidently the world acts crazy.

We try to contribute to communication. Bombs are not the right way. They cause new streams of refugees.

We wish you merry Christmas holidays and a happy new year 2016. Christina und Rolf

From: Ira
To: we 3 (Jan 12, 2016)

Dear Sheri, Jeffrey and Gail,

Thank you very much for your present! So surprising ... and touching. A really good starfish-story. Thank you for your touching words, too. I am very glad about it and proud... The picture got the best place in the room (where I can always have a look at it). ...

Wed, Jan 13, 2016 2:40 pm
From: Rolf
To: we 3
Subject: Thanks for the Gift!

Dear Sheri, Gail and Jeff, many thanks for your email from December 23. and 24., and especially for your parcel with the gift, the frame with the wonderful story and your warm words. It reminds us, that we all can do great things, although it seems that

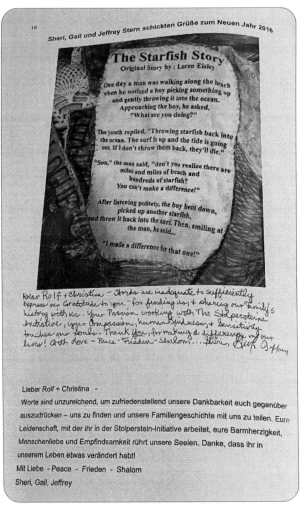

Starfish Story Gift, sent to our Significant 4 sometime after we'd returned home from our 2014 Germany Journey.

we are doing nothing important but it can make a contribution to peace between people. I hung the picture on the wall in my office and together with the stone in front of our door with „Shalom", it reminds us of you....

On January 21. 2016 the members of the 'Initiative Stolpersteine Meinerzhagen' come together to make plans how to celebrate the commemoration of the Holocaust on January 27, the day the Russian soldiers liberated Auschwitz...

In love and embracing you, Yours, Christina and Rolf

Von: Sheri
To: our Significant 4
Gesendet: Samstag, 16. Januar 2016
Betreff: received MEINHARDUS 12/2015 edition

Just picked this up at the post office today; thank you for sending. Though I cannot interpret the German words, I recognized the pictures from our time together with you all in 8/2014, and Gail's return 9/2015. Truly a life-altering experience for us, in so many dimensions. Shaked – what's up? Miss hearing from you – give us an update!

As I reviewed the special edition, while I do not profess to "know" any of your pain, shame, and guilt that some of you have expressed regarding the Nazis' past actions – what I DO know is that you did not carry out those actions, nor are any of you standing by silently even now 70-75 years later, as evidenced by your ongoing passionate work with The Stolpersteine Initiative as well as welcoming tens of thousands of Syrians seeking safety and peace into your homeland. As each of us must travel our own Path towards Peace in our Mind, Heart and Soul, and Reconciliation with what "was", I know I cannot relieve anyone's residual shame, guilt, or pain.

What I CAN do, though, is let you know from one human being to another that I feel no animosity, blame, anger, or hatred toward any of you – NONE OF YOU ARE RESPONSIBLE FOR WHAT HAPPENED! And furthermore, while you cannot bring our millions of loved ones back, you ARE doing what IS within your power in this 21st Century to make amends, heal old wounds born of man-made tragedy, and offer "the olive branch" of Peace and

Reconciliation to us and many other Families – which we have accepted. DAYENU (Hebrew) – as Gail wrote to you – 'It would've been enough for us'.

I still recall the retired German teacher who cried with me while we embraced at the dinner ceremony the night before the laying of the Stolpersteine, the Stolpersteine group's sensitivity to our kosher dietary laws in their labeling of the foods prepared for us at that dinner, Christina and I crying in each others' arms in the bathroom at the Museum when I was so overwhelmed with sadness and grief, the many cemeteries we visited, Rolf's passionate 'We should NEVER forget!' as well as his motivating 'Come, come, we go' (when we couldn't keep up with his brisk pace!) and his polishing our Family's Stolpersteine for us, looking over Ira's work table at papers/artifacts from that time in history and her understanding my initial concerns about traveling to Germany, Herbert's initiation of the Stolpersteine Initiative and driving us back to the airport for our return home, Oliver's interpreting German into English for us, Rolf and Christina's inviting us into their home, my goodbye to Ira, Oliver, Rolf and Christina at our last dinner together 8/2014, and of course all of our lively dinners breaking bread together and getting to know each other while in Germany.

So I say to each of you and the Stolpersteine Initiative Members, with all respect for each of your personal experiences – if any of you are still carrying any shame and guilt:

DAY (pronounced in Hebrew, 'dye'), ENOUGH, and LA'AZOV – LET IT GO (the pain and shame and guilt). While none of us should ever forget what happened, I hope you continue to do your Peace-building work with Passion, and see how much lighter your Hearts will feel when you let go of the shame and guilt. Please accept "the olive branch" we extend to you across the miles.

I leave you with The Four Things That Matter Most: A Book About Living (by Ira Byock):

I forgive you.
Please forgive me.
I love you. Thank you.
With Hugs and Love, Sheri

BE the Change you wish to see in the World.

Mahatma Gandhi

From: Ira
Subject: AW: received MEINHARDUS 12/2015 edition
Date: Sat, Jan 23, 2016

Dear Sheri, dear all, Thank you very, very much for your warm words. I am still impressed and I had to think about your thoughts before answering, but every answer seems to be so inadequate (specially in English).

I thank you, because you had the willingness to come to the country, which murdered your family. You have the greatness to look on your family history without hate, or bitterness, with sadness and with a look on the future, that such things should not happen any more. You call us – the children and grandchildren of the perpetrators – 'mishpacha'.

To search and to think about the Holocaust is not possible without tears and a deep sadness. My motive is not a bad conscience. I never felt guilty. Because to be guilty is something individual. Everyone has to do in his one life. And – it would mean to think like a Nazi – they called it "collective punishment" (kin liability – I don't know the right English word). If I did something wrong to you, please forgive me.

But I feel deeply ashamed about the barbarity, which happened in our country. Our fathers and grandfathers were the perpetrators and were responsible for those crimes against humanity. That makes a difference. You can visit the places, where it happened and it was in the name of Germany. As you said – we can not change the past. But we can shape future. What can we do, that such things never can happen again?

How was it possible that a majority of a cultured nation voted against their democratic rights, agreed to a dictatorship, agreed to separate a part of their population, agreed to violence and inhumanity? In these days of populists I can understand better how it works (to discriminate a group of people – Muslims, refugees..., to spread hate).

Many things are going worse at the moment. It splits our

society. On the one hand: to take one million people (Author's note: Syrian refugees) in a short time is only possible by volunteer work of citizens. That's really great. So many people are engaged. It's getting popular to call them "do-gooder" or "starry-eyed idealists". It is not meant in a friendly (way). On the other hand: many are in fear that refugees will be competitors for their jobs and their housing. Many think that they pay for the refugees without being asked. Yes, it costs. But no one of us would have one Euro more without refugees. Facebook and other media are full of hate and racism. I never thought to hear such things again. New is: these are not only some Neo Nazi idiots. It is a furious middle-class, feeling like underdogs, for fear for globalization and social decline, without any trust in the political system, which rescued the banks but not their pension. They are angry that they hear every day that our economy is booming, but they don't have the feeling that they are involved. Many problems we had before so many refugees were coming.

Now politicians began to speak, what they think, that their voters want to hear. Discrimination begins with words – you know ___ – and language is traitorous. They are 'intellectual arsonists'. After that, others think they have the right to set homes of refugees on fire or to attack people on the street. Sometimes it is really crazy. In Dresden 2 Israelis were attacked. Not because of being Jews, but of looking like Arabs. In my hometown someone wants to found a civil defense going their rounds to protect 'our' women against the bogy man on the streets. It's calming that only a few wanted to follow. After Cologne some are hysterical. They don't distinguish. Not all refugees are criminal – some are. It doesn't matter if they are Buddhists, or Muslims, or Christians, Germans or Arabs or what else. All are equal before the law. If they overstep limits, they have to take the consequences. But they are individuals.

They complain that 70% of the refugees are men. Many are married and have children. Now they want to prohibit that their families will come, too. On the other hand: they should learn German fast, they should work, they should build a new life. Without their families? How does that work? I don't want to keep secret, that there are problems. Most of them are coming from a cultural milieu where authoritarian family structures, no equal rights of women and anti-semitism are usual. They will change our country. They have to accept rules – and many are willing to do so. It is no reason to denounce them all. Many refugees – I know only some from the German lessons – are really willing to assimilate. They want to learn – and not only the language. They need our willingness, too. Integration is a both sided process. To respect each other is a basic requirement.

It is not long ago that many Germans were refugees. The German (and European) right of asylum is a lesson from history. It is an achievement. The law knows no limit, but there is a limit our society can carry. Now we want and we need the solidarity of Europe. For many years it was the problem of Italy and Greece on the external border of Europe without our solidarity. What goes around, comes around. The eastern-european countries signed common European values, they profit from the European-Union, but they don't want to help to solve a common European problem. The refugees will come – with or without a border or wall. What is an alternative? To shoot on unarmed people? To scuttle rubber dinghies?

Here extreme-right-wing parties have 10% or 12% at the moment. But it is growing. The mood shifts. Sorry for talking so much about the refugees, but that is our job at the moment. What we can learn from Auschwitz is to oppose discrimination and violence and to protect those who are fleeing from persecution, war and terror. I really think that those values are in danger – not only in Europe.

I think that shame is not only negative. I wish many people would be ashamed for the hate against others they spread. Sometimes we should be ashamed. You are right; peace has to begin in our heart, in our family, so it can go in the world. It is wonderful that we – on different sides of the world – work together. I am sure – there are more.

With Hugs and Love, Ira

Ira really made me think, and process her thoughts. She's right – "shame is not only negative". It's the outward expression of our conscience, our moral compass. It's what stops many of us from inappropriate, illegal, and/or unethical behaviors. Some people confuse "shame" and "guilt" as the same thing, when in fact they are similar but not the same. I remember learning decades ago in grad school that guilt is a feeling triggered by an action that one takes, or inaction that someone chooses. For example, I might feel guilty if I ate a bowl of ice cream, knowing that it would elevate my blood sugar and add pounds. This is an example of an action I took that may've triggered guilty feelings. I would feel guilty if I was walking down the street and saw someone having a seizure, but didn't go over to help him (I'm a Nurse, so I know what to do.) or call 911 to get him help. That's an example of guilt stemming from my inaction. However, my inaction in this case would additionally cause me to feel shame, ashamed of myself/ me for "who I am as a person" because I did nothing to help that person having a seizure.

Did any of the Nazis feel shame about themselves for what they did, and/or for bearing witness to other Nazis' inhumane actions without trying to stop them? Did any of the Nazis feel guilt about their actions, or inactions – standing by and watching others treat human beings heinously without attempting to stop it? Were they capable of feeling shame and/or guilt? They were "regular" people before Hitler came into power. What does this demonstrate to us about what "human beings" are capable of doing? What did 911 demonstrate? What do all the mass shootings and terrorist attacks show us? What has George Floyd's murder shown us? What did 1/6/21 at our US Capitol teach us?

And what do natural disasters demonstrate to us about what human beings are capable of doing? Time and again, post-disaster, Americans gratefully see people pitching in to help their neighbors from all over the country, whether it be by donating money, clothes, food, or helping to clear debris and rebuild.

So clearly, history has shown us the good, the bad, and the ugly about what human beings are capable of doing – both for ourselves and for each other. So I agree with Ira, and Nigel Dunkley's previous students (chapter 3), that there is not reason for Germans today to feel "guilt" about what their countrymen did during the Nazi regime, for they themselves neither perpetrated nor ignored it. And I now better understand the feelings of "shame" that Ira spoke of – not about shame of herself, but shame stemming from her countrymen's barbarity and inhumanities. For I feel shame stemming from my countrymen's barbarity and inhumanities, not just from the past but ongoing in this 2021 year.

So what do "we" do with this shame? If left untended, it will grow, fester, and make us sick. If instead, positive actions are taken in response, just like I described above post-disasters, it fosters good will and helps both the givers and the receivers. As well, I can now better understand our German Mischpacha's feelings of "responsibility" and "duty" to do something in response to their countrymen's reign of atrocities, because I, too, share those same feelings of responsibility and duty to do something in response to my countrymen's shameful behaviors.

Together, sharing shameful histories, both we American Mishpacha and our German Mishpacha are taking positive actions to help prevent the hatred and intolerance that have contributed to our countries' caste systems, slavery, lynchings, and genocide. We each work collaboratively – even across the ocean – to build a kinder gentler world for all of us to share, in Peace and acceptance.

From: Gail
To: international@stolpersteine.eu
Subject: Minsk – Stern Family
Date: Thu, Feb 18, 2016

Dear Mrs. ___, I saw recently that Mr. Demnig will be laying stones in Minsk on April 15 and 16. I met Mr. Demnig in 2014 when my dear friends, Rolf and Christina, Ira, Oliver and others from the Stolpersteine Initiative in Meinerzhagen coordinated the laying of stones for my Dad and many others from our family in Meinerzhagen, Hohenlimburg and Meckenheim. I returned to Germany last year to visit my friends and to learn more about my family.

With their help, I sadly learned that my grandparents and aunt, together with another 1,000 Jews, were transported on July 20, 1942, from Cologne to Minsk, where they were immediately marched into the forest and murdered. I saw on your website that Mr. Demnig will do 'group' Stolpersteine, or stumbling thresholds, for large groups of people that were murdered in one place, and was wondering if it is possible, since he will be in Minsk in a couple of months, if Mr. Demnig could do one in Minsk for all of the people taken from Cologne to Minsk and killed? I know it is very last minute, but it would mean so much to us.

My family and I, of course, would be willing to pay all of the costs for the stone, and make a donation, if this could possibly be arranged. If it could, I would go to Minsk for the installation.

Many, many thanks for your consideration, and for the wonderful work that your group does. Gail (Author's note: This unfortunately did not come to fulfillment. However, a memorial to Holocaust victims in Minsk is being planned.)

In February 2016, our friends sent us an article in the local newspaper about the Hohenlimburg Alte (old) Synagogue, and translated it for us into English:

A Memorial site for almost 30 years

Private initiative in charge of the synagogue in Hohenlimburg / The history of the Jewish community goes back to the 14th century.
...
In 1984, the city Hagen bought the building, which was in a bad condition, and had it completely renovated. On September 15, 1986, the Old Synagogue was inaugurated as a memorial site in order to commemorate centuries of Jewish history in Hohenlimburg.

During the pogroms on November 9, 1938 (the so-called Kristallnacht), a Nazi mob passed through Hohenlimburg and damaged houses and shops of Jewish owners as well as the synagogue in Jahnstrasse.

Members of the NSDAP and Nazi sympathizers tore off the David's star from the roof of the synagogue and destroyed the roof, windows, doors and the interior. The Jewish community was forced to sell the building, whose walls had remained intact, to an entrepreneur from Hohenlimburg. He transformed the building into a factory. When, in late 1975, a fire broke out in the building used as a warehouse for furs and the roof structure was hit as well, the building was threatened again in its very existence. In

1980, however, citizens from Hohenlimburg founded the initiative Hohenlimburg Synagogue, which was fighting for the preservation of the former synagogue and its renovation. With the expulsion and assassination of a part of the 70 Jews, who had still been living in Hohenlimburg in 1931, almost 600 years of Jewish-Christian coexistence came to an end.

A remarkable document gives us an account of the beginnings of Jewish life in Hohenlimburg. A charter issued by the Count of Limburg in 1350 granted Jews the right to collect outstanding money and to go to court in that matter, the safe passage for them and their messengers to and from Dortmund as well as protection: Cheating and fraud against these (Jews) are to be forbidden, and they are to be safe from any violence.

Since about 1650, the settlement of Jewish families in the County of Limburg became permanent. The Counts of Bentheim-Tecklenburg encouraged the settlement of Jewish families in their territory not because of humanitarian or religious, but economic reasons. This tolerant settlement policy had the effect that the proportion of the Jewish population among the total population was much higher than in neighbouring Hagen, Iserlohn or Altena.

In 1782, the Jewish community was allowed to build the first synagogue in then Eggestrasse (present-day Jahnstrasse). When this building was no longer sufficient in the 1860s, the Jewish community had a new synagogue built between 1868 and 1870. A third of the donations for the construction of the synagogues are said to have been provided by Christian inhabitants of Hohenlimburg. Next to the synagogue, there was a Jewish elementary school, which was closed in the 1920s, however, because there were not enough Jewish children left.

Due to the diaspora context, the members of the Jewish community had to overcome their differences. The synagogue district of Hohenlimburg, which comprised Berchum, Letmathe and Oestrich as well, was a so-called 'Unitarian' community with Liberal and Orthodox tendencies alike. In the Hohenlimburg synagogue, they celebrated the traditional service together and in Hebrew. ...

Von: Sheri
Gesendet: Dienstag, 22. Marz 2016 (Tuesday, March 22, 2016)
To: all
Betreff: Grieving… again

ENOUGH – ENOUGH – ENOUGH! I know we are sharing grief for today's tragedies in Belgium, and standing in Solidarity to create a safe world for each other and our children/grandchildren/ and future generations. Same recurrent tragedies, different city/ country, more cherished loved ones murdered senselessly, more grieving… again.

Thinking of you and your families, keeping you in our Prayers, holding you in our Hearts. Be safe. … Love, Sheri

From: Sheri
To: all
Sent: Sun, Jul 17, 2016 10:58 pm
Subject: Elie Wiesel quote (original source unknown)

We lost a great soul yesterday, Elie Wiesel, Holocaust survivor, writer, humanitarian, and Nobel Peace Prize winner. We can honor his memory, his bravery and his love of humanity with our deeds. As he once said: 'There may be times when we are powerless to prevent injustice, but there must never be a time when we fail to protest.'

Sheri

En date de : Mer 8.3.17, Sheri Stern a écrit :
Objet: My message
À: all

Dear all – I wrote this in response to someone's posting that she used to believe that 'Germans were evil', but now she 'knows there is evil everywhere'. I clearly needed to educate her and others viewing her comments: "I can tell you from personal experience, ___ and everyone, that it was NOT 'the Germans' who were evil – but 'the Nazis'. I didn't even realize that I, too, believed it was 'the Germans', until I learned from the examples of my dear German friends in Germany and my trip there, through the members of the Stolpersteine Initiative (google it), all NON-Jews, who volunteer for their Mission of placing 'Stolpersteine', 'stumbling blocks', brass plates bearing the names/dates/etc of those who died/committed suicide/or were able to escape from the Holocaust – placed in the sidewalks in Germany, Austria, Poland, etc at the last known residences of those individuals and families before they were deported – to memorialize the significance of their lives. I know it was 'the Nazis' who did evil and were evil, not 'the Germans', because I witnessed our German friends (We call them 'Mishpacha', Yiddish for 'family'.) lovingly placing those Stolpersteine for my father-in-law's entire family in 8/2014 in his small German town (He got out via Kindertransport at 15 yrs old, emigrating to the USA 2 months before Kristallnacht – and the rest is history; his family never got out.) This was and is a life-altering experience for me and my Family.

I am sorry for your losses, __, and everyone's losses. PLEASE – let us learn to stick together and speak out together for ALL of us. This affects ALL of us, and we are ALL members of the ONE SAME Family – HUMANITY! Sheri"

In 2017, I created and facilitated a workshop entitled "Getting Unstuck". Included was my brief summary of our experiences with our German Mishpacha and the Stolpersteine, so I'd asked our Mishpacha to please share their perspectives about our journeys together. Here is Ira's response, 7/13/2017.

Experiences: Being a German historian I am doing research on German history for many years. Albeit I know what crimes Germans committed in the past – to Jews, but also to others, the extent of brutality and inhumanity for me is still unbelievable. Together with a Jewish friend of mine (Author's note: Gail) I visited Minsk, Belarus, the forest of Blagowtschina, where her grandparents and her (in 1942) 15-year old aunt were murdered by the SS. Belarus, where 25% of the population were killed for racial and political fanaticism.

I don't feel guilty personally, because I think that I am not guilty for something my father did or did not (I don't know exactly) long before I was born. I think that guilt is something individual. Collective punishment was what Nazis did. They called it kin liability.

But anyway we are Germans and as Germans we stay responsible for what our ancestors did and how we deal with this horrible history today. First we have to accept the facts. We can not change history, but we are obliged to face it. This heritage is our common heritage and it must never be forgotten. We have to endure it. The wounds still remain and hurt. But we can do steps to heal one another.

I think that the remembrance of the victims and the survivors is meaningful in itself. Doing research on their lives and telling what happened to them may give them back a part of their dignity, that was stolen from them in such a horrible way. We could experience how important it is for the descendants of the victims to know what happened to their families – as sad and tragic their fate was. They intend to know every sad detail and have a deep right getting to know it at least.

To meet survivors was and is very important for me, too. It touched my heart and my soul that the descendants of Holocaust victims were and are willing to visit a country, which expelled or murdered their fathers and mothers, their grandparents, their aunts and uncles. That they are willing to speak, eat, drink, sing, laugh and shed bitter tears with us, the sons and daughters of the perpetrators. We could and can talk about our lives, our problems, our dreams and even have fun together. It is a miracle that deep friendships could and can grow albeit both sides are carrying terrible heritages.

There is one more important point. Germany was a cultured nation before the Nazis took over. A permanent view at our history is essential. It is necessary to learn and to understand which conditions and circumstances made 'normal' people becoming mass murderers. It is necessary for a better future.

It is terrifying to see how fast a democratic system could entirely collapse and how fast hate and violence could overcome a society supposed to be civilized. We all have to take care of our current societies. It is our responsibility to fight for democracy and human rights, in order to give hate and racism no chance at all but love, peace and understanding.

On Nov 10, 2017, at 8:03 AM, Christina (Dietmar) wrote:

... Dear Sheri and Jeff, Dear Gail, Dear ____,

... I just wanted to tell you that we had something special prepared for last night.

Some weeks ago the Stolperstein-Initiative went to Cologne to visit an exhibition on the occasion of Gunter Demnig's 70th birthday about the history of the Stolpersteine called 'The project Stolpersteine – a work of art turned into a citizens movement'.

It has been 25 years now since his first laying and more than 61000 stones have been laid in 21 European countries. Apart from historical dates, facts and figures, publications in the press and scientific research on the project there were also many examples of how citizens put effort in making the idea more public in Germany by offering flyers and self-guided tours to the places where stumbling stones have been laid in their city.

One display case in this exhibition even showed the equipment for keeping the stones clean and shining while in another I caught sight of a poster called 'Der Grindel leuchtet'. It showed some Stolpersteine being illuminated on occasion of the 75th return of the 'Reichspogromnacht' in 2013 in a part of Hamburg. Since then every year residents of this quarter illuminate the Stolpersteine in their street to remember the vanished neighbours of the past. The Motto is 'No stone is being left alone tonight'. About 5000 Stolpersteine have been laid in Hamburg so far, more than 2000 of them in the Grindel. I also learned – when contacting the fotografer mentioned on the poster – that in 1925 about 20000 Jewish people lived in Hamburg, most of them in the quarter 'Grindel' called 'Little Jerusalem' at that time and having a lively Jewish community with two synagogues. Since 2003 life has come back to the Jewish community in Hamburg by the new Rabbi ____ who opened the ____ ... Meanwhile 156 children of different beliefs are attending it.

I was very touched by the foto and told the other Stolpersteiner about the idea to illuminate our Stolpersteine in Meinerzhagen, too, open for the public on the night of 9./10. November. We had already planned a public meeting for that night with Ira telling us about her travelling to Minsk with Gail (Spurensuche in Minsk) and ___ showing fotos (collection on DVD) of the layings on July 7th in Meinerzhagen and Kierspe. We would like to send you this DVD, too. To do so we are in need of your postal adresses (alternatively Diemar could put the pictures in a dropbox).

Unfortunately Dietmar and me were not able to attend yesterday for reasons of health. Nevertheless we wanted to let you know about it today. I think there will also be a report in our local newspaper which helped us announce the illumination and meeting. I took the foto on the attached poster at the Buchhandlung Schmitz, so Sheri can find her grandmother's stone in the above middle. We also chose the motto 'Kein Stein bleibt diese Nacht allein' (No stone is being left alone tonight) and kept the candles burning till this morning.

Hoping you all are fine and sending you a warm hug, Christina and Dietmar.

From: Christina (Dietmar)
To: all
Sent: Sat, Nov 11, 2017 6:40 am
Subject: No Stone is being left alone tonight

Dear All, ... Attached you will find today's newspaper article in the Meinerzhagener Zeitung. ... about fifty people took part in the walk. Many of them brought candles with them (which we collected on Friday morning and will keep maybe for next year).

You can see Rolf and Christina on the upper photo as fourth and fifth from left. They had illuminated the Stolpersteine in Kierspe beforehand.

___ gave a very touching speech partly quoted in the article and said that candles are often used to remind of the dead and also to remind of victims of accidents or brutal crime – as applying here. On the Reichspogromnacht it had been revealed/ became strikingly obvious to everyone that murder in the name of antisemitism and racism became appropriate official means of the German government. He ended by pointing out that that night had been the official start of the biggest genocide in human history... After the walk most of the people listened to Ira's lecture about Gail's and her travelling to Minsk and looked at the photos of both layings back in July.

Sending warm regards and wishing a relaxing weekend to each of you, Christina

From: Dietmar
To: all
Sent: Sun, Nov 19, 2017 9:49 am
Subject: Just a note

Hi all,... Today, we commemorated the people who died in the wars, and the victims of the terror regime of the Nazis in Germany („Volkstrauertag"). In a separate email, I send you a few pictures that Christina took of the wreath ceremony at the memorial for the deported and murdered Jewish citizens of Meinerzhagen at Kirchstraße. There the Protestant minister who gave the commemorative address explicitly mentioned the Stolpersteine, too. He also said how touching he found the lights and candles reminding of „Kristallnacht" making true that „no Stone was being left alone" that night. The Initiative Stolpersteine at the end of the ceremonies also visited the Jewish Cemetery.

Warm regards from Meinerzhagen, and „Shalom" from Christina and Dietmar.

In the Spring of 2018, it had been four years since I'd seen our Mishpacha, though Gail had returned almost annually to visit and learn more about our family – always sharing news of everyone and details of her trip when she returned. Jeffrey and I were planning a trip to Italy with friends, and since we'd be so close to Germany – I'd suggested that we also return to visit our Mishpacha, and then I'd also be able to travel further north to visit my Skype-pal Beate!

Of course, our Mishpacha welcomed us with open arms. I'd shared with them that although I'm always interested in learning more about our family's history, I personally wanted this trip to be less about the Holocaust and more about having fun hanging out with our Mishpacha seeing the tourist sites that they'd normally take other friends and family to see (If they could hopefully arrange their work schedules.). This was a conscious effort on my part not to continue to define Germany solely by its

Holocaust history, but also for its beautiful architecture, culture and customs, good food, wine and beers, and its people. As you can see below, they listened – and created a custom-designed itinerary to accommodate Gail's, Jeffrey's, and my interests. As it turned out, our trip to Italy was cut short halfway through because we needed to return to the states with our friends. As a result, Jeffrey remained back in the US and did not return to Germany with me this time. So Gail and I were the only Mishpacha returning to visit our German Mishpacha for this trip.

From: Dietmar
Subject: Schedule for your visit
Date: April 19, 2018

(By this time in 2018, he and "his" wife Christina were now the new Leaders of the Meinerzhagen Stolpersteine Initiative chapter, as the initial leaders (Rolf and Herbert) had passed the torch on to younger members. Dietmar and "his" Christina, as I called her – because Rolf's wife is also a Christina, were the singers at the Meinerzhagen Stolpersteine Initiative's dinner on 8/28/2014 – the evening before our families' Stolpersteine Ceremonies on 8/29/14, during our initial Journey to Germany. They also sang and provided touching musical accompaniment to each of the 3 Stolpersteine Ceremonies on 8/29/14. We did not get to know them during our initial trip in 2014.)

Dear Gail, Sheri and Jeff:

Here, finally, are our plans for your visit. Let us know if that's all right. It's all about having time together while seeing places of interest. Meanwhile, we hope that Sheri and Jeff are enjoying their time in Italy. We are so much looking forward to having you here soon! Best regards from all the others, too ...Dietmar

Schedule for your visit April 28 – May 2, 2018

Sat, April 28
Driving from Frankfurt International Airport to town with your rental car meeting at Ira's home approx.. 10/10:30 a.m. (address: Ira will send written directions.)

Enjoying a short walk around town and/or visit in the city of Siegen, with Ira and family, Dietmar and Christina, stopping for lunch at some nice little restaurant... closing with tea or coffee at Ira's home.

Later in the afternoon: driving to Meinerzhagen, check-in at Hotel Wirth. Coming together with Rolf and Christina, Oliver and maybe others in a nice beergarden having a beer, or wine if you prefer, for the evening.

Sun, April 29
9:30 a.m. Leaving for Meckenheim with Rolf and Christina, Ira, ... Dietmar and Christina, and maybe others. Visiting Meckenheim (Author's note: And as I'd requested, walking to the train station there from where our family was temporarily living in Meckenheim, following in Dad's footsteps with his parents when they said their goodbyes to send him to America and safety. Gail had already done this "walk" on a prior trip with them.), and after lunch, Bad Godesberg (Burgfriedhof cemetery, Stolpersteine) on the trails of your family. Opportunity of closing the day in Rheinhotel Dreesen on the riverbank. Driving back to Meinerzhagen.

Mon, April 30
9:30 a.m. Leaving for Hohenlimburg with Rolf and Christina, Ira, ... Dietmar and Christina, and maybe others
10:30 a.m. Meeting at the Synagogue. Talk with students from a local high school still in the Synagogue
11-12 a.m. – Meeting at the town hall. Having lunch, then driving back to Meinerzhagen.
4 or 5 p.m. "Stolpersteine tour" in Meinerzhagen
6 p.m. Meeting with the Initiative Stolpersteine at Gemeindehaus (Protestant Community Center, near the church) in Meinerzhagen, having a nice evening with buffet and talk (Local press and/or a local TV team will be present for part of that.)

Tue, May 1 (Labor Day in Germany)
10:15 a.m. Leaving for the River Rhine with (probably quite a

few) members of the Initiative. Visiting the medieval Marksburg Castle overlooking the River Rhine (guided English tour); quick lunch; River cruise on the Rhine from about 3 till 6 p.m., passing the famous Loreley and deboarding at the beautiful winery village of Bacharach before heading back.

Driving back to Meinerzhagen.

Wed, May 2

(The morning being still open); at about 2 p.m., visiting a small local museum in Siegen presenting, among other things, the history of the Nazi years in Siegen (with Ira, on your way to Frankfurt Airport)

During our April/May 2018 return trip to Germany, there were many more wonderful experiences, including Ira's generous offer for us to stay with her and her family while visiting. I enjoyed staying with her, meeting her family and getting to know her husband and sons, sharing American colloquialisms with her husband who collects them, and being thoroughly spoiled by Ira who got up early each day to go to the neighborhood bakery before I came downstairs ... so that I could have fresh baked German breads and treats at her breakfast table! Four additional special experiences stand out in my mind.

During one of Gail's previous trips, she'd noticed that the inscriptions on the Weil's parents' tombstone had eroded and were no longer readable. So she arranged through Rolf and Christina for that to be fixed by a local community member. Rolf and Christina, Ira, and now Dietmar and "his" Christina joined us in a drive to the cemetery to see the newly re-engraved stone. We thought we were going "simply" to see it and pay our respects. However, when we arrived, Rolf's Christina motioned us all to the trunk of her car and asked us to help carry the contents to the gravesite. We carried ground-covering perennial plants, shovels, fertilizer, soil, and gardening gloves to the gravesite. Our Mishpacha had not only seen to the "fixing" of the actual tombstone engravings, they'd also decided that the surrounding overgrown area needed to be beautified. So together, these five German mensches along with Gail and I went to work making our family's great-grandparents' gravesite dignified and beautiful. Our German mensches had the foresight and compassion to do this for our ancestors, for us. We have pictures and videos of us working together towards a common goal in this cemetery plot, working together to continue to heal each other and create an oasis of Peace in the world we inhabit.

Another memory was our cruising on the Rhine River with Ira, Rolf and Christina, and Dietmar and "his" Christina. They took us to visit a medieval castle followed by a day-cruise, so we could see for ourselves Germany's rich history and beauty! And they gave us their scarves and hats, because it was quite cold and windy that day. And together, we continued to forge our friendships – with fun and light hearts, not only tragedy.

An emotional experience was walking alongside Gail in Dad and his parents' footsteps, from their forced-residence

Fresh ground plantings to beautify great-grandparents' Sophie and Berthold Weil's re-engraved tombstones (Auguste and other siblings' parents; Jeffrey and Gail's great-grandparents). They both died before WWII and the Holocaust, and therefore were able to be buried privately.

in Meckenheim to the train station there – where Dad and his parents said goodbye to each other ... forever, never to see each other again. As a human being, and especially as a mother – I could not then nor now fathom the pain of their making that difficult decision, taking that walk, knowing what they'd already lost by that point in time because of Hitler and the Nazis, fearing what the future held and what more might happen. Perhaps his parents (and sister) truly believed they would be able to join Dad in America. Perhaps his parents knew deep in their heart from what they'd already been forced to experience that that was unlikely to happen. Since there wasn't enough money to sponsor all of them, his parents were forced to "choose" which one of their children to save! How Dad and his parents and sister must have clung to each other, not knowing what the future would hold, memorizing and drinking in each other's faces, each other's touch, the color of each other's eyes, their smiles, their love for each other. I think of them, our own children and grandchildren, and the pain of their situation is unbearable.

There was an especially touching moment when we visited the Meckenheim Stolpersteine for our family. These were the stones that were laid in October 2014, after we'd already returned home from Germany the previous month. We had only been able to see these stones laid out on the carpet of the Meckenheim official's office during our August 2014 journey. Now they were installed, and there was one Stolperstein for Dad (this now his second), Margot, Julius and Auguste, and Aunt Jenny, as well as Max, Selma, and Susanne with whom they'd lived briefly before all (except Dad, who had escaped to the US by then) were sent to the Convent in Bonn-Endenich to await their deportation. So again, Dad was "together" with both his nuclear family and some different relatives of his extended family – now in two different towns where they'd lived: Hohenlimburg (their last freely-chosen home) and Meckenheim. You may recall from Chapter 2 that this placement is not the usual location according to Stolpersteine protocol of placement at victims' last freely-chosen residence. That said, you can imagine that we are forever grateful that these stones have been placed here as well. We had nothing to do with this particular placement; it was completely the decision of the Stolpersteine Initiative. Now we were seeing the stones already laid in the pavement, outside the last place that Dad had briefly lived together with his family. It was from here, Meckenheim, that he'd walked to the train station with his parents (and possibly his sister) on September 7, 1938, to begin his journey to America, to escape the horrors of the Shoah, believing that his parents and younger sister would soon follow and join him in America.

As is their usual routine, members of the Stolpersteine Initiative have several ceremonies throughout each year at historical moments (i.e., Kristallnacht) in which they remember and honor the memories of the victims of the Shoah ("No stone shall be left alone tonight."), light a candle, and shine the brass Stolpersteine plaques that are "planted" in the ground. This time, Dietmar was down on his knees shining our family's Stolpersteine, while we were watching. This time, I felt like I should help, lend a hand,

Meckenheim Train Station: Dad's parents, and possibly his sister Margot, walked him to this train station on September 7, 1938 to escape to America via a Kindertransport arranged by HIAS. It was the last time they saw each other. L-R: back row: Rolf, Ira, Christina (Rolf's wife), and Dietmar. L-R: front row: Gail, Sheri.

and thus signify our working together to "Never forget". When I asked Dietmar if I could help him, he paused before politely responding, looked up at me intensely and said, "You may ...but it is our duty." I was speechless. I silently nodded my understanding, stepped back, and continued to watch him perform his duty, his responsibility – not wanting to interfere with his personal process of shining our family's Stolpersteine, and perhaps – his own ongoing healing.

From: Christina (Dietmar)
Date: April 27, 2018 at 1:32:34 AM EDT
To: we 3
Subject: Have a Save Trip! / Fotos?/ Kippa-Day

Dear Sheri and Gail,
We are very much looking forward to your visit and hope you will have a safe trip and a soft landing ✈ ...
... For I am not sure it was broadcasted in the USA I've also wanted to tell you about the KIPPA DAY in Berlin and many other German Cities on Wednesday this week, (sharing) a post for solidarity, tolerance and peace and against antisemitism.

https://www.thetimes.co.uk/article/germans-unite-on-kippa-day-to-fight-antisemitism-bnmctzx9t

https://www.haaretz.com/world-news/europe/berlin-jews-organize-wear-a-kippah-demonstration-in-response-1.6026552

Last but not least : We are so very much looking forward to you and are sure that we will spend some unforgettable days together again. Please give Jeff a warm hug, too. We all hope to have him here again some time not too far from now.
Christina

From: Christina (Dietmar)
Date: September 22, 2018 at 6:13:39 PM EDT
To: Sheri Stern USA
Subject: Jüdische Allgemeine II

Translation of the short extract of the article on the front page: Jüdische Allgemeine "ANGST SOLLTE NICHT DAS BEHERRSCHENDE GEFÜHL SEIN – 'Fear shouldn't be the dominant feeling'.

Memorials for the victims of the Nazi concentration camps and Jewish Museums have been reporting rising numbers of visitors since years. Thousands of non-Jewish citizens put on a kippa to show solidarity. After a smashed window in a synagogue in Gelsenkirchen the parish received many letters of solidarity. More than 60,000 people visited the spontaneous 'concert against right' (in Chemnitz a week ago)."

(From Christina): Such examples could be continued. They often don't make headlines but only when you take them into account you get a complete picture of the situation. ...

To: Beate (my Skype-pal friend in northern Germany, whom I met online. She called me her "Sister of my Heart" and I echoed the same to her.)
From: Sheri
Subject: interpretation of Rolf's letter
Date: 2/25/2019

I found your attachment/interpretation of Rolf's letter. Thank you so much.

It's very endearing to "see" how Rolf began to advocate for our family so early on in January of '14. Within "weeks" of "finding" us in America, he knew how important it was to us that our family be "all together" in the last place they lived and laughed and loved together in Hohenlimburg – before Hitler came into power. Rolf's was not an easy path to advocacy, but he chose it anyway, repeatedly, for people he didn't even know, as the decision-makers were not always cooperative – especially since there were already Stolpersteine existing at other locations for

Julius/Auguste/and Margot. In the end, he persevered, and gave us a bittersweet Gift we will never forget.

Those Stolpersteine in Hohenlimburg represent 1 commemoration/memorialization of the 4 of them together, the very first one installed for Dad as well as together with his family. As well, shortly after our trip, Dad and his family had another set of Stolpersteine installed in Meckenheim 10/2014, where he lived shortly with his immediate and some extended family before he escaped to the USA on 9/7/1938. Thank you for giving me that Gift with your interpretation, Beate, from your Heart. Priceless . . .

In all the years between 2014 and the present, emails still continue to flow back and forth. We've met Oliver twice in the US, when he came for international conferences where he was featured as a speaker. One time was in Washington, DC, and we were thrilled to have him be a guest in our homes during his brief visit. During this trip, we traveled with him to show him the US Holocaust Museum in DC, and Gail had arranged for a private docent tour and conversation afterwards. As well, Jeffrey had recently attended a wonderful local program featuring an author who'd written a book about the Holocaust. The author was selling her book, Jeffrey purchased it for Oliver, and requested the author please sign it personally for Oliver – which she did. The other time, we drove to Philadelphia to meet him for dinner, as he only had a short time in-between his conference responsibilities.

It was during one of Oliver's trips to the US that we presented him with a Gift – and we also mailed that same Gift to Ira, Rolf and Christina. We framed a copy of "The Starfish Story", I handwrote a brief note at the bottom of it stating what a difference our Significant 4 have made in our lives, and Jeffrey, Gail, and I each signed it. Each of them have told us that it's prominently displayed in their homes.

Since returning from our initial 2014 journey, some of us:

~ have lost loved ones,
~ have gained new grandchildren,
~ have gone through chemotherapy,

~ have given birth (Well, actually his wife did!)
~ have been hospitalized, and/or
~ have had surgeries.

In March 2021, since we had to do a second Zoom Passover Seder due to ongoing COVID-19 restrictions – we invited our Mishpacha from Germany. We were thrilled that Ira and one of her sons were able to join us, drink the traditional four cups of wine with us, and read passages from the Haggadah along with us (Prayer book for Passover that shares the Biblical story of the enslaved Israelites gaining their freedom from slavery and their exodus from Egypt and Pharaoh's cruel reign).

During these past seven years since our initial journey to Germany, we've all unfortunately experienced international terrorism, repeatedly, and we here in the US have experienced multiple episodes of domestic terrorism as well, repeatedly. On 6/14/21, I received an email update from ADL reporting this:

"Two new ADL reports shine a spotlight on the soaring levels of antisemitic incidents, including violent attacks in our streets, and their damaging impact on the American Jewish community. Alarm in the Jewish community is soaring along with a 115% rise in antisemitic incidents since the beginning of the conflict between Israel and Hamas, compared to the same dates last year." [2]

Our Significant 4 have experienced an influx of many Syrians that Germany has welcomed into their country as a safe haven due to the humanitarian crisis in Syria. One of our German Mishpacha told us that it's the first time since WWII and the Holocaust that she actually feels proud of Germany – for taking in immigrants, especially those fleeing from war and violence. Immediately after the Biden-Harris Administration was sworn in on January 20, 2021, we Americans continued to experience an influx of many individuals at our borders seeking asylum and safety from the violence and poverty in their countries of origin – especially unaccompanied children. A bright light was reported on the news on 5/3/21: 4 families seeking asylum here in the US in 2017 who were cruelly separated from each other, parents

2   ADL email report, 6/14/21

from children, by the prior US Administration's policies, will be reunited tomorrow per our Biden-Harris Administration's policies and sleuth work in just the past few months! Both we Americans and those abroad have lived through the USA's prior Administration's policies of racism, bigotry, antagonism, blatant lies, no centralized government approach to the COVID pandemic, pulling out of major alliances like the Paris Climate Accord and NATO, and years of the absence of strong healthy national leadership.

In January 2020, I participated in a "Bridges Trip" Mission to our Arizona – Mexico Border with my Sisters from our Sisterhood of Salaam Shalom organization to learn and see for ourselves exactly what was going on at the border as well as what actions we could take to implement HIAS's Mission to "Welcome the Stranger. Protect the Refugee." This was another life-altering experience for me. As has been my lifelong ritual, I felt called to write about that experience and share it with others. Below is the piece I wrote about going to our Arizona-Mexico border, which I shared with friends and family, and with my fellow synagogue congregants one Shabbat morning in April 2020 – by zoom, of course, by that time.

Bearing Witness ... at our Arizona-Mexico Border

First they came for the socialists, and I did not speak out – because I was not a socialist.

Then they came for the trade unionists, and I did not speak out – because I was not a trade unionist.

Then they came for the Jews, and I did not speak out – because I was not a Jew.

Then they came for me – and there was no one left to speak for me.

Martin Niemöller (1892–1984) wrote those words after WWII, the Holocaust, and his imprisonment in a Nazi concentration camp. Tragically – they could still apply today.

G-d commands us in multiple texts how we should respond to "strangers":

Exodus: *You shall not oppress a stranger, for you know the feelings of the stranger, having yourselves been strangers in the land of Egypt.*

Deuteronomy: *You too must befriend the stranger, for you were strangers in the land of Egypt.*

I went on a Mission in January (2020) with fifty of my Sisters from our Sisterhood of Salaam Shalom (an international organization of Muslim and Jewish Women coming together in Peace to rise up and respond against hate and intolerance of any kind.). My objectives for this Shabbat program are the same as our Sisterhood's purpose for that Mission: (1) to see and tell others what is really happening at our Arizona-Mexico Border, and (2) to learn about AND take effective ACTIONS so we can be a part of the Solution, rather than remaining silent – for we ALL know from the Shoah what silence begets.

Day 1: Operation Streamline at the Tucson courthouse:

I witnessed 75 human beings, 5-point-shackled, from 18 – 60-something years of age, male and female, being factory-like-processed per the plea bargains they'd "agreed" to at their 30-minute-allotted meeting that morning with a court-appointed-lawyer (NOT an immigration lawyer!). For crossing the Mexico-Arizona border to seek a better life, to seek asylum – safety, NOT through a legal Port of Entry – because all of them have been closed by the current US Administration – each shackled human being received a US-prison sentence of 30-105 days, followed by immediate deportation either back to their own country or to another country entirely (Guatemala, Honduras, far from their families, and with the same poverty and safety risks existing there!). By the way – these are private prisons they're being sent to, which make a lot of money off of the detained refugees! Just so you know the facts, restrictions on immigration did not begin with this current administration, but rather with Presidents Bush, Clinton, and Obama. However, the current administration has increased restrictions for crossing the Border, and "criminalized" it.

The Judge repeated the same litany of 5-6 questions for each of these 75 people, the max for each weekday day (that means potentially 375 people weekly). These are the 75 people for whom I accepted the awesome responsibility to "Bear Witness": Jesus, Raciel, Raul, Junielis, Fabiana, Camerina, Segundo, Yordi, Cupertino, Eligio, Benjamin, Marcos, Hugo, Abraham, Jose, Francisco, Victor, Martin, Eduardo, Jose, Juan, Ignacio, Jose, Martin, Rogelio, Eduardo, Yoen, Marcos, Antonio, Abel, David, Minerva, Yolanda, Adolfo, Oscar, David, Delmar, Hilsias, Hector, Pascual, Jose, Yomar, Leonel, Feliciano, Eliazar, Baudel, Mauricio, Jose, Eber, Karen, Emerson, Angel, Santiago, Jose, Maria, Juan, Simplicio, Irma, Antonino, Roberto, Patricio, Obed, Marcos, Jose, Lester, Enrique, Celso, Francisco, Eduin, Martha, Juan, Deonicio, Maynor, Natividad, and Inocente: each one, somebody's brother, sister, child, mother or father, gramma or grampa.

I choose to mention each of their first names because each of them is a Human Being who matters – just as each of our family members who perished in the Shoah mattered; I choose to omit their last names, out of respect to preserve their dignity – though they'll never know I did so ...but I know!

I want to share 3 of those 75 people's words, that still ring in my ears:

With his shackled hands in prayer mode, one man looked at the Judge and said sincerely:

"1000 pardons for breaking your United States laws". It's important for everyone to know (per our training from HIAS) that "seeking asylum" is not illegal.

Whispering into his appointed-lawyer's ear, so the lawyer could speak it aloud to the Judge in English – this man's request was to receive his diabetes meds back, which had been confiscated by Border Patrol; he'd been without his meds for 10 days already. It's routine policy that Border Patrol Agents confiscate EVERYTHING these people have when they cross the border – their ID, their money, medications, papers ...and shoelaces – to prevent any self-harm while detained imprisoned; none of these are returned to them. So when they are deported, they have no ID, money, meds, papers ...or shoelaces. Besides those dehumanizing measures (sound familiar, i.e. the Shoah?), having no shoelaces makes these people "easy targets" for human traffickers and cartels once deported to a remote town or different country – because "no shoelaces" means "no connections". The US "Remain in Mexico" Policy actually delivers families into the hands of cartels and traffickers.

Also whispering into his lawyer's ear for translation, this third man had crossed the border several times; his message to the Judge was: "Judge, I just want you to know that the reason I keep coming back ... is to see my four children."

That was my breaking point. I wanted to stand up and scream with the tears running down my cheeks: "THIS IS WRONG; STOP IT NOW!" ... I'm ASHAMED that I didn't.

Since my return, I had lunch with a Maryland woman I volunteer with for something completely unrelated to the Border issues. Turns out, her future son-in-law is a 20-something Border Patrol Agent at our Texas-Mexico Border. She mentioned that he works on the "front lines" of the Border Crisis, often being assaulted, needing to restrain some individuals who cross that Border carrying knives, sticks, and/or illicit drugs. So to be fair and show all truths of which I am aware, not everyone who is crossing our Border is doing so with good intentions.

Day 2, Morning / Desert Walk:

The purpose of this Walk was twofold: (1) to Bear Witness to the treacherous, lengthy, courageous journey these refugees take (often in the dark of night, extending to daytime sun/heat!), and (2) to provide Humanitarian Aid for those who make that journey. As we carried jugs of water, and boxes of snacks to leave in designated places in the desert, we walked on uneven ground with steep inclines and drops, climbed over logs, rocks, and slippery pebbles for several miles; there were no markers showing us where to go – only our Guides. There are people who don't welcome anyone crossing our Border, and they slash the water jugs so all the water leaks onto the desert floor, and take the snacks. All of us were thoroughly sunscreened, with plenty of water, wearing wide-brimmed hats, sunglasses, and sturdy comfortable walking shoes, none of us fearing for our lives or worrying about the outcomes of the journey. None of the refugees come with any of those luxuries, but they do come fearing for their lives, their health, and the uncertainty of the outcomes. Some never complete the journey, including their children, because they die in the desert from the heat and dehydration.

As the water and snacks were left at the designated unmarked spot (By the way, some Americans have been imprisoned for providing humanitarian aid for refugees.), Muslim and Jewish Sisters prayed together for the people who cross the Border.

Day 2, Afternoon / (name), at The Wall:

The Wall itself is ugly, concrete, tall, full of barbed wire – much like the ones in the Nazis' concentration camps. It's literally down the middle of a street: think ___ Road in this town having a Wall dividing the Northbound and Southbound lanes. Just imagine that for a moment, and that you're not being allowed to cross.

___ lives in Mexico. He's crossed the Arizona-Mexico Border many times, and was always deported back. Here's what he wanted us to know, and to carry back to Americans: (1) All Mexicans do not deal drugs or kill people (just as all Americans do not); (2) Crime in Mexico does not occur as often as it's portrayed in the media; in fact, the media rarely – if at all – tell the "other side" about the Mexican people; (3) Mexican people are hard workers who like to earn their money – just like Americans; and (4) Mexican people also have dreams – for the same things Americans want: freedom, safety, security, a stable roof over their heads, and the opportunity to work to provide for their families ...but they are not able to obtain that in Mexico. They want to come to America legally, but those options have all been cut off.

Day 3, HIAS Training:

(**H**ebrew **I**mmigrant **A**id **S**ociety, which was created after WWII as the Jewish Response to the Holocaust and the many Survivors displaced without a safe homeland.): This training was full of hard facts and statistics, as well as practical training on how to contact legislators, write op-eds, engage in dialogue, and stand up and speak out for refugees. Most asylum seekers now in the US are from Guatemala; you may recall I just mentioned that our government often deports refugees BACK THERE – REALLY?! The "Remain in Mexico" Policy forces Mexicans to remain in Mexico until the date for their immigration hearing.

Seeking asylum in the US IS LEGAL according to US and

International law. Similarly, any effort to deter or block individuals from seeking asylum is ILLEGAL according to US and International Law, per the Refugee Convention of 1951. Therefore, the current (2016-2020) US administration's orders surrounding asylum-seeking are UNLAWFUL, and our government has now CRIMINALIZED seeking asylum. We need to be the Moral Voices.

Day 4, last day – a Ray of Sunshine, at Casa Alitas Welcome Center in Tucson:

Casa Alitas is a program of the Catholic Community Services. There, "the lucky ones" are allowed to stay in the USA until they can go to live with their family somewhere in the USA while awaiting their asylum hearing (3-4 months for scheduling). Casa purchases bus tickets for them to travel to their families, provides food and water for them on their journey, and takes them to the bus station to interpret instructions and assure they get on the correct bus to their destination. They also offer legal assistance, food, clean water, laundering facilities, and safe shelter, a room for each family – that purposely has no locks on the doors, a clinic with volunteer physicians, and a sign posted on the door of the building stating: "It is strictly prohibited by law for any Border Patrol, ICE, or any policing agencies to enter this building at any time." We saw this same sign on a number of other buildings in Tucson.

We were each allowed to select an area to help in for the day. Just before we began, one of our Sisterhood members presented the staff member with lots of COSTCO gift cards that we'd brought with us; we'd all asked our family and friends to donate to purchase these. Staff use the cards for items for their Guests: toiletries, food, supplies, and prescriptions. Some of you in the (synagogue) community gave from your hearts when I asked for donations to purchase the COSTCO cards. I can assure you – you each performed a tremendous Mitzvah!

My job there was playing with the children – OHHH, that was the BEST! You know, human beings are human beings, and parents are parents no matter what religion, nationality, skin color, or language they speak. When we asked in Spanish for permission to play with their children, they each readily smiled, nodded their heads and said "Si" (yes), and gestured with their hands to "get to it, POR FAVOR / **PLEASE!**" The children quickly became engaged and forgot about their parents and their circumstances for a few hours, while we cavorted, made silly faces, built with Legos and blocks, and hugged them. Volunteering at Casa Alitas was an experience filled with hope and joy, a stark contrast to our first day at the courthouse filled with 75 sets of shackles, prison sentences, and deportations.

Finally, I'll talk about **ACTIONS** each of us can take in order to support refugees seeking asylum (as many of our Family members were refugees seeking asylum during and after the Shoah, and as you recall, many of them were denied entry into the USA, Palestine as it was called then, and other countries). There will be some handouts available after Shabbat, that (synagogue) staff can email you, listing resources and these effective actions each of us can take to protect and support refugees:

- VOTE in every election.
- Contact your legislators.
- DONATE money – a handout with organizations will be available after Shabbat via (the synagogue).
- Write op-eds to your local papers supporting refugees, sharing what you heard today from an eyewitness who was there, and sharing practical ACTIONS that people can take to help.
- Educate yourself about this topic. Many resources are available.
- Organize a fundraiser for a nonprofit of your choice: Casa Alitas, Borderlinks, and other organizations that fight for Social Justice everywhere – like HIAS.org, ACLU, Southern Poverty Law Center, ADL.
- Talk to your friends, family, and coworkers about what you've heard here today from someone who was there.

Add even one item to your virtual Seder this year about the plight of refugees all over the world: HIAS suggests that after we dip our finger in wine for the 10 plagues that G-d brought upon the Egyptians, we add these 10 plagues that exist for refugees and asylum seekers all over the world: Violence, Dangerous Journeys, Poverty, Food Insecurity, Lack of Access to Education, Xenophobia (fear of "the other"), Anti-Refugee Legislation, Language Barriers, Workforce Discrimination, and Loss of Family.

In conclusion, this Mission to our Arizona-Mexico Border was: intense, angering, devastating, sad, and embarrassing, but also: humbling, powerful, enlightening, educational, empowering ... and necessary. It was filled with Grace and Hope – and the Spirit of the Human Soul seeking Freedom, Safety, Opportunity, and Justice – just as our Ancestors did.

This is a message from the HIAS Haggadah this year (2020): *Jewish tradition teaches us that we are G-d's partners in the continual act of creating a more just world in which all human beings are treated with dignity and compassion. As we recall the strength that G-d extended to the Jewish people in the season of our escape from oppression, we extend our arms to embrace those in our world still experiencing persecution because of who they are. May next week's Seders inspire each of us to take action on behalf of today's refugees and asylum seekers, as we join and strengthen the Jewish response to the Global Refugee Crisis at this critical moment in history.* [3]

As Mark Hetfield, President and CEO of HIAS says: "We started HIAS to help Jews. We continue the work of HIAS... because we are Jews."

And of course – all of us here in the US along with all of our Mishpacha across the ocean in Germany and Paris continue to live through the COVID-19 pandemic and it's local and global impacts, thankfully improving in the Spring of 2021 because of effective preventive measures which now include vaccinations (Although some countries continue to struggle.)! Thankfully, despite some of us experiencing other serious health issues during these past seven years, none of us have contracted COVID-19. Thankfully, many of us in America, Germany, and Paris (and globally) are already partially or fully vaccinated at the time of this entry on 3/29/21, though there remains much work to do to get more vaccinations into arms locally and globally!

One thing in particular about COVID-19 that I continue to

---

3   www.hias.org, from their 2020 Haggadah

believe passionately is that it could become a unifying instrument instead of just one more derisive and dividing one – globally, but especially for Americans, some of whom have objections to necessary COVID-19 restrictions as well as vaccinations which are based on scientific evidence ("It's a hoax; I'm not wearing a mask; You're taking away my rights.").

"Derisive and dividing" had become well-known adjectives that described America and our prior 2016-2020 Administration's four years, not only related to COVID-19 – but also to just about any other major and even minor American concern.

As a human being and a Nurse Psychotherapist, I knew that grief and mourning had already touched so many Americans and their families due to COVID – whether through contracting and surviving the disease and/or through the loss of their loved ones to the disease. I knew that grief, mourning, and COVID-19 had no regard for whether you were a Democrat or a Republican or who you voted for in 2016 or in 2020. Grief, mourning, and COVID-19 are all "equal opportunity employers".

Therefore, I knew in my neshama that before or during the January 20, 2021 inauguration of our new American Administration, especially in light of the January 6th insurrection at our Capitol, we Americans needed a national mourning and healing ritual, led by our newly elected President and Vice-President. And so, shortly after the Presidential election in November 2020, I rolled up my sleeves, googled leaders of the Inaugural Committee, contacted them and my own Maryland Legislators, and shared my concise Vision and plan for such an event with the right people to hopefully make that happen. I do know that my letters and phone calls reached their destinations, although I do not know whether they made a difference and led to that event.

What we all know now is that on January 19, 2021, the evening before the Inauguration, a brief but powerful Memorial Service, socially distanced, outside, with masks, led by our incoming President Joe Biden and Vice-President Kamala Harris – did occur. It doesn't matter whether my input made a difference or not. What matters is that others recognized the need for such a critical "life passage" event that allowed Americans the opportunity to grieve together for all of our loved ones as well as prior freedoms, jobs, incomes, and feelings of "safety" that we'd all lost due to COVID, blue and red alike, no matter where you were born or your political views. Though our Nation thrives on differences of opinion and beliefs, I'd like to believe we did all come together towards the common goals of grieving and working towards healing – even if only briefly, and virtually at that – on that January 19th evening in Washington, D.C. at that National COVID-19 Memorial Service. I am grateful to those who created it and made it happen.

On June 1, 2021, President Biden spoke at the Centennial Commemoration of the Tulsa Massacre. Two of his passages in particular hold great significance for me, for they relate to our family's experiences, and to all people's experiences of hatred and intolerance. President Biden said, "With truth comes healing, justice, and repair. ... We can't just learn what we want to know. We must learn what we need to know."

Through it all, since 2014, we Jewish-Americans and these Christian-Germans have sent each other flowers, gifts, wine, condolences, compassion, prayers, Shalom / Frieden (Peace, in German), mazel tovs (Hebrew: literally means "good luck", but is commonly used by Jewish people on the occasion of important events and life passages, i.e. weddings, birth of a child, graduations), hugs, and love – like the Mishpacha we are for each other, helping each other weather the tough times, and celebrating each others' joys through the good times – together.

This portion is being added in June 2021 because of recent exciting news of which I just became aware. While there were 10 homes filled with loving Jewish Meinerzhagen families who became victims of the Holocaust, only 8 of these families had Stolpersteine laid in that town as of 2017. The endeavors of the Meinerzhagen Stolpersteine Initiative since 2011 had made it possible for 38 former Jewish citizens to be commemorated with Stolpersteine in front of those houses, laid in 2013, 2014, and 2017. The last two families' Stolpersteine have not been laid due to conflicting factors, despite the best efforts of the Initiative members in the years since. Gail and I also stood up and spoke out in support of these families' Stolpersteine being laid when we returned to Meinerzhagen in 2018, noting how much it means to us that our family's stones were laid in 2014; the local newspaper printed it. As well, the remaining living family member of these two related families wrote to relevant officials in 2015 requesting the laying of their Stolpersteine – to no avail. [4]

Fast forward to June 2021. As part of their "optional" High School Independent Study course entitled "Jewish Life in Meinerzhagen" (Each student chose to take this year-long course.), taught by Dietmar, 19 students learned of this and knew it was neither "right" nor "completed".

According to Dietmar, this course teaches about the roles Jews played in Meinerzhagen for more than 125 years since the first Jewish families settled there early in the 19th century, what happened to them during the Nazi regime that destroyed Jewish life in this town, and how Germans can learn from this history so that "Never again" will this happen to any human being.

Upon learning this, these 19 students decided to take action on what they perceived as wrong and unjust. They developed and sent a petition to the Meinerzhagen City Council requesting the *Stolpersteine Verlegung* for these remaining two families, 9 stones in total (English: Stolpersteine that are set/placed in the ground). [5]

These 19 passionate, compassionate, courageous students have finally achieved what seemed to be a dead end, after 10 years of continuing struggles by the Stolpersteine Initiative: The last two Meinerzhagen Jewish families will indeed have their Stolpersteine laid, planned for the fall of 2021 (depending on COVID status). This will finally complete the circle for all of Meinerzhagen's Jewish victims of the Shoah to be remembered and commemorated!

---

4   Per Dietmar's clarifications, June 2021
5   The students' Petition, dated March 23, 2021, here digitally filed for the Agenda of the City Council. This document can be downloaded from the homepage of the City of Meinerzhagen. https://meinerzhagen.ratsinfomanagement.net/sdnetrim/UGhVM0hpd2NXNFdFcExjZSr0Yr7gM5wXMmckiRBc3Y-AR-3PdEOBhgr1a_HK6kbr/Antrag_vom_23.03.2021.pdf

Because these 19 students believe this is their duty as the next generation, their responsibility to acknowledge and do what they can to "right" the "wrongs" of the past, to remember and commemorate the victims of the Shoah, to "Never forget" – they were able at this crucial point to urge the City Council members involved in the decision-making process to create a "consensus of Humanity". [6]

Mazel Tov (Congratulations in Hebrew) and Ich gratuliere, den Schülerinnen und Schülern! (Congratulations to the students in German)! [7]

Thank you for who you are and what you've accomplished, for the HOPE that you give us – knowing that the future is in your caring capable hands. You inspire us to stand up and speak out for what is right and just, to take action against ALL hatred and intolerance, and to work together to make our world a kinder gentler one.

Students' Petition, English Translation (by Dietmar)
[Students' addresses omitted due to data protection]
58540 Meinerzhagen

To the City Council of Meinerzhagen
58540 Meinerzhagen
Meinerzhagen, 3/23/2021

"Citizen Petition" in accordance with section 24 of the Municipal Regulations for North Rhine-Westphalia, for the Laying of Stolpersteine at Zum Alten Teich 2 and Hauptstrasse 32

Dear Mayor Jan Nesselrath,
Being aware of the [i.e. City Council's] decision of 2012 [i.e., that the contemporary owners have to agree that Stones be laid on the City's sidewalks in front of their houses = "the compromise"], we herewith apply for the laying of the remaining nine *Stolpersteine* for our former Jewish citizens in front of the

---

6 Dietmar's phrase, 6/2021
7 With Christina's translation (Dietmar's wife).

houses "Zum Alten Teich 2" and "Hauptstrasse 32."

In our Independent Study course "Jewish Life in Meinerzhagen" at the local High School *Evangelisches Gymnasium* we have dealt with the fate of the Jewish citizens of our town, and with the *Stolperstein Project* to commemorate them. It means a lot to us to also honor these remaining nine victims of Nazi terror and to give them a last remembrance.

So far, 38 *Stolpersteine* have been laid [i.e., in our town], and we cannot understand why the remaining nine Stones may not be laid. [By laying these Stones] we would pay tribute and the appropriate respect to them as well as to their families' descendants, which is long overdue. In particular, we are thinking here of Yvonne, the granddaughter of Nathan Stern.

We, as young people, feel it is our responsibility to commemorate **all** these people, and that those terrible times may never happen again.

Sincerely

[Signed by all 19 students of the Independent Study course]

•••

"I shall pass through this world but once. Any good therefore that I can do or any kindness that I can show to any human being, let me do it now. Let me not defer or neglect it, for I shall not pass this way again."

Mahatma Gandhi

As I write this in June 2021, Yvonne, Rene, Gail, Jeffrey, and I have just booked our airline tickets and hotels to join our German Mishpacha again in Meinerzhagen this fall – pending travel advisories based on COVID status. We want to support Yvonne and Rene, gather again and embrace our German Mishpacha, see more of Germany, and bear witness to "completing the circle" of all of the Meinerzhagen Stolpersteine *Verlegung*.

In July 2021, Ira was researching information about Rene's family, at his request. What she found was astounding: several members of his family were also forced to live in the monastery in Bonn-Endenich, where our family members were forced to live – all awaiting deportation, together. As well, she found that his family and our family were together on the same deportation train from Cologne to Minsk on 20.July 1942. And finally, tragically, she found that his family was murdered – together with our family – in the exact same forest of Blagowtschina on the exact same day – 24.July 1942.

Chapter 10

NEVER, EVER THE SAME

How wonderful it is that nobody need wait a single moment before starting to improve the world.

— Anne Frank

Wednesday 9/29/21:
Aboard the plane to Frankfurt, Germany

Unbelievably, here I am again – on my third flight to Germany, seven years after our original journey, three years after my second one. Is anything the same this time? Is anything different? I don't know that *anything* is the same in 2021 compared to 2014 and 2018, other than the fact that I'm in an airplane again about to fly over the Atlantic Ocean more than 4000 miles to Frankfurt, Germany. It's unbelievable to me *this* time, because I've actually set foot on an airplane – complete with my tools: hand sanitizer, three 2021 vaccinations, and wearing a mask for several hours already from the minute I entered the airport . . . during a one and a half-year ongoing global pandemic! I am reminded of my two-fold rationale for stepping onto this airplane by Friedrich Nietzsche's quote, which also appears in Viktor Frankl's book *Man's Search for Meaning*: "He who has a *why* to live for can bear almost any *how*."

In his book, Frankl applied Nietzsche's quote to his own survival in several concentration camps. While imprisoned, Frankl realized that there was an important task he needed to finish: the completion of a manuscript he'd been working on before his life was traumatically disrupted and endangered by the Shoah. Viktor Frankl said: *"The meaning of life differs from man to man, from day to day, from hour to hour. What matters, therefore, is not the meaning of life in general but rather the specific meaning of a person's life at a given moment. To put the question in general terms would be (akin) to the question posed to a chess champion: 'Tell me, Master, what is the best move in the world?' There simply is no such thing as the best or even a good move apart from a particular situation in a game and the particular personality of one's opponent. The same holds for human existence. One should not search for an abstract meaning of life. Everyone has his own specific vocation or mission in life to carry out a concrete assignment which demands fulfillment. Therein he cannot be replaced, nor can his life be repeated. Thus, everyone's task is as unique as is his specific opportunity to implement it. As each situation in life represents a challenge to man and presents a problem for him to solve, the question of the meaning of life may actually be reversed. Ultimately, man should not ask what the meaning of life is, but rather he must recognize that it is he who is asked. In a word, each man is questioned by life; and he can only answer to life by answering for his own life; to life he can only respond by being responsible." [1]*

For me, in this life moment, my two-fold "why" that spiritually and physically propelled me to "bear the how" of walking into Dulles airport and buckling my airplane seatbelt during a global pandemic, is:

1. To visit and embrace – at least once again – our German Mishpacha, before it is too late to do so, for we have all aged and experienced a variety of health challenges over these past seven years.

2. Like Frankl's (though there is no comparison to surviving the Holocaust), my Mission, my "calling" that demands fulfillment in this chapter of my life is also to complete my manuscript for publication with this last chapter.

So "what's different" for this 2021 journey to Germany? This time:

- Everyone needs to wear masks, for hours, throughout the departure and arrival airports and our flight to Frankfurt – not to mention throughout our week's journey in Germany.

- We had to complete 2 online forms pre-flight, a "sign of

---

1 Frankl, V.E., "Man's Search For Meaning". First published in German, 1946, by Verlag für Jugend und Volk.

the times": an EU digital entry form, and an airline form with our uploaded Covid-vaccination card and other information.

- We asked our German Mishpacha to arrange approved pre-departure covid-testing for us in Meinerzhagen, so that we can bring the required results to the Frankfurt airport in order to be allowed on the plane returning to the USA.

- Besides showing our passports at Dulles, we had to show our actual Covid-vaccination cards. A negative Covid-test 2-3 days prior to arrival in Germany is *not* required for entry in September 2021, although it *is* required prior to our arrival back into the USA.

- I'm traveling with our son this time, and he's a delight! We've probably talked more in the past week and on this flight than in the past couple years – not because we're estranged, but because he's not usually much of a talker.

- Tonight at Dulles airport was only the third time since March 2020 that I've eaten *IN*side a restaurant! Still, despite being fully vaccinated and having received my booster shot several weeks ago, I put my mask back on in the restaurant as soon as I'd finished eating. It still makes me feel safer, along with the vaccines. Weaning OUT of the original lockdown restrictions into lesser restrictions has been a challenging process for me, despite the welcomed freedoms we've gained.

- Because we're all older and some have experienced significant health challenges over the years, I'm acutely aware that this may well be the last time I see some of our German Mishpacha – not just because none of us knows how much time we have left on this earth, but also because I don't know if I'll return to Germany again, nor that any of our German Mishpacha will be coming to the USA.

- I'm traveling from one high-risk country, my own USA, to another high-risk country – Germany!

- There are no more Stolpersteine Verlegung for our own family this trip, but rather for a friend's family. However, it's possible that we *are* family because her family's last name is also Stern! Of course we'll do the Stolpersteine circuit and visit all of our family and others' Stolpersteine as well as gravesites for those who died pre-Shoah and had proper burials and tombstones.

- I've written this book that will be published soon! I'm so excited to meet Dietmar's students who developed the petition that made *this* journey's Stolpersteine Verlegung finally possible after 10 years! I'm so excited to share my "pre" book copy, which doesn't include the final chapter 10 yet because I'm beginning to write that chapter as we take off!

- Although I've experienced anxiety before this 2021 trip, too – *this* time it is *only* related to my concerns about Covid, *not* about meeting "strangers", getting in their cars, being harmed by Germans, or being separated from Gail. And still, I've boarded the plane!

- Dietmar's picking us up this time, and he's rented a VAN because now there are SIX of us Americans flying in – Gail, me, and Steve (previous trips), and Ryan, Yvonne and Rene (first trips).

- I just turned 68 last week, I stopped coloring my hair at the beginning of the pandemic – so it's all-natural-white now, I wear hearing aids which make a significant difference in my quality of life, and I've just completed a course of physical therapy before this journey.

What *hasn't* changed since 2014 and 2018? Most of all, I look forward to embracing and reuniting with our Significant 4 and additional Mishpacha. We still haven't heard whether Oliver is joining us this time. I hope so. As well, my passion for being a part of the solutions to people's acceptance of one another as brothers and sisters, and collaborating together for sustainable Justice and Peace for ALL – continues. To that end, I sincerely hope that this book will touch your neshamas, move you, and propel and continue to propel your neshamas into positive actions – for each of us is capable of being a positive change agent in our own unique way.

Off to sleep now!

Thursday 30.September: arrival in Germany, dinner and wine (Time zone: six hours later than EDT in the USA)

I can't believe it's still Thursday, our arrival day in Germany (I'm writing this at 10:30 pm Germany time in our hotel room, after dinner and wine.)! We arrived on time in Frankfurt. The van Dietmar rented for us – and our luggage – was perfect. A two hour drive to Meinerzhagen, which I just learned that I've been pronouncing incorrectly for seven years! Dietmar taught me today that it's pronounced as if it was spelled Meinertzhagen, although there is no "t" in the spelling. During our drive, there was never a moment of silence in the van! Yvonne shared some of her family's history, and additional information was shared by Dietmar – from Ira and her comprehensive research. I sat up front with Dietmar, and we spoke nonstop about German and American politics, current events, our families, and our visit here. He told us that unfortunately, Oliver could not make the trip this time. We miss him already! Ryan was sitting behind me in the third row, and Gail was behind me in the second row. I turned to her and said, "This trip, I'm not worried about being separated from you because *now* our people are Mishpacha, and because you're here with me in the same van – so I don't have to keep turning around to make sure you're behind me!" Nor was I worried about being separated from my son Ryan. My, how I've grown!

Dietmar shared a beautiful story about the van he'd rented. When picking up the van, he told the staff the reason he was renting it – to pick up six Americans (three of whom were returning for the third or fourth time) whose families had been victims of the Holocaust, who were coming to Meinerzhagen for the Stolpersteine Verlegung for one of the American's families – Jewish former Meinerzhagen citizens. After Dietmar returned home with the van, he received a call from the manager stating that he was impressed with the Stolpersteine Initiative's mission to remember and commemorate Jewish victims of the Holocaust and their company wanted to contribute to the mission. Therefore, their company was going to pay for the costs of the rental, insurance, and gas for the entire week!

Once we checked into our hotel (wearing our masks), where we've stayed during previous journeys, we had some time to unpack, shower, and relax for awhile. Then we walked about two blocks to dinner at a local café, where Dietmar and "his" Christina had reserved it just for our group of 13 vaccinated-Mishpacha. I still wore my mask inside, but as soon as Gudrun found me and we hugged – I removed it. Then the rest of our group commenced with a mutual rotating hug-fest! It was as if we were malnourished and starved for it, both from not having seen each other for several years as well as a result of the pandemic. Rolf and "his" Christina were also there, along with Herbert, and a City Council member we hadn't met before – Ingolf. During dinner, Rolf's Christina shared some history about how Rolf had passionately persevered, meeting with each City Council member individually to introduce and urge their support for the Stolpersteine Verlegung in Meinerzhagen long before the first commemoration ceremony occurred in 2013. It was difficult initially, but he prevailed. What a meaningful legacy he and Herbert gifted to the world, to us and the other families with Jewish ancestors from Meinerzhagen.

The owner of the café did an outstanding job at taking care of our lively group, having prepared both a delicious meal and a striking presentation. She shared a German colloquialism that we'd never heard, and there are similar American ones. When describing her English language skills, she said, "My English is not the yolk in the egg." Our Mishpacha explained that it meant she believed that her English was *not* the best, comparing it to the yolk that *is* considered the best part of the egg! We Americans have similar ones: not the brightest bulb in the pack, not the sharpest knife in the drawer, implying similar descriptions of "not the best". The next day, I decided to walk back to her café and present her with a copy of my "pre" book (without chapter 10) with an autographed personalized note. She was clearly touched, thanked me, and told me that now she would work on her English so that she could read and understand it.

Once we were having dessert, Dietmar got everyone's attention to announce that I'd like to present some gifts honoring who they are and what they've given us through their dedication and passion to the mission of the Stolpersteine Initiative. Gail, Ryan and I gave 1 kippah each to Dietmar, Herbert, and Rolf (and saved one for Oliver, to be mailed later), a "special" kippah from Ryan's Bar-Mitzvah engraved inside with his name and Bar-Mitzvah date. Before coming to Germany, I'd written each of them a note to accompany the kippah – explaining the significance of *this* particular kippah and why we were presenting them with it. I explained that Ryan was only able to be born, and continue in the traditions of his Jewish grandfathers, L'Dor v'Dor, because his Pop-Pop Rolf/Ralph Stern was able to escape from Germany to America in 1938. We wanted them each to have this kippah because of all they've done personally, as well as to inspire others, to remember and commemorate our loved ones who were not able to escape, who subsequently became victims of the Shoah. They were each visibly touched, thanked us, knew exactly what a kippah was, and placed it on their heads. They wore them on the day of the Stolpersteine Verlegung for Yvonne's family members. In addition, I presented each of them and all of the others with a copy of my "pre" book, complete with a personalized note and autograph. Reuniting with some of our Mishpacha on our first evening back in Germany, with our son with us this time, was a beautiful beginning to this 2021 journey. It was a reuniting of *our* neshamas, Christian German and Jewish American, together again.

Friday 1.October: A cemetery, a memorial, our first of many Kaddish Prayers; personal time with Gudrun and her husband, the Stolpersteine circuit, and dinner, dialogue (and more wine) with Dietmar's students

This morning, along with Rolf and Christina, Dietmar and Christina, and Gudrun and her husband Gerd, we drove a short distance to the new Meinerzhagen Jewish Cemetery. What a surprise they had in store for us! Just 2 days prior, a memorial that had been discussed for many years had just been erected – with the names of those Jewish citizens whose tombstones had been desecrated, stolen, and used for paving sidewalks by the Nazis during their regime of terror. Although those individuals are not actually buried here, there is now a memorial sign with each of their names so that they can be respectfully remembered as valuable individuals – not just as a number or statistic, which was Hitler's plan. Originally, when Gail, Jeffrey and I came to Germany in 2014, we had discussed with our Mishpacha that we'd like to provide a monument with these individuals' names – both to "remember" them, as well as to honor Rolf by fulfilling his dream he'd shared with us to do so. Despite a number of starts and stops over the past seven years, a monument had not yet come to fruition.

The Meinerzhagen Stolpersteine Initiative members have demonstrated numerous times in numerous ways that they won't take "no" or "inaction" for a final answer. As well, they are persistent in their actions to create the desired outcomes, and if one action is ineffective – they switch gears and try "Plan B" to obtain their goal. Dietmar's Christina explained that the two of them had originally designed the signs for this memorial, after they and other Meinerzhagen Stolpersteine Initiative members saw similar ones in a neighboring town – Attendorn – two years ago. In fact, they'd also contacted a printer at that time about creating this memorial. Step by step, they designed the signs with the help of a local man doing the technical aspects of the maps, but without other professional assistance! Just as we've experienced here in the USA, because of coronavirus, there were delayed schedules for receiving orders and increased costs for wood. They actually had to order the wood frames for the memorial sign as well as the actual nine Stolpersteine for Yvonne's family earlier this year, BEFORE the final decisions for each of those projects had even been made! Talk about Faith!

Following a newspaper article this year describing the pending Meinerzhagen Stolpersteine Verlegung for Yvonne's family on 2.October, a local bank called Dietmar and "his" Christina asking how they could support the laying of the Stolpersteine (which Stolpersteine and the memorial sign were also made possible because of Ira's comprehensive research of the individuals' names, dates, and places of birth and death). Subsequently, the local bank made a donation. Therefore, the memorial costs were completely covered! So while our Mishpacha thanked us for offering our donation to pay for the memorial – they did not need it at this time.

We were blown away at their surprise for us, we shared our gratitude for their remembering and commemorating, and then we six Jewish Americans said Kaddish together. Although we didn't know any of the individuals, still – they were *our* people, people of our Jewish Tribe, who likely no longer had anyone to pray Kaddish for them. Rene explained that whenever one recites Kaddish for an individual, it elevates that individual's soul / neshama to a higher level – and that's a mitzvah, a good deed. It was a powerful experience, even more so because we prayed together "in community", six American Jews (All of us are descendants from three separate Jewish families – all victims of the Holocaust from Meinerzhagen and other neighboring German towns. We would likely have never met each other any other way – but for our shared Holocaust history and our Significant 4.), with our German Mishpacha standing beside us, supporting us, "remembering" together with us, and adding additional love, dignity, and respect to our mutual experience of remembrance, commemoration and healing.

As pre-planned by Gudrun and me prior to our journey, our group separated at this point. I went with Gudrun and Gerd to their home for some special time together and "to see how we regular people live in Germany", according to Gudrun! The others did the walking Stolpersteine circuit, going to visit each Jewish Meinerzhagen family's Stolpersteine (which I'd done twice on prior visits). Then Gudrun and I would meet back up with the group somewhere along the Stolpersteine circuit. Her husband told me privately at their home that since they were both leaving Saturday morning for holiday, Gudrun had been quite upset that she wouldn't be able to spend more time with me – so she was really glad, and so was he, that I'd be together with them in their home. So was I.

Once there, I toured their beautiful home where they've lived some 50 years. Then we had coffee, tea, and some sweets, and talked and talked and talked, sharing photos and stories of each others' families – mostly our grandchildren! Gerd recommended a tasty treat that he enjoys, so I tried it: soft cheese (not cream cheese) spread into a small individual-portion-size pie-crust-filling and topped with their homemade Himbeer-gelee (raspberry jam). The two flavors of the cheese and tart jam complement each other – delicious!

We did not talk about our shared histories. We talked as if we'd been long-time friends, about the same things other friends talk about. Normal. Though the initial "bond" between us and our German Mishpacha <u>was</u> our shared traumatic histories, for we would have never met otherwise, perhaps that bond occurred more quickly and more intensely *because of* our shared histories. But together, over time – we've discovered that we have so much more than that in common, and so much more than that shared history defines us, which is clearly the glue that keeps our bond strong. Perhaps that bond has also been able to continue so strongly because of the deep emotions we've shared with each other in such a condensed period of time initially in 2014, during the 8-months of developing email relationships during which we shared our emotions and our vulnerabilities with each other, as well as during our initial journey to Germany. And most certainly, our bond has continued strongly – because at the end of the day, our German Mishpacha are kind, decent mensches with whom we share our common values and humanity. We all brush our teeth, put our pants on one leg at a time, love and are loved, experience sadness and joy and many emotions, grow old, experience challenges, enjoy "giving back" to others, stand up and speak out for justice, adore our children and grandchildren, and celebrate holidays (although different ones) with lots of family, food, and wine, etc., etc., etc.

Then Gudrun and I rejoined the others towards the end of the Meinerzhagen Stolpersteine circuit, and I joined the others in reciting Kaddish at each of the remaining family's Stolpersteine. Once we'd completed the circuit, our group disbanded to complete preparations for this evening's plans with Dietmar's Independent Study students at their high school, and we went back to our hotel for a little down time (where I continued writing this chapter).

In the early evening, we went to the local high school where Dietmar teaches – among other courses – the academic-year-long Independent Study course: Jewish Life in Meinerzhagen. These students, 17-18 years old, had been in classes all day since 7:30 a.m., yet they stayed there to set up, to meet us, to hear our stories, to ask questions, and to dialogue together. In preparation for the evening, I brought a number of my books to give to them, my traveling Shabbat candlesticks and candles, and my kippah – to light the candles for Shabbat as I do weekly at home. This would be the first time ever that I would wear my kippah in Germany, not to mention light the Shabbat candles!

Dietmar told me that there was no specific schedule or end-time for tonight's program (a dangerous thing to tell ME, because I can talk on and on when I'm passionate about something!). His agenda was simply that we all meet each other (which I'd also requested over the summer), share a bit about our family history, and answer any questions the students might ask. Of course, it quite naturally and easily flowed from that into so much more. Once again, I wore my mask inside to begin. Once inside, I reminded myself silently that these students had just self-tested that morning, and they would not be allowed to be here right now if they'd tested covid-positive. As well, I looked around at every adult in attendance – they were the same who were with us at dinner last night – and I knew they were all vaccinated. Once again, I removed my mask shortly after arriving, deeming it unnecessary in these safe circumstances. I did this on my own this time, without any gentle reminders from anyone else.

After each student told me their name, I introduced myself and lit the Shabbat candles, explaining the blessing and the purpose as well as my kippah. I made sure to tell them that this was my first time bringing my kippah to Germany, and how friends and family had told us in 2014 not to bring anything to *any* European country that would clearly identify us as Jews – because of the risks of ever-present antisemitism. I felt brave and proud to wear my kippah here, and unafraid. To be fair, I knew I was in a safe environment with safe like-minded people. In fact, I felt safe in this cocoon of individuals not only with regard to my religion – but also with regard to covid. While vaccinations for students remains voluntary, all are required to perform rapid-self-testing for covid three times weekly on Mondays-Wednesdays-and

Fridays, right in their classroom with their teacher supervising, with results available quickly. No whining, no complaining about nasal discomfort, no impassioned cries about their rights being taken away. They just DO it as a necessary fact of life, a small price to pay to keep themselves, their families and their friends as safe as possible. Couldn't WE in the USA learn from Germany's safe practices and duplicate them?!

Next, I shared the following. "Mazel Tov (Congratulations, Hebrew) und Ich gratuliere den Schulerinnen und Schulern (Congratulations to the students, German)!

Danke schoen (Thank you very much, German) for who you are: passionate, compassionate, courageous students who chose to stand up and speak out rather than be complicit in your silence, who chose to be the moral voices, who developed a petition for the last two Jewish Meinerzhagen families – victims of the Holocaust, the Shoah in Hebrew – to be remembered and commemorated with a Stolpersteine Verlegung tomorrow. And you've also shined our loved ones' Stolpersteine.

You give us HOPE for the present and the future, by accepting the responsibility and the Stolpersteine Initiative's mission of remembering each individual Holocaust victim as a person who mattered, who loved and was loved, and whose life made a difference. Know that you are already doing the work at your young ages of Tikkun Olam – repairing the world (Hebrew).

You inspire us to stand up and speak out for what is right and just, to make our world a kinder gentler one. As noted author and Holocaust Survivor Elie Wiesel said, 'There may be times when we are powerless to prevent injustice, but there must NEVER be a time when we fail to protest.'

And now, it is my pleasure to present one of my books to your teacher Dietmar – to be placed in your library here at school, as well as seven other books to be shared amongst each of you in Dietmar's 'Jewish Life in Meinerzhagen' class, and with others after that if you wish. Danke schoen."

Then I shared the title of my book and what it's about, what motivated me to write it, and some of our relevant family history. I would often say, "Can you imagine that?", when describing how Hitler's persecutory regime and laws impacted Dad and his family, i.e. he couldn't play with his non-Jewish friends anymore, his father's business failed since they no longer had any income because it was against Nazi laws to do business with anyone Jewish – so they were forced to move because they could no longer pay for their home. Gail added more information, as did Steve, Yvonne, and Rene about their families' experiences, and we all thanked them for what they've given us. All of us were tearful at times, and we could see that some of the students were as well. The students asked thoughtful questions, especially once they were told they could ask in German if they preferred (even though they spoke English very well, but of course it is not their first language) – and Dietmar's Christina translated for us. It was a beautiful dialogue that some students said made all the difference, compared to their reading and learning about it in their history books, because now they were hearing that history come alive through descendants of the loved ones who were victimized and persecuted.

Dinner that the students were responsible for preparing, and wine, followed. As I saw the students nonchalantly pouring themselves wine, and some adults actually pouring wine for them, I was astonished! I asked what the drinking age is in Germany: it's 16, for beer and wine only!! Wow!

When I went to the restroom, one of the students and I were washing our hands at the same time. I took the opportunity to thank her for her candid participation in the program, and to ask her a personal question: "May I ask where you were born? To my ear, I don't hear any German or any other accent. You actually sound to me like you're American." She beamed a beautiful smile, thanked me, and readily explained. She shared multiple hurtful experiences on social media when talking to peers globally. She explained that inevitably, each peer would ask where she was from. Sometimes she would talk around that, so as not to give her nationality away. But when peers pressed, she of course told them that she's from Germany. Whenever she did so, one after the other, her adolescent peers from around the globe would make a negative face and comment – sometimes including, "I mean, are you actually proud to be a German?" Ultimately, her peers would each abruptly end the conversation and further contact.

Because of the discrimination and negative stereotyping she felt from her global peers because of a shameful part of her country's history, she had vowed to do whatever it took to "lose" her German accent – spending hours and months watching and listening to American songs/YouTube – "to speak like Americans." While *she* was flattered that I'd thought she was American, because it meant she'd indeed lost her German accent – which was her goal, *I* was saddened and scared – and shared why. To me, at my age and per my life experiences, I crave cultural diversity – different languages, different accents, different colloquialisms/ food/music/traditions than my American ones. To me, that's what makes us and the world so interesting, so beautiful, so colorful and vibrant. But I still remember my adolescence too, wanting to "fit in", to "belong"; that's a normal life stage we all go through. I felt sad that her global peers were judging her SOLELY on a part of her country's history that occurred decades before she was born, dismissing her without even taking the time to get to know HER. And I felt sad that because of part of her country's history, wrong as that history was – she believed she needed to "lose" her German accent in order to hide her identity, especially in light of the fact that she's chosen to be a part of the *solution* by standing up and speaking out with her fellow students via the petition they wrote to their local government officials! Perhaps part of it is their age, but that actually makes it *more* painful AND frightening to bear witness in 2021 to how some people – especially some young people – "define" and judge others based on only one singular fact, or more often on misinformation and inaccurate stereotypes (which we know from repeated history and the present is exactly what feeds hatred and intolerance, and can lead to violence and genocide), when in fact, this young woman standing in front of me is defined by so much more. It makes me wonder if people judge me as an American, before they get to know me, based on *my* country's shameful parts of history, some of which are ongoing – slavery, racism, a caste system, poverty, homelessness, and more. When I asked her if I could please share her story in my book (without her name, although she told me it would be okay if I used her full name), she readily said "yes" – and that she would feel honored if I did so.

Saturday 2.October: Two Stolpersteine Verlegung for Yvonne's family – at last! Dinner with the Meinerzhagen Burgermeister (Mayor) and guests at City Hall

Today is Yvonne's day – the day of her family's two Stolpersteine Verlegung at 11 a.m. – finally, after 10 years of the Meinerzhagen Stolpersteine Initiative members' struggling to make this happen! Despite the cold overcast day, it did not rain. Yvonne's family was able to escape Germany (before she was born) at a time when few countries would allow Jews to immigrate, among them China, Cuba, and Argentina. Her family escaped to Shanghai, China, and years later immigrated to the USA. Therefore, she was able to grow up with her parents. We walked to Yvonne's family's first of two home sites, which our Mishpacha had shown us yesterday. Since this family's home no longer exists, just as ours no longer exists, these Stolpersteine will be set in the street pavement in front of where their home last stood (which is a double-garage now).

As the crowd begins to thicken, I'm trying to stay socially distanced, even though we're outside. I move closer to Rolf and our other Mishpacha who I know are "safe", i.e. vaccinated. I don't know who else is vaccinated or not. Some are wearing masks, many are not. Sheri, I say silently to myself – it is "okay" because we are outside. Yes, but there are many young children here as well, so I know they're not vaccinated yet. I remind myself to relax, that I am triple-vaccinated, and we are outside – even as the crowd is growing. I have not been with this many people for a year and a half! This is like a visceral shock to my system. I remind myself to be patient, that coming "out of" stricter covid restrictions that were scientifically evidence-based as necessary more than a year ago is a weaning process for me, and our Mishpacha would never place us or themselves in any unsafe situation – covid-related or otherwise. Just then, we six Americans are ushered under an open tent as special guests. Looking out at the growing crowd, I put my mask on to feel safer – although no one else around me is doing so. Soon after, Dietmar comes to my side and softly whispers so that only I can hear, that because we are outside – there is no need to wear a mask. I tell him that I "understand"

and thank him for the reminder, but that I will keep it on for now because it makes me feel safer. He kindly says okay, and carries on with his preparations for the ceremony. Within a short time, I silently rationalize to myself with facts and science, including the fact that I am sitting under this open tent with "only" my own family and the other Americans – all of whom are vaccinated and tested negative before coming to Germany (even though testing was not required to enter Germany). The "crowd" is "out there", well more than 6 feet away from us. It's okay, I'm safe, we're safe. I remove my mask.

Now I concentrate on the ceremony. Wow, I think there's more than 200 townspeople here, more than in 2014! This is fantastic – more than 70 years after WWII and the Holocaust ended in 1945, this many people in this small town remain interested and committed to remembering and commemorating their town's Jewish former citizens who were victims of the Holocaust! Christina, co-leader with Dietmar, shares her opening speech.

"Good morning to all those present, and a good morning it is: we are happy and grateful that today at our fifth installation, the last 9 of 47 Jewish former fellow citizens will receive a special and individual memorial of their life among us through these 'Stolpersteine': the families of the Meinerzhagen brothers, Nathan and Emil Stern, married to the sisters Rosa and Paula ...

As organizers, and in consideration of the recent events in Hagen, we thank (our Stolpersteine installer) for the considerate street closures, as well as the local and regional police for providing security at our event.

In the name of the 'Stolpersteine Initiative' of Meinerzhagen/ Kierspe, I'd like to extend an especially warm welcome to our six guests, who have undertaken the long trip from the USA (in spite of the Coronavirus restrictions, which made this whole event into a bit of a nail-biter up until just 10 days ago): (our six names).

A warm welcome also to our Mayor, Jan Nesselrath, and all of you who have made the journey here today, since you have supported the 'Stolpersteine' project and many of you have likely taken part in installations already. I'd also like to welcome the students of the special course 'Jewish Life in Meinerzhagen', who made these last two installations possible through their proposal to the city government. Thanks to their enormous dedication, we are today able to say: 10 years for the 'Stolpersteine Initiative', 10 'Stolpersteine' at the 10 final places of residence for our Jewish former fellow citizens. I'd say we deserve a bit of applause."

(Paraphrased: Pastor offers a prayer. The middle school choir of the EGM sings. All are invited to attend the luncheon in the congregation hall after the ceremonies.)

"5 Stones   5 Menschen   5 Names

Nathan and Rosa Stern (Yvonne's grandparents), their son Hugo and daughter Hedwig (Yvonne's mother), and Nathan's cousin Paula. These five people represent the options: hauled away and murdered, forced into exile, or driven to suicide.

I would like to relate what our neighbor once told me decades after the event and still visibly shaken: on the morning of November 10th, 1938 (Authoress: Reichspogromnacht), she saw from the window how Yvonne's mother, Hedwig, sobbed and cried out in disbelief, as local SS-men robbed, trampled, and then burned all the sacred objects (Torah scrolls, candle sticks, and furniture) … before her eyes, RIGHT HERE on the street. She would never forget Hetti's screams, she said, nor the horror and fear that she herself felt from that moment on. Two months after this event, Hetti fled … to Shanghai, the only port at that time that accepted Jewish refugees without extensive document-processing. Yvonne was born there in 1944.

Hetti's brother Hugo had already fled to Buenos Aires in 1936. Two years ago, my husband received a letter that Hugo had written in 1966 to his neighbor... In the letter, Hugo wrote, 'Dear (neighbor)... I saw you in the Meinerhagener-Zeitung from December 24th (I still receive the papers, though six weeks later.) … I have now been here (in Buenos Aires) for 30 years and am already 54 years old. And every night, in my dreams, I am in Meinerzhagen; I still long to return. I can never forget my Meinerzhagen.' (The neighbor's) granddaughter had found this letter in the attic and asked us to give it to Yvonne, whom she knew would be coming for the installation of 'her' Stolpersteine. And today is the day. (The letter is given to Yvonne.) …

(History of the Stolpersteine-Project in Meinerzhagen, discussion beginning more than 10 years ago, including Ira's 'careful and determined research which showed how Jews lived in Meinerzhagen since 1810.') ... Many of the Jewish families (in Meinerzhagen) first lived in very impoverished circumstances until they managed a remarkable socio-economic leap into the middle class, and thereby integration into Meinerzhagen society. Integration meant that Jews belonged to the voluntary fire department and, in time, also to the Schutzenclub, gymnastics club, choir, and of course the numerous neighborhood associations.

It was only after the coup of the National socialists that a systematic ostracism began – at first through denigration and slander, then through employment and business prohibitions, which robbed them of any ability to conduct their lives. In the end there was imprisonment, forced emigration, and finally deportation to concentration camps for their murder. Through Ira's telling of the fates of the Stern (and other families, in 2011), our city Archivist (Ira) made this history real and gave it even more than a face. ... Allow me here to make a comment on the theme of ostracism: it begins small, perhaps with looking away and not greeting someone at a chance encounter. Someone in the store, pub, or at a party makes derogatory or derisive comments, makes sweeping generalizations. If no one challenges this, an impression can be made, which becomes the general opinion and then the danger exists that, bit by bit, one's individual thinking is shaped, all according to the motto 'when everyone thinks something, there must be something to it'. It is important in such situations to overcome one's inhibitions, to take courage and to challenge the idea. It only takes one statement, such as 'I've got my own opinion about that', or 'I don't see it that way.' The listeners of Ira's lecture were so deeply moved, that in the discussion that followed, it was decided to form an initiative for the installation of Stolpersteine. On March 28th, 2011, the initiative met for the first time. At the time, we did not think that it would take 10 years to install the Stolpersteine at the 10 locations.

Our first installation took place on June 26th, 2013 at Hauptstrasse 15 in front of the earlier residence of the R family. All 15 surviving descendants of Walter had flown in from Israel. At this opportunity, our same neighbor delivered two silver pastry forks to the daughter and granddaughter of Walter, which she had kept safe for 70 years at the request of her Jewish neighbor. I was deeply moved by the words of one descendant at that time: 'It's like a homecoming; now my father's soul can find its peace. He is no longer just a number among six million victims. With his name, he has his worth again. He will be seen. As a person with an individual fate.' And it is precisely this that makes the difference between Stolpersteine and other memorials or plaques. Stolpersteine make the data of history personal and therefore tangible, comprehendible. Their focus is less on death, rather they bring the victims back into their lives among us, with their own history, their preferences and talents, their profession here in their true home, which often they never found during their lives abroad. (Description of installations two, three and four between 2014-2017.)

Which brings us to today, September 2021, the fifth and final installation of Stolpersteine 10 years after the start of our initiative. I must admit: we still find it incomprehensible how much fear and resistance these little stones can arouse. It has been for me equally surprising, that nearly all the descendants of our Jewish former fellow citizens have come here – to the land of the perpetrators – have returned again and again, and have opened their ears and their hearts for us. The friendships that have developed are a sign that reconciliation between the generations, even after such atrocities, is possible. It is a gift of inestimable worth, perhaps a gift from the one G-d, whom we share."

The Independent Study course students also gave a speech: "In memory of all the Jewish victims of national socialism who lived in Meinerzhagen.

Today we are especially thinking about Nathan, Rosa, Hugo, Hedwig and Paula Stern (Zum Alten Teich 2; their home address) and about Emil, Paula, Hans and Herbert Stern (Hauptstrasse 32). Right now we are standing at a very special place. This is where the families Nathan and Emil Stern had their last freely chosen residence. We are finally able to pay our last respects and thoughts towards them by laying their very own stumbling blocks with which we are able to remember them.

Stumbling Blocks in Meinerzhagen are memorials to remind us of all the victims of the National Socialism. In 1992 the Cologne artist Gunter Demnig created them. Nowadays more than 75,000 stumbling blocks can be found in Germany and 21 more European countries. Stumbling blocks are small eye-catchers in the pavement. You will not stumble and fall physically, but your heads and hearts will stumble. Every victim is referred to so that they will never be forgotten. The goal of the National Socialists to erase all the memory of these victims is reversed by Gunter Demnig's action, they give remembrance. With the motto 'One Block. One Name. One Person.', the data is engraved into the brass plate by hand, and after that the stumbling blocks will be put in the ground at the very last freely-chosen residence of the victims.

In Meinerzhagen, 38 stumbling blocks have been laid so far. The victims' names were brought back to their hometown, and the place that was stolen from them can now be given back to them.

In our project class 'Jewish Life in Meinerzhagen', we have been intensively dealing with the destiny of the Jewish citizens in Meinerzhagen since November 2020. We started digging into the history and got to know the stumbling blocks in January 2021. When we started to research about the 38 stumbling blocks here in Meinerzhagen, it did not take us very long to find out that there were nine blocks missing because they had not been laid down yet. We were devastated when we found out about that.

How could this injustice be justified of denying these remaining nine people their last honor? We did not see any reason for these last stumbling blocks not to be put in the ground and not to pay tribute towards the last victims. We could not understand how the stubbornness of individual people was able to fulfill the goal of the national socialists to forget about the affected.

As a young generation, we feel responsible to remember all of these people so that this horrible past cannot be repeated. We have to learn from the past! The only possibility for that is with knowledge about history and thinking about the victims. This is why we wanted to pay the honor and the necessary and long overdue respect to the nine remaining victims by standing up for the laying of these last stumbling blocks in Meinerzhagen.

After intense preparation, we sent a citizen proposal to the City Council of Meinerzhagen in March (2021) about the laying of the remaining stumbling blocks in front of the houses 'Zum Alten Teich 2' and 'Hauptstrasse 32'. In the next council meeting, our proposal was approved.

It is important for us to give back the robbed Jewish citizens of Meinerzhagen their so long denied place in their homeland, and to present to them a place which remembers them. Now we are finally here, and the remaining stumbling blocks can be put in the ground – in memory of Emil, Paula, Hans and Herbert Stern from 'Hauptstrasse 32' and in memory of Nathan, Rosa, Hugo, Hedwig and Paula Stern from 'Zum Alten Teich 2'.

We are very happy about the presence of Yvonne, the relative of these nine family members, who stands here with us after a long journey and shares this important moment with us." (end of speech)

The children are led by their accordion-playing teacher in singing Shalom Aleichem and several other songs – in Hebrew! All of this was happening while Gunter Demnig's assistant was "planting" Yvonne's family's five Stolpersteine in the pavement, silently and reverently – just as Gunter Demnig did for our family seven years ago. Yvonne gave a tearful speech, mostly in German – which was actually her first language, sharing her gratitude for the townspeople's remembrance and Stolpersteine commemoration and sharing how much her mother always spoke lovingly about Meinerzhagen as her "home" – despite the persecution and her family's need to escape to Shanghai to save their lives. When the laying was completed, we Americans looked upon her family's Stolpersteine and recited Kaddish. At the end, I'd prepared one sentence in German to share with all those in attendance – just as I'd done in English in 2014: "Liebe, vergebung, heilung und frieden . . . Das ist mein wunsch – fur euch alle, fur uns alle – zusammen. Love, forgiveness, healing and peace . . . That is my wish, for all of you, for all of us – together."

After this ceremony, we walked a short distance to the former home site of the rest of Yvonne's family for those last four Stolpersteine to be laid. Now, the circle is completed! All Jewish Meinerzhagen families, all victims of the Shoah in that town, all respectfully remembered and commemorated now. And they will not be forgotten after today, nor will our family or others' in Meinerzhagen, Hohenlimburg, and Meckenheim – for our Mishpacha will remember, visit them and polish their Stolpersteine with love regularly, and pass that responsibility and duty to their younger generations – who are already picking up and accepting that responsibility and duty, L'Dor v'Dor – from generation to generation.

Next, we all walked to the local church (the same as in 2014) where we enjoyed lunch prepared by the Stolpersteine Initiative chapter members and the company of many people. I met friends from 2014, including the young woman who still wears her beautiful star of David ring! We each remembered each other immediately, embraced, and talked and talked. I enjoyed some 1:1 time with one of Rolf's sons. Several chapter members told me they are looking forward to reading this book. Today I saw Gretel for the first time since our arrival, Herbert's wife. We both share heads of white hair now. Ahhh, it is good to be with Mishpacha!

Later this evening, we went to the Meinerzhagen Rathaus – their City Hall building. We had cocktails and dinner with the Burgermeister Jan Nesselrath and his wife (both of whom we knew from our previous trips), his administrative assistant, and the two students who'd come to the Rathaus to deliver and share their petition for Yvonne's family's nine Stolpersteine Verlegung. I presented the Burgermeister with a copy of my "pre" book. I sat next to one of the students (one is Rolf's granddaughter, and the other is a young man – both classmates in Dietmar's Independent Study course), and marveled at several things in particular about him: his vast international traveling experiences already at the age of 17, his interest and commitment to continuing to work with the Meinerzhagen Stolpersteine Initiative members and fulfilling their mission ongoing – even now that all the town's Jewish citizens have been commemorated, his outstanding grasp of English – both speaking it and understanding it (and I talk pretty fast!), his willingness and interest in both speaking and listening to me, and his question about where and when he can purchase a copy of my book. "When something is as important as the content in your book, it's not important what the price is. It's important that I read it, so I will buy it."

I enjoyed another unexpected gift when Rolf's oldest son came to pick his daughter up (Rolf's granddaughter) at the end of the evening. We had the opportunity to catch up and hug, as I had done with his younger brother earlier today at the Stolpersteine Initiative luncheon at the church. So let me just take a moment here to add two other unexpected "gifts". This 2021 journey has so far been more than another journey of Stolpersteine Verlegung, cemeteries, Kaddish, remembrance, commemoration, mishpacha and healing, and of course – wine, as our previous trips have been. It has now become a journey "to the other side" for me: feeling safe, comfortable, and at ease with eating INside restaurants (We were always socially distanced from others. We often had our own separate dining room because we were a larger crowd. All restaurant staff wore masks at all times – covering their mouth AND their nose!), being *in-person* with more than two to six people at a time, and hugging "safe" others, both INside and outside, withOUT wearing a mask. I could never have imagined this a month ago, nor the day we arrived. I've eaten IN more restaurants, and hugged and cheek-kissed more "safe" people in these first three days in Germany than I have in the past year and a half in the USA, and boy – does the hugging nourish my neshama! And the second unexpected gift: I realize that this journey has also become a reuniting of "our" neshamas, Christian-German and Jewish-American, Mishpacha, for the people and the events of this journey continue to touch my neshama – and reunite mine with theirs.

Sunday 3.October: Rene's parents' two hometowns, and Meckenheim

Today is Rene's day for his family. However, no Stolpersteine are being laid for them today because that process has not yet begun. It can take months for the research to be completed and verified as well as further time for the individual Stolpersteine to be hand-made and engraved by Herr Friedrichs-Friedlaender. We visited each of Rene's parents' home sites in their nearby towns: Heimerzheim (his mother's birthplace) and Kirscheim (his father's birthplace). The Mayor of Heimerzheim greeted us warmly outside with her team of City Council members. One of the Council members shared his own eyewitness story from after the war. He recalled the day he watched 12 Nazis being forced (by Allied troops?) to return to Heimerzheim to re-install a number of Jewish tombstones that the Nazis had stolen during the Holocaust. The tombstones had been stored with plans to be desecrated and recycled into pavement stones and roads. Instead, they were re-placed securely in the ground, and we were eyewitnesses to seeing them today – 76 years later!

We met the Heimerzheim Archivist, Ira's colleague, who'd prepared a thick binder with family trees, photographs, and detailed information about Rene's parents and family; his parents were able to escape to the USA, and therefore he was able to grow up with them. She is "our Ira", who through extensive research helps to "return families" to descendants by finding often-previously-unknown "puzzle pieces" of their lives. She presented Rene with a framed photograph of his mother (His father had passed away previously.) and other family from the early 1980s when his mother had returned for a visit to Heimerzheim. They took us to see the location where Rene's mother had gone to school, as well as the previous Rathaus-City Hall where his parents had gotten married. Rene said it was like "walking in my parents' footsteps". Of incredible note, the Archivist was able to search, collect, and organize all this information for Rene within only a couple of months before we arrived. That's because there was a fire in their building, the sprinklers went off, and many archived documents and photographs were found wet afterwards. They placed the wet items in the freezer, and that preserved them in decent condition! Who knew?!

I told Rene privately, with a hug: "Watching you today, Rene, is like watching a little boy opening his Chanukah presents in wonder and awe! It's bringing me such nachas (Yiddish: joy; pleasurable pride, often in others' achievements), despite its bittersweet nature! And it brings back our own 2014 bittersweet emotions – when Ira and Oliver's research, and Rolf and Christina (our Significant 4) were able to fill in many blanks in our own family's stories."

Yesterday, Dietmar and "his" Christina had recommended to Rene that if he wanted a Stolpersteine Verlegung for his family in their hometowns, he should request it today while we were with the Mayor. At the end of our day, Rene was so filled with emotions that I was concerned he might forget to ask. So I intervened and boldly told the Mayor that I knew Rene wanted a Stolpersteine Verlegung to remember and commemorate his family, and asked her what he needed to do to help them make that happen. We know from experience that this can be quite a long process, months to a year, which involves a City Council vote and more. Without so much as a blink, she turned to Rene and asked if he wanted Stolpersteine laid for his family members in Heimerzheim. He replied, "Yes, very much, and we would return here for that." Without a moment's hesitation, without so much as even asking any of her City Council members if they agreed, without delaying the process by stating she'd need to meet with her Council members and take a vote, she quickly replied, "Then that is what we will prepare to do, and we will be in touch with you for the details of when you can return to Germany for the laying of the stones." DONE!

Wow! That Dietmar and "his" Christina, they've "been around the block a time or two". "This ain't (isn't) their first rodeo" (meaning they're experienced and prepared for the situation), as we say in America! In American slang, this means that Dietmar and "his" Christina are well-versed in knowledge and people-skills, have clearly observed, listened and learned from Rolf, Herbert, and the Meinerzhagen Stolpersteine Initiative members' mentoring and collaboration over the years, and they hoped that Rene's wish for his family's Stolpersteine would be granted.

Then we had a picnic lunch outside that our Mishpacha had packed for all of us, because there were no restaurants re-opened yet as a result of the severe summer flooding that had occurred. A few Stolpersteine chapter members had kindly prepared some additional food for us to bring, including pizza-rolls which were delicious. Following that, we drove to Meckenheim to visit our family's Stolpersteine, and for Ryan and I to walk in Dad's then-15-year-old-footsteps with his parents from their temporary home in Meckenheim to the train station – where Dad, Ryan's Pop-Pop, and his parents had hugged each other good-bye as

Dad boarded the train to escape Nazi Germany, to eventually arrive in the USA safely to live with relatives. That was the last time they saw each other. Although I'd done this walk with Gail and some of our Mishpacha in 2018, I imagined the idea to walk it with Ryan – privately, just the two of us – before we left the USA to come to Germany this time. Dietmar had told me that we could make time for this.

Why did I want to do it? Why did I choose to place myself and our adult son in such a tragic "imagined" experience? I'm not sure I can explain it, actually put it into words. Maybe I thought it would make me feel "closer" to Julius and Auguste, by "fake"-imagining what they were forced to do in real life? Maybe I thought it would make me feel "closer" to Dad? Maybe I thought it would make me feel "closer" to Ryan? Maybe I thought it would remind Ryan again how much I love him and can't "imagine" my life without him, though he already knows that from 40 years of experience. It was more of a visceral, gut feeling than something I can describe. I just "knew" that I wanted to do it. When I'd told Ryan I wanted to take "the walk" with him, he'd readily agreed.

Christina walked us to the corner just to show us where to go. Then it was just Ryan and me, mother and son. The train station looks different now than in 2018. Now there's a restaurant, and people were dining inside and outside. Several trains passed by, but none stopped. As we walked towards the station, I began to cry. I told Ryan what was in my heart: how much I love him, how I couldn't imagine the pain and worry that Julius and Auguste experienced saying goodbye to their first-born child, knowing they would likely never see him again, but leaving him with the hope that they and his younger sister would reunite with him in the USA as soon as they could. I told him I didn't know how they were able to make that incredulous traumatic decision that no parent should ever have to make: to choose which child to save, since there was only enough money to save one. What strength, and Faith, Julius and Auguste had to have to do the impossible, in such an impossible life circumstance that was thrust upon them because of hatred, intolerance, persecution. I told Ryan I didn't know how I could ever choose between him and Michelle. He said, "Hopefully you'll never have to." As we rounded the corner before returning to where the others were waiting for us, I dried my eyes, hugged Ryan, and told him I loved him again. "I love you, too", he said. Whatever it was that I'd viscerally wanted and/or needed from this walk, spiritually wanted and/or needed, I feel like I experienced it. It touched my neshama, and connected with Ryan's. As I write this days after returning home, I am crying again at this special memory.

Upon returning to the others, Dietmar was on his knees shining our family's eight Stolpersteine that were laid in October 2014 (Dad, sister Margot, parents Julius and Auguste, Aunt Jenny, Aunt Selma and Uncle Max, and Max's sister Susanne), just as we'd watched him do in 2018, just as we'd watched Rolf do for Aunt Jenny and Uncle Wilhelm's Stolpersteine in 2014. Dietmar looked up at me and asked if we'd had a good walk. I nodded yes. Then he asked, "Do you remember, Sheri, asking me last time if you could help me shine these same Stolpersteine?" Sheri: "Yes, I remember. And you looked up at me intensely and said, 'You may, but it is our duty.'" Dietmar: "I offer you to help now, if you would like, but my answer is the same: You may, but it is our duty. And besides, it makes me feel good to do this." Once again, as in 2018, I chose not to help shine, not wanting to interfere with his process. This time I asked if this is therapeutic for him, polishing the Stolpersteine. He said, "No, I never felt or feel guilty. That is not why I do it. I don't think too deeply about it – it just feels good."

After Dietmar had completed shining the Stolpersteine, we gathered and recited Kaddish. I was tearful. And while I've thought of Oliver and Ira every day since arriving, at this particular moment I viscerally missed them. As Dietmar was cleaning up the supplies to return to the van, he said, "You were right, Sheri. I guess it *is* therapeutic after all."

Upon our return to Meinerzhagen, we had dinner at a restaurant, and our same City Council member, Ingolf, joined us again. He's Mishpacha now, too! We ate (I had Wienerschnitzel.), we imbibed, we laughed, and we pleasantly argued over who would have the privilege of paying the bill. I shared some stories about Jeffrey and I in our early adolescent years together; they laughed. We were all pretty rowdy. It was okay – by now, we were the last customers in the restaurant! We ordered more drinks and desserts. We clearly entertained each other. And in the midst of this, Gail shared some very kind thoughts about me with everyone. Together, we walked back to our hotel escorted by our Mishpacha City Council member.

Monday 4.October: Covid-testing, Dad's Hohenlimburg Stolpersteine and Synagogue, Glockenspiel

Today is Covid-testing day – the day "the rubber hits the road" (Another American colloquialism: when a theory or idea is put to the test to see if it actually works. In this case, covid-vaccinations!). We'll find out the results within 15 minutes. We're leaving Wednesday, and all require a negative test for each of our different destinations. When I tell you that this testing center is efficient, I mean it's like mega-efficient! Not to mention that it's FREE (for another week, after which they start charging) AND just 1 block from our hotel, so we walk there. Incredibly organized, in and out in less than 30 minutes with a link for a digital result as well as a print-out of your result in your hand, organized skilled professionals in full PPE including visors over their masks. Though I've not needed to be in an American covid-testing center, I understand from friends that we're just as efficient in our own American town.

YAY – we all passed! Baruch Hashem (Thank G-d, Hebrew) for vaccinations – they work!

After some down time (Dietmar and Christina are still working this week in addition to all their Stolpersteine responsibilities!), we are picked up to drive to Hohenlimburg – Dad's hometown, 26 miles from Meinerzhagen. First, we meet Stefan again and hug, at the Hohenlimburg Rathaus. We'd met him briefly in Hohenlimburg in 2014 after Dad's family's Stolpersteine ceremony, when he played the Star-Spangled Banner for us on the town's Glockenspiel (bells, chimes). The music is audible throughout the town for all to hear. Today, he plays not only our American National Anthem, but also Hatikvah – Israel's National Anthem. He shares that he's pleased to be able to play Hatikvah for us, even though he knows that we are not Israelis, because he thought we would appreciate it as Jewish people – which of course we do and we thank him for doing so. I gift him one of my "pre" books, and he is visibly surprised and moved. The Mayor is there and welcomes us with a speech in English. There is also a newspaper reporter with pad and pen who will come along with us throughout the afternoon.

With notes in hand, Stefan surprises us by taking us on the Hohenlimburg Stolpersteine circuit – something none of us have ever experienced in Dad's hometown. We've only ever seen Dad's family's Stolpersteine here. As we stop at each family's Stolpersteine site, Stefan personalizes it and makes it "real" by sharing some information about the family who'd once lived there, the family we're "remembering" and commemorating by visiting. We say Kaddish together for each family and place stones on their Stolpersteine. At two different locations, there is only one lone Stolperstein for one person. Though he doesn't know for sure, Stefan hypothesizes that these individuals had either hidden there until they were discovered, deported, and murdered (each of their individual Stolperstein note both deportiet and ermordet), or that their Stolperstein were laid in the early years (? 1990s) at a time when family members from different towns did not have their Stolperstein placed together in one location.

Along the Stolpersteine circuit, the newspaper reporter is asking relevant questions and taking notes. I share how our Significant 4 and other Mishpacha have made such a difference in our lives that I've written a book about it – to thank them, to honor them. Once I write the final chapter upon my return home, the book will be published. Stefan shows him the "pre" book I've given him, and the reporter wants to borrow it for awhile. I ask the reporter if he's ever walked a Stolpersteine circuit. He says yes, but this is the first time he's ever done it with descendants whose family members were victims of the Holocaust. He adds that this time, it's totally different walking alongside us. He doesn't need to explain; I know what he means. THIS, I think to myself, is how we create Peace: walking alongside each other, sharing our stories, sharing our common humanity.

By the way, I think it wasn't until Saturday or Sunday that I first became aware that Ryan was reciting the Kaddish aloud along with us, word for word. He's never had to say Kaddish yet, and yet he knows it. I am amazed! He touches my neshama. I am moved to tears.

Finally, we come to Dad's family's Stolpersteine at their last freely-chosen home. Clearly, this is the most moving Kaddish we recite, after which we place stones on their Stolpersteine. Stefan shares with us that in anticipation of our visit, he has polished our family's Stolpersteine, and he hopes they look good to us. Of course they do, and we share our gratitude for his kind neshama-touching gesture. As we're chatting, the "new" next-door neighbors came out to meet us, and they joined us in the synagogue for awhile. Also, the previous next-door neighbor shows up. Although he has moved elsewhere nearby since we last saw him in 2018, and no longer lives next-door to where Dad's home was, he tells us that he walks by their Stolpersteine on his way to work and always stops to say hello to our family. And then, he offers to polish their Stolpersteine routinely for us since he lives nearby! Another neshama-touching moment, for which "thank you" feels so inadequate.

Next we go to the Hohenlimburg synagogue – a Jewish museum since before we were originally here in 2014 – next door to where Dad's home was, the synagogue where he became a Bar-Mitzvah in 1936. Gail and I have been here before; it's Ryan's first time. We stand at the very place where Dad stood 85 years ago becoming a Bar-Mitzvah, and have a photo taken of us to "remember". Dietmar is wearing his kippah which we gifted him. Once again, touching my neshama.

This evening is our last dinner all together, because tomorrow Dietmar will make the two-hour drive each way to the Frankfurt airport hotel where we'll stay overnight for our flights on Wednesday. To say we ate, imbibed, laughed, and sang together is quite an understatement! And once again, we were the last customers in our private room. Though it was not verbalized, clearly none of us wanted to leave – the restaurant, the fun, the love . . . each other. I have beautiful fun videos of the 15 of us creating lasting memories on our last evening together during this 2021 journey together, for it has been a journey not only for us – but for our German Mishpacha as well. And what better type of journey to embark on, and complete, than one with Mishpacha. Although I know that tomorrow morning I will see Rolf and Christina at our hotel for a surprise birthday celebration for Yvonne, just in case – I walk over to Rolf and privately ask him for his special goodnight. He knows exactly what I mean. We hug, and then he places his hands on each side of my face, and gently kisses my forehead – just as he did in 2014. I am tearful again at this special memory that touches my heart and neshama.

Tuesday, 5.October: Happy Birthday, Yvonne!, packing, visiting Ira, returning to Frankfurt airport

This morning, the hotel owners have arranged rose petals, candies, and a birthday card at our breakfast table before Rene and Yvonne arrive for breakfast, in celebration of her birthday today. Yvonne is touched. Prior to this morning, we'd collaborated secretly with Dietmar, Rolf, and "their" Christinas for their idea for a special birthday surprise for Yvonne. As she unsuspectingly walks into our hotel lobby, we are all there awaiting her: several of the students we've met – including Rolf's granddaughter and the young man I'd chatted with at the Burgermeister's dinner, Dietmar and "his" Christina, Rolf and "his" Christina, and we Americans. We sing Happy Birthday in English, and the students also sing it in German. She is surprised and delighted. Once inside the dining room, there is a beautiful chocolate-filled cake and champagne to celebrate Yvonne together. Dietmar has granted special permission for these students to take a break from school and miss their physics class in order to participate. Though we didn't see Stefan this morning, he dropped off several copies of today's Hohenlimburg newspaper with the journalist's article and photos of our visit yesterday. So sweet that he wanted us to have these in hand before we leave Germany.

When the celebration concludes, it is time to say our last 2021 goodbye. How do I do this? With my heart and neshama, I say a silent "see you again" (auf wiedersehen, German) to Julius, Auguste, Dad, Margot, Aunt Jenny, Uncle Wilhelm, Aunt Selma, Uncle Max, and Susanne. As well, to Oliver who was deeply missed this time. I'll be saying "hallo" and auf wiedersehen to Ira and her family shortly when we stop to visit them on our way back to the airport. Finally, I embrace Dietmar, Rolf, and their Christinas as if I may never see them again, with ongoing danke schoens for .... they know why. And once again, Rolf shares his special goodbye as he did last night, and every night during our

2014 journey. Though this is the end of our 2021 physical and geographical return journey to Germany, it is most definitely not the end of our spiritual journey nor our ongoing relationships with our Mishpacha. At the time, I didn't cry. Now I am, as I write this into the book from home. In fact, I've been quite weepy since our return to the USA. Still missing our time together, still missing them all.

Wednesday 6.October: Aboard the Dreamliner airplane with Ryan, returning home, and back in the USA

Though I miss our Mishpacha already, and I love to travel – it is always good to come home.

Tears quickly flow as I reflect on this – my third journey to Germany.

Missing Ira and Oliver's daily presence with us this time, missing all of our German Mishpacha already, remembering who they are and what they've given us.

Remembering the reasons we originally came in 2014, and how they "found us".

Remembering our loved ones whom we never got to meet, whom we never got to hold, be held by, or celebrate life with – because they were murdered in cold blood almost 80 years ago.

Remembering those we never knew, but said Kaddish for anyway – because we are Jews.

Remembering my paranoid fears that almost prevented me from coming to Germany in 2014 (By the way, while in Germany this third time, I've often seen and heard dogs barking as well as the two-tone sound of their ambulance and police sirens. And while I still have the "thought" of "Nazi Germany" sometimes, there is now a complete and beautiful absence of any physical or emotional anxiety – every time. Finally, my post-traumatic hardwiring has been desensitized, eliminated, and re-wired in a healthy way. Baruch Hashem!).

Remembering my real fears about covid that almost prevented me from coming this time (By the way, I also tested negative again five days after returning home! YES – vaccines WORK!).

Remembering what a gift it is that our son Ryan came with us this time, and watching and discussing his reactions together.

Remembering hearing our son recite Kaddish at multiple cemeteries and multiple Stolpersteine.

Remembering that I purposely did not bring any Jewish objects to publicly identify myself as a Jew in 2014.

Remembering that during *this* journey seven years later, my beautiful lavender kippah sat proudly, and safely, atop my head.

Remembering the G-d-given blessings of our ongoing relationships with our German Mishpacha that grew from the ashes and empty holes in our hearts, that continue to grow from their compassion and kindness – relationships made possible ironically *only* because of the tragic history we share. While we all clearly wish that tragic history had not occurred, I continue to marvel and delight in the seeds of friendship and mishpacha that we've each mutually planted across the ocean ("across the pond," as Oliver says!), watering, nourishing, and nurturing them to become the blooming garden of love that we each continue to carefully tend – still today, amidst the ongoing recurrences and rise of global antisemitism, amidst the ongoing pain of old inaccurate stereotypes of "all Germans" as "Nazis" (as that teenage student taught me from her social media experiences).

Through it all, I still believe it boils down to "people", and Love + Forgiveness = Healing and Peace – no matter our religion, skin color, or language. When we realize that, the path becomes clear on how to create that: one person + one person, one action at a time – together, zusammen.

We must each continue to repeat this humane cycle of Tikkun Olam (Hebrew, repairing the world). It is our responsibility, our duty – to our world, our planet, ourselves, to our children and our grandchildren, to future generations. For during our lifetimes, we all must look at our own reflections in the mirror. And even after we die – it is said that we will each be judged upon Judgment Day, both for what we "did" with our life on earth, as well as what we "did not" do. Because in every moment that we take a breath, we always have the choice.

I will always remember, never forget the tragic lessons

learned from our family and all who were lost – to hatred, intolerance, the dark evil impulses that lurk beneath the surface in each of us, which history has shown time and again can be triggered as "simply" and quickly by imparting and implanting misinformation-propaganda repeatedly until some believe it as "truth" – which we have seen can turn "normal, regular" people into inhumane monsters void of empathy and humane values, instincts, and behaviors . . . into mass murderers.

I will remain vigilant to current events, both at home and across the oceans, and continue to take action. From the ongoing mass shootings in the USA, the January 6th insurrection at our Capitol which threatened to overturn our democracy, our ongoing caste system and racism, ongoing genocides, the unwelcoming responses and sense of threat felt by some people globally to the influx of thousands of immigrants to multiple countries (including the USA) in the face of dire humanitarian crises in their own countries . . . to the even more recent teenager's thwarted plan for an explosives attack at the Hagen synagogue in Germany on Yom Kippur weeks ago, and the removal of an Israeli flag flying at the Hagen town hall – I will always "remember", "never forget" that history *can* and *does* repeat itself, so we must respond with many courageous, loud moral voices and actions against injustice.

We can all learn, and be filled with gratitude, from one of Stefan's courageous examples below: a letter he wrote as a solidarity address upon seeing the Israeli flag flying from his town hall removed at the request of a group of people.

"Ladies and Gentlemen of the Society for Christian-Jewish Cooperation,

I am horrified by the attacks on Israel. I am equally horrified by the attacks on Israeli and Jewish people, signs and buildings in Germany.

I am completely disconcerted by the decision ... to remove the flag of Israel hoisted on the town hall at the request of (some people) ... (One writes) like a warning, yes threat also for the future. It reminds me of what is reported about the beginning of worst times in our country.

I see with great sadness how the situation of Jewish people in

Germany continues to worsen. (Some groups) are harassing their community ... and putting pressure on it. It is appalling, however, when representatives, while formulating solemnly devout words, abandon our Jewish citizens and signs of 'their' state.

Today, in the ... church congregation ... to which I belong, prayers were said for the Jewish people. And for 'that we do not sin against them, our brothers and sisters, once again and never again'.

But in my opinion visible signs should follow. Perhaps the Society for Christian-Jewish Cooperation can and will give impulses here? As far as a vigil or a common prayer in front of the synagogue is planned, I am gladly ready to participate in the preparation. ... Also, if you would like to assign people to the non-violent defense of the synagogues ..., I am ready.

Thank you very much for your work in the society! All the best to you and especially to the Jewish citizens! With kind regards! Stefan"

(Authoress note: Per Stefan's social justice activism and idea for a Solidarity Rally, this Society organization called for a rally supporting the Jewish community – and many people of different faiths attended. As well, Stefan made a comment aloud at the rally in support of the Jewish community. Danke schoen from our neshamas (souls) to yours, Stefan, and to the people of the Society for Christian-Jewish Cooperation!)

After we arrived home, Stefan forwarded an email to us from a humanitarian activist who wanted to make sure that the descendants of Rolf/Ralph Stern (Dad) were aware that since June 2018, there *is* a memorial at Maly Trostenets in the Blagowtschina Forest, where our family and Rene's were murdered by the Nazis along with many other Jewish people on July 24, 1942. This is the memorial that was being planned when Gail was there several years ago. We are grateful for this memorial, and grateful that Belarusians and Germans were committed to collaborating on this project – in order to remember and commemorate our loved ones and others. Despite that tragic history, and/or perhaps precisely because of it – I choose to see this collaboration and commemoration as a hopeful sign of Peace, with the fervent shared hope that "never again" should such hatred, intolerance, and genocide occur.

Also after our return home, Barbara and Heinz shared this example of hope, growing acceptance of one another, and collaboration for sustainable Justice and Peace for ALL, from our younger generation. As part of a German-Israeli Youth Guide Exchange 2020-2022, students from both countries have been collaborating on a virtual project entitled: *Pieces of Memory: Children in the Shoah and Us*, expected to be completed next Spring. This speaks for itself, and makes my neshama sing and dance!

So what about Ryan's perspectives about this journey? We discussed them both during our journey as well as once we'd returned, naturally – because I'm a Jewish mother, an educator, and a previous nurse psychotherapist – so I ask a lot of questions! Initially, he shared that his decision to come to Germany was a spur of the moment decision – only when Gail brought it up at dinner together in June, which he thought was a good idea. After further thought, he realized that he'd really like to see the "stones" we've talked about so often as well as "see" Pop-Pop's history that shaped him. He denied any concerns about traveling to Germany or anywhere in Europe as a Jewish man, "because there's anti-semitism here in the US, too, and I didn't expect it to be much different there. I wasn't worried about the possibility of me actually facing it in Germany any more than I am about that possibility here at home." Three things pleasantly surprised him:

"It was amazing that 'the whole town' turned out for Yvonne's family's Stolpersteine!

I couldn't believe that the children were singing songs IN HEBREW, about Peace! It was kind of cathartic for me, and maybe for the German people too, that now love is growing in a place where such hatred had been before.

I don't think I've ever experienced such hospitable, gracious and welcoming hosts anywhere else. They were so friendly and forthcoming, so honest about the facts of the Holocaust, so committed to the mission of the initiative and creating better relationships between people. They're helping to assure that future generations *will* "remember," and "never forget." And the high school students – they are amazing in their efforts and commitment to that, too. I really feel like I bonded with Dietmar that week. I left Germany feeling like he is a true friend, if not brother. And we talked about getting together again in the future."

As well, he now realizes that he wants to travel more internationally, including returning to Germany to do the tourist things too, i.e. Berlin, see where "the wall" was built and later finally torn down. This journey "re-emphasized how important Pop-Pop (Rolf/Ralph Stern) was to me, and that I want to follow in his footsteps and do good things." Writing in the guestbook at the renovated Hohenlimburg Synagogue, he thanked the townspeople for restoring it. It was special for him to stand where his Pop-Pop had stood 85 years ago becoming a Bar-Mitzvah – despite the difficulties for Jews at that time, just as Ryan did in America 27 years ago when both sets of grandparents were able to celebrate with him – thankfully without the persecution and anti-semitism his Pop-Pop and their family endured. Does he feel different Jewishly after this journey? "No, but I look back now on my Hebrew school education, and my trip to Israel and Eastern Europe as a teen, as having prepared me for *this* journey." The Meckenheim train station walk? "It was an emotional experience for me, imagining how Pop-Pop must have felt at only 15, how his parents and sister must have felt in those circumstances." Does he "see" Pop-Pop any differently now after this journey? "I feel like I 'knew' him my whole life, especially since I lived with him during the last year or so of his life – and we talked a lot, but I realize it was only about 'the good stuff' – understandably. Now seeing where he grew up and what he experienced when he was only a teenager, this journey has completed my picture of him."

In my life, I will remember Martin Niemöller's prose, with its lesson to stand up and speak out against injustice to *any* of our sisters and brothers – because it is the right thing to do, and because if I do not – when they come for me, there may be "no one left to speak for me". I will remember Elie Wiesel's belief, that "There may be times when we are powerless to prevent injustice, but there must *never* be a time when we fail to protest." I will remember Helen Keller's belief, that "I am one, but I am only one. I cannot do everything, but I can do something. And because I cannot do everything, I will not refuse to do the something that I can do."

And while I will "never forget" what Hitler and the Nazis did to our loved ones and many more, I *will* always "remember" the gifts of kindness, compassion, reparative actions, remembrance, commemoration, and the loving neshama-touching healings of these "old but present traumas" from our shared histories – "gifted" by our German Mishpacha, standing beside us in solidarity.

To our Significant 4 Mishpacha, Rolf and Christina, Ira, and Oliver: More than seven years ago, at our last night together on 29.August, 2014, I made you a promise – that I would tell others back in the States about you, because the world needed to hear "this" – now more than ever. I have passionately fulfilled my promise to you, sharing who you are – mensches – and what you've given us, with people back in the States. With this book, I hope to reach so many more, in the USA, Germany and globally. I have turned my pain and paranoia from the Shoah – to purpose, as a Peace Ambassador – through this book as my instrument. For it is both sad and frightening, in 2021, that so many *still* need to hear and heed the calls – for acceptance of one another, and collaboration for sustainable Justice and Peace for ALL – in our words AND our actions.

Liebe (Dear) all of our Mishpacha:

Some people come into our lives and quickly go.
Some people move our souls to dance.
They awaken us to a new understanding with the passing whisper of their wisdom.
Some people make the sky more beautiful to gaze upon.
They stay in our lives for awhile, leave footprints on our hearts, and we are never, ever the same.

Flavia Weedn

The "Surprise" Memorial at the New Jewish Cemetery in Meinerzhagen: Remembering and Commemorating those Jewish individuals whose tombstones were stolen, desecrated, and turned into sidewalks/roads. Friday, 1.October, 2021.

Left side, from L to R: back row: Gerd, Rolf, "his" Christina; front row: Sheri and Gudrun, looking at each other.

Right side, from L to R: back row: Dietmar's Christina, Steve; front row: Gail, Yvonne, Rene, and Dietmar.

1.October, 2021: Meet, Greet and Eat with the students who developed the petition that led to the final Meinerzhagen Stolpersteine Verlegung on 2.October, 2021 (Yvonne's families).

Left to Right, back row: Christina (Dietmar's wife), Christina (Rolf's wife), Jessica, Shadia, Laurin, Ryan, Maik, Raphael, Laurenz, Steven.

Left to Right, front row: Sheri, Yvonne, Rene (behind Yvonne), Gail, Steve, Rolf, Lilli (Rolf and "his" Christina's granddaughter), Leonie, Louisa.

4.October, 2021: Dietmar and Gretel "Remembering" Dad's family, polishing their Stolpersteine in Hohenlimburg.

Ryan and me (Sheri, the authoress) at the Restored Hohenlimburg Synagogue, standing where Dad/Pop-Pop stood at his Bar Mitzvah in 1936.

Maskless Memories of our last night together in Meinerzhagen:
Left side, front to back: Ryan, Dietmar's Christina, Sheri, Rolf's Christina, Rolf, Yvonne, Dietmar and Rene in front, with Gail and Stefan (standing).
Right side, back to front: Ingolf, Beate, Bathseba, Gretel, and Herbert.

Epilogue: Mishpacha Gifts

Born of tragedy and ashes, nurtured by compassion and courage. Bearing Witness alongside us. Bearing our pain, and theirs. The Gifts of Family. Commemorating and validating that each of our loved ones' lives had worth and mattered. Remembering. To "Never forget". Researching, interpreting, and sharing more of our personal family history, thus "returning" our family back to us – if only spiritually. Advocating successfully for Dad to have two of his own Stolpersteine, and "reuniting" him with his sister and parents. Reuniting their neshamas, as well as theirs with Gail's, Jeffrey's, and mine, after 76 years almost to the day that they said goodbye at the Meckenheim train station: priceless.

And in their process of gifting us by advocating, remembering, valuing, and commemorating, by acknowledging that Hitler and his Nazis' hatred and atrocities were wrong, by making amends for their countrymen's reign of terror, by dialoguing together ... perhaps we began or continued to mutually heal from the pain and appropriate shame borne of the inhumanities, perhaps more than we ever had before we met each other, perhaps without ever realizing that we'd needed healing (which was the case for me). And in their process of gifting us ... together, we became role models as a group of individuals, along with the Meinerzhagen Stolpersteine Initiative members, demonstrating what *can* be done between motivated compassionate individuals and groups when we rise up and respond nonviolently against hate of any kind, make amends when it has occurred, work together towards healing, and work together for Peace – locally and globally, so that "Never again" will such things occur, and "Never again" will people be complicit in their silence.

And in their process of gifting us... we fell in love, "adopted" them, and they *became* family. We are honored to call them "Mishpacha".

ACKNOWLEDGMENTS

There are many individuals who contributed in some way to the birth of this book, to whom I am grateful.

My husband Jeffrey: for accompanying us on our initial 2014 journey to Germany, filling in details of our experiences, never once complaining about how much time I was spending on conceiving and birthing this book (which was time not spent with him!), *kvelling* about my achievements, and continuing to be my best friend and first and only love since adolescence.

My sister Gail: for accompanying us on that 2014 journey to Germany, for her support, for sharing pictures, and for graciously giving me the gift of saying "yes" when I asked her to please write the chapter about her personal experiences in Minsk – which enhances our family's story.

All individuals included in this book: for giving me your "carte blanche" trust by granting me permission to use your names, emails, and rich stories about you.

Israela, Carmela, and Rae: for sharing their experiences with editing and publishing.

"Cousin Carol": for believing in me and helping with some initial editing years ago.

To our Significant 4 (Ira, Oliver, Rolf and Christina), Christina and Dietmar, Herbert and Gretel, Gudrun, Barbara and Heinz, Stefan, and the Meinerzhagen Stolpersteine Initiative chapter members: Thank you all for who you are – Mensches – and what you do. Additional thanks to Ira and Oliver for their vast historical and personal-family research and translation of family letters written in German, before-during-and beyond our initial 2014 Germany Journey.

Gunter Demnig: for his creative Art Project: The Stolpersteine Initiative, for personally planting our family's Stolpersteine in Germany, and for his permission to use selected content from the Stolpersteine Initiative's website in this book.

The many organizations who've sponsored Peace-building and Social Justice webinars and trainings that I've devoured for years, increasingly more during the first year of the global COVID pandemic (2020). I met my dear friend Beate when we both participated in training and became Certified Peace Ambassadors in 2016 (theshiftnetwork.com: Peace Ambassador Training 2.0).

Penguin Random House Publishers: for granting permission to use selected excerpts (relevant comparisons and contrasts between the caste systems of India, America, and Nazi-Germany) from Isabel Wilkerson's #1 New York Times Bestseller: "Caste: The Origins of our Discontents".

My editor and publisher, Chaim Mazo, for believing in me, for having patience, for granting permission to include two Holocaust witnesses' testimonies, for helping create this polished version of the book, and for believing that our family's stories need to be heard – now, more than ever.

My Morning Gratitude Peeps, who continue to nurture and sustain my neshama throughout the pandemic (even in a virtual platform).

HIAS: for all individuals past, present, and future within this organization – for who you are, for implementing your Mission to "Welcome the Stranger. Protect the Refugee.", for what you continue to accomplish despite marked obstacles, and for unquestionably saving my father-in-law Rolf/Ralph Stern's life by bringing him to America to escape the horrors of the Shoah. How very different all of our lives would have been ... had you not chosen to take that action. How very different many people's lives are today... because you continue to take action.

Dietmar's Independent-Study High School Students of 2020-2021, for having the courage and conscience to be the "moral voices", for initiating your petition to your local government to "complete" the laying of the final two families' Stolpersteine in Meinerzhagen. You've already made a difference in individual people's lives and the World through your courage and your actions. Pass it forward!

References

Adams, C. (March 26, 2021). Evanston is the first U.S. city to issue slavery reparations. Experts say it's a noble start. NBC News. https://www.nbcnews.com/news/nbcblk/evanston-s-reparations-plan-noble-start-complicated-process-experts-say-n1262096

ADL email update. (June 14, 2021). Increase in anti-Semitic incidents.

Anti-Defamation League (ADL) Press release. (May 13, 2020). https://www.adl.org/news/press-releases/adl-welcomes-senate-passage-of-never-again-education-act

ben Maimon, M. Translated by Bell, B. Immersing in a Mikvah (Ritual Pool), Positive Commandment 109. Retrieved Spring 2021, from https://www.chabad.org/library/article_cdo/aid/961505/jewish/Positive-Commandment-109.htm

Biden, J. (June 1, 2021). Speech at the Centennial Commemoration of the Tulsa Massacre.

Brutal anti-Semitic rape. In The Independent, UK online news. Retrieved December 2014, from http://www.independent.co.uk/news/world/europe/brutal-anti-Semitic-ra

Byock, I. (2004). *The four things that matter most – A book about living.* James Bennett Pty Ltd.

Clifford, R. (January 27, 2016). Who is a Holocaust Survivor? https://www.thebritishacademy.ac.uk/blog/who-holocaust-survivor/

Corbach, D. (1999). The Transport to Minsk / Trostenez on 20.7.1942 VI. In *Departure: 6.00 a.m. Messe Köln-Deutz: Deportations 1938-1945, Cologne* (German/English) (p. 545, 734, pp. 744-747).

Facing History and Ourselves. (Last updated: 2021, April 16). Genocide still happens: Help students understand warnings for the future and echoes from the past. https://www.facinghistory.org/educator-resources/current-events/genocide-still-happens

Frankl, V.E., *Man's Search For Meaning,* Verlag für Jugend und Volk. German edition, 1946.

Genocide Watch. Copy of current genocide watch alerts. Retrieved 6/19/21 from, https://www. genocidewatch. com/copy-of-current-genocide-watch-aler

Germany's Ban on Jewish Emigration 1941. Archive Sta Meinerzhagen, B 1.3 file 217b. With permission by Ira at Meinerzhagen Archives.

Grinberg, E. (May 1, 2019). How the Definition of Holocaust Survivor Has Changed Since the End of World War II. Smithsonianmag.com/history/what-and-who-defines-being-holocaust-survivor-180972076/

Hebrew Immigrant Aid Society. https://www.hias.org/who/history

HIAS. (2020). HIAS Haggadah. https://www.hias.org

History.com Editors. Nuremberg Trials. (updated: June 7, 2019. Original: January 29, 2010). https://www.history.com/topics/world-war-ii/nuremberg-trials

Kranz, M. (2017, November 22). 5 genocides that are still going on today. *Business Insider.* https://www.businessinsider. com/genocides-still-going-on-today-bosnia-2017-11#darfuris-in-sudan-5

Ochab, E.U. (2021, January 18). Simon-Skjodt Center for the Prevention of Genocide of the Holocaust Memorial Museum in Washington, D.C., in cooperation with Dartmouth College's Dickey Center for International Understanding. Countries at risk for mass killing 2020–21: Early warning project statistical risk assessment results. *Forbes Magazine.* https://www.forbes.com/sites/ewelinaochab/2021/01/18/what-are-the-countries-at-risk-of-mass-killings-in-2021/?sh=4ed1cde93c35

Renewal of the Avenue of the Righteous Among the Nations. (October 23, 2005). Yad Vashem, The World Holocaust Remembrance Center. Retrieved June 2021, from https://www.yadvashem.org/press-release/23-october-2005-10-33.html

Santayana, G. (1905). Reason in common sense. Archibald Constable and Company.

Social Security Administration. (December 21, 1999). https://secure.ssa.gov/apps10/poms.nsf/lnx/0200302327

Sönnert, I. & Pertz, D. (2013). *Ihre Namen werden bleiben! Dokumentation zur Geschichte der Meckenheimer und Rheinbacher Juden und ihrer Friedhöfe, Zeugnisse jüdischer Kultur im Rhein-Sieg-Kreis*, Band 5, Siegburg, p. 31-32.

Stolpersteine Project Website. Retrieved April 8, 2021, from http://www.stolpersteine.eu/en

The Kindertransport Association. www.kindertransport.org/history09_FAQ.htm#1

United States Holocaust Memorial Museum. In Holocaust encyclopedia. https://encyclopedia.ushmm.org/content/en/article/jewish-badge-during-the-nazi-era

United States Holocaust Memorial Museum. www.ushmm.org/remember/holocaust-survivors

United States Holocaust Memorial Museum. Days of Remembrance Resources. Remembrance Day Calendar. Retrieved 6/19/21, from https://www.ushmm.org/remember/days-of-remembrance/resources/calendar

Wilkerson, I. (2020). *Caste – The origins of our discontents*. Random House.

Appendix

RISE UP AND RESPOND: ACTIONS FOR PEACE

1. Peace begins within.

a) List your triggers for stress, intolerance (including views that are "different" from yours), and "other-isms".

b) List your early-warning signals (physical, emotional, behavioral, spiritual) of (a) above.

c) List at least 5 effective coping strategies for (a) above (include a routine Gratitude practice if you don't already have one, i.e. journaling/listing who and what you're grateful for; include educating yourself via webinars/books/etc and getting to know people from different cultures/religions/ethnicities/genders, etc; yoga, music, meditation, exercise, prayer, community worship, self-care)

d) Practice above consistently.

2. Practice compassion, empathy, and patience for yourself and others.

Dalai Lama: "Be kind whenever possible. It is always possible."

Ian MacLaren, Scottish author 19th century: "Be kind, for everyone you meet is fighting a hard battle."

John Bradford, 16th century: "There but for the grace of G-d go I."

Sheri Stern: "Create a goal to say one kind thing/compliment to at least one person daily."

3. Self-monitor to see how often you may "label" people unnecessarily, i.e.

"The black woman at the salon", "the Asian guy at the parking lot", "the Hispanic girl who's the manager", rather than "the woman, the guy, the girl". **Then change your practice**.

4. *Make a list of the top 3 local / global issues that touch your soul* ... i.e. hunger, poverty, systemic racism, gun violence, domestic violence, civil rights, social justice, voter suppression, genocide, infant mortality, vaccine and medication availability for all people, gender equality, healthcare reform, homelessness, the prison system, making a living wage, immigration reform, disability rights, reproductive rights, the environment, etc. **Then actively work towards solutions!** "Think globally, act locally".

5. *Volunteer And Donate!* (thewaterbearers.org)

6. If you don't already know who they are, **look up your state legislators and their contact information: www.congress. gov; www.senate.gov; www.house.gov; U.S. Capitol, general:** 202-226-8000; 202-224-3121: Switchboard Operator can connect you directly with your Congressman or Congresswoman.

7. Then contact your legislators by phone, email, or mail, or leave a concise message with their staff member - to share your thoughts and feelings about issues important to you, to urge their support or opposition to critical bills (First, educate yourself about the bills.).

8. Break Bread Together: within safe CDC Guidelines. (You can do it virtually if you have those resources.) Invite someone to dinner who is of a different faith, culture, skin color, etc. to learn about each other, and share one of your cultural meals and conversation... When you get to know others, you reduce fears and misunderstandings.

"You can't hate someone whose story you know."
– Margaret Wheatley

9. *Participate in protest marches / vigils for ideals and values that are important to you. See #4 above.*

10. *Research, join, and/or support organizations that are already well-established with* ... Missions that reflect and enhance the values you live by and choose to promote, i.e. you can check these out, and/or google "organizations that help (enter your mission of choice, i.e. homelessness, hunger, poverty, voting rights, etc.)". You are encouraged to check Charity Navigator (charitynavigator.org) to evaluate any nonprofit organizations where you're considering donating and/or volunteering. In full transparency, these organizations below have not been checked by the Author on Charity Navigator.

- (LWV) League of Women Voters: lwv.org
- Feeding America: feedingamerica.org
- Reginald F. Lewis Museum: lewismuseum.org
- National Museum of African-American History and Culture: nmaahc.si.edu
- NAACP – National Association for the Advancement of Colored People: naacp.org
- Support Black Businesses: supportblackowned.com
- Support Native American Businesses: sba.gov/business-guide
- Support AAPI Businesses: nbcnews.com/shopping/lifestyle/aapi-owned-businesses
- ADL (Anti-Defamation League): adl.org
- ACLU (American Civil Liberties Union): aclu.org
- Bend the Arc: bendthearc.us
- Genocide Watch: genocidewatch.com
- Sharaka: The Gulf-Israel Center for Social Entrepreneurship: sharakango.com
- Catholic Charities: catholiccharitiesusa.org
- The Stolpersteine Initiative: stolpersteine.eu/en
- The US Holocaust Memorial Museum: ushmm.org
- HIAS (Hebrew Immigrant Aid Society): hias.org
- End Homelessness: endhomelessness.org
- Natural Resources Defense Council: nrdc.org
- Environment: blueandgreentomorrow.com
- LGBTQ: diversitybestpractices.com

- Everytown for Gun Safety: everytown.org
- MoveOn: moveon.org
- SPLC (Southern Poverty Law Center): splcenter.org
- SOSS (Sisterhood of Salaam Shalom): sosspeace.org

11. When you see something, say something.

Don't put yourself in harm's way. Do call the appropriate professional resource for the incident (i.e. police, fire department, 911). Do not stand by and simply "watch" as someone else is being harmed in any way.

12. Check your "privilege" at the door, but first - in the mirror.

This bears repeating here from an earlier chapter. The best definition of privilege that I've ever heard was given by one of the speakers I heard at the peaceful 1/21/2017 Women's March on Washington, DC. She said (paraphrased): "The definition of privilege is not paying attention or being concerned about something – because it doesn't affect you personally."

Perhaps ... number 12 above holds the meaning of the phrase that came to my mind as I was drifting off to sleep in the airplane flying home from Germany on 8/31/14: "and you having the mirror". In my "having the mirror", I can use that mirror as one instrument along with my one authentic voice to collaborate with others to create positive change.

1. First, I need to look into the mirror I'm holding and ask: "What am **I** doing to take actions against hatred and intolerance, and for acceptance of all my brothers and sisters, and Peace?

2. Then, and only then, may I turn the mirror around and offer it as a gift to you - so that if you choose, you may look into it and ask yourself the same question.

3. And together, my authentic voice, plus yours and others joining in ... can and will create a Symphony of Acceptance and Peace for all.

Remember: "Never forget."

First they came for the Socialists,
and I did not speak out ...
because I was not a Socialist.

Then they came for the Trade Unionists,
and I did not speak out ...
because I was not a Trade Unionist.

Then they came for the Jews,
and I did not speak out ...
because I was not a Jew.

Then they came for me ...
and there was no one left to speak for me.

Friedrich Gustav Emil Martin Niemöller

Made in the USA
Columbia, SC
10 November 2021